European and Native American warfare, 1675–1815

European and Native American warfare, 1675–1815

Armstrong Starkey

University of Oklahoma Press : Norman

Starkey, Armstrong.
European and Native American warfare, 1675–1815/Armstrong Starkey.
p.   cm.
Includes bibliographical references and index.
Index 0-8061-3074-1 (cloth: alk. paper). — ISBN 0-8061-3075-X
(pbk.: alk. paper)
1. Indians of North America – Wars — 1600–1750.   2. Indians of North
America — Wars — 1750–1815.   3. Indians of North America — Warfare.
I. Title.
E82.S7   1998
973 — dc21   98-24425
CIP

University of Oklahoma Press edition published by special arrangement with UCL Press,
UCL Press Limited, 1 Gunpowder Square, London EC4A 3DE, UK. Copyright © 1998 by
Armstrong Starkey. All rights reserved. First printing.

1 2 3 4 5 6 7 8 9 10

Contents

List of maps

Preface

European and Native American warfare is well travelled ground in North American historiography. Captivity narratives and accounts of Indian campaigns were popular reading during the colonial era and controversies over frontier warfare helped shape an American nationalist tradition. In the nineteenth century Francis Parkman portrayed the Anglo–French struggle for the continent on a broad canvas against a chiaroscuro background of savagery and untamed wilderness. Parkman's history captured the spirit of Anglo–American manifest destiny to rule a continental empire. The French and their Indian allies were its inevitable victims.

Like most Americans of my generation, my sense of frontier warfare was founded upon Parkman, fortified by the work of novelists such as James Fenimore Cooper and Kenneth Roberts. Indeed, when I first naïvely approached this subject as a military historian, I was unaware how much things had changed. This book reflects significant historiographical developments over the last 25 years: the overthrow of Parkman's thesis by the historian Francis Jennings, whose own work is best captured in the title of his book *The Invasion of America*. Not only did Jennings portray the Anglo-Americans as brutal invaders, but he discredited Parkman as a reputable historian. Jennings has also contributed to the development of ethnohistory, a discipline combining historical and anthropological methods, which seeks to understand Native Americans on their own terms. For the first time the Europeans' opponents have been given a voice of their own and with that a point of view. I have profited enormously from the work of experts in the field who have given me an understanding of and appreciation for the lives of native peoples and the Indian way of war.

This book is about warfare and I view it as a work of military history. It is about conflict on the frontier, a zone in which Europeans and Indians engaged in conflict and co-operation. This was as true of warfare as of any other aspect of life. Europeans and Indians fought with one another and allied with one another; they learned one another's way of war and those who adapted best were most successful. Europeans arrived in North America at a time when Europe is sometimes said to have been undergoing a "military revolution", a concept that has generated considerable debate among scholars. European soldiers brought the new weapons and techniques associated with this revolution with them to North America and by 1675 had provoked a military revolution of a sort among Native Americans, a revolution that for 140 years gave them a tactical advantage over their more numerous and wealthier opponents. European success in the frontier wars depended on their ability to strike the right balance between their own military traditions and the Indian way of war. Thus, as I hope this work makes clear, European military developments in themselves did not guarantee the conquest of the continent.

In addition to the many scholars acknowledged in my notes, I wish to give special thanks to those who read part or all of my manuscript: Jeremy Black, who suggested that I begin the project in the first place, Colin Calloway, Francis Jennings, whose good-humoured response to my comments about his own work I greatly appreciated, and an anonymous reviewer. I also thank my colleagues in the Adelphi University History Department who read parts of the manuscript and made helpful suggestions. I would also like to acknowledge the assistance provided by the staffs of the Adelphi University Library, the New York Public Library, the British Library, the William L. Clements Library of the University of Michigan, the Huntington Library, San Marino, CA, the Scottish Records Office, Edinburgh, and the Public Records Office, Kew.

Chapter One

Introduction: raiders in the wilderness

Fort Bull

On 27 March 1756, a starving and exhausted raiding party of French, Canadians and American Indians emerged from the forest near Fort Bull, a fortified Anglo-American storage depot located at the great portage on the way from Schenectady, New York to Fort Oswego on Lake Ontario. The detachment of 362 men under the command of Lieutenant Chaussegros de Léry had made an arduous 15-day march from Lachine struggling through heavy snow, ice and torrential rains. Despite the deer shot by their Indian hunters, the men had been without food for two days.[1]

Now they found themselves astride a much travelled military supply road linking Wood Creek with the Mohawk River. At 10.00 am Léry's Indian scouts captured two sleighs loaded with provisions and the party broke its involuntary fast. Learning that a servant accompanying the sleighs had escaped to give the alarm at neighbouring Fort Williams at the far end of the portage, Léry determined to attack Fort Bull immediately. The Indians in his force protested this decision. They argued that they were fortunate to have captured sufficient food to see them home and that it would be tempting fate to try more. "If he desired absolutely to perish", they said, "he was master of his Frenchmen."

Léry was an experienced frontier commander. Born in Canada, the son of a French military engineer, he had been commissioned as an officer in the *troupes de marine*, French regulars stationed in the colonies and commanded by colonial officers. Although following in his father's footsteps by qualifying as an engineer, he had cut his teeth in frontier warfare during raids on the New England frontier in 1746–8. Now he demonstrated his ability to lead Indian warriors. Recognizing that Indians seldom risked an assault on a fortified

1

position, he replied that he did not wish to expose them, but asked for only two volunteers to serve as guides. Eventually, some 20 of the 103 Indians, aroused by drams of brandy, agreed to join in the assault. The remainder posted themselves in ambush along the road from Fort Williams.

Léry hoped to surprise Fort Bull without firing a shot. His French and Canadian troops, a mix of regulars (*troupes de terre* recently despatched from France), colony regulars and Canadian militia, fixed bayonets and advanced quickly upon the fort. But the Indians, on flushing a small English work party, emitted a war whoop which alerted the garrison, who managed to bar the gate. Fort Bull was not a proper fort in the eighteenth-century European style. Rather it was a stockaded supply depot and the garrison of 60 men was armed only with muskets and grenades. When the French-Canadians gained possession of the loopholes in the fence, they were able to fire into the fort and the enclosed area became a killing ground. Under the cover of this ferocious fire, the gate was soon battered in. One account of the engagement indicates that Léry summoned the English commander to surrender, promising quarter to the garrison, but was answered by a volley of musketry. Such an offer and refusal could be used to justify the subsequent event. Breaking into Fort Bull during a bitter struggle of almost an hour, the French-Canadians bayoneted nearly the entire garrison. No more than three or four prisoners were taken.

On hearing the sounds of battle, the British garrison at Fort Williams despatched a relief force. They promptly fell into an ambush by the Indians posted on the road. Seventeen of the Fort Williams party were killed before they could regain the protection of their stockade. One of the Indian chiefs asked Léry if he now proposed to attack the other fort. He replied that "he would do so forthwith if the Indians would follow him. This reply drove this Chief off, and all his party prepared to go after him."

Léry himself may have had no intention of attacking Fort Williams, which he knew to be provided with cannon and more strongly built than Fort Bull. The latter had caught fire during the battle and the powder magazine exploded, destroying all of the supplies accumulated within the depot. Aware that large Anglo-American reinforcements would soon appear, he led his men back into the forest for the trek to Lake Ontario. Again food ran short. The raiders subsisted in part upon horse flesh and "had even devoured a porcupine without any other dressing than sufficed just to scorch off the hair and quills". All depended upon meeting supply boats at the appointed rendezvous. After a march of seven days, they arrived only to find the bay empty. This cast the raiders into despair as once again they faced the prospect of starvation. They kept a cold and hungry watch until M. de la Saussaye arrived with the rescue bateaux on 13 April, 17 days after the attack on Fort Bull.

Léry had executed a remarkable winter raid with the loss of only three dead and seven wounded. He had exposed the fragility of Fort Oswego's supply line and dealt a severe blow to Anglo-American preparations for a summer offensive on Lake Ontario. Aside from the material damage, this successful deep strike into British territory sapped Anglo-American morale. Indeed, it may be said to have been the opening move in the Marquis de Montcalm's capture of Fort Oswego in August 1756, a victory which strengthened the French grip upon the Ohio country.

Aside from its strategic significance, this little campaign offers insight into the issues of this book: European versus North American Indian styles of warfare. As should be evident from the preceding account, the two styles were not necessarily incompatible. Léry's force included a large party of allied Iroquois, Algonquin and Nepissing Indians who played an indispensable role as scouts, hunters and skirmishers. The French-Canadian raiders, striking out into the forest in the midst of winter without an assured source of food, had adapted themselves to an Indian way of war which demanded tremendous physical endurance and indifference to deprivation. Still, it is unlikely that they would have risked such a march without Indian support. Once the battle for Fort Bull erupted, the two styles of war parted: the Europeans fixed bayonets and assaulted a fortified position while the majority of the Indians withdrew into the woods to prepare an ambush. The latter reminded Léry that he was master of the French, but not of them. They considered themselves allies rather than subordinates bound to follow orders not to their liking. He was intelligent enough not to force the issue, but rather found a way by which they could render useful service. The outcome of the assault upon the fort was a "massacre". Indeed, more people were slain at Fort Bull than during the celebrated "massacre" at Fort William Henry in 1757. But the slaughter at Fort Bull was carried out by French-Canadian troops who gave no quarter to the hapless garrison once they stormed the gate. If it is true that Fort Bull's commander had rejected Léry's summons, the killing of the defenders was consistent with European military custom and the laws of war. This should be kept in mind when one considers the "barbaric" martial customs of eighteenth-century North American forest Indians.

Léry's achievement may be contrasted with that of his contemporary, Major Robert Rogers, whose rangers were the most famous Anglo-American frontier fighters of the time. Although he was a bitter enemy of the French-Canadians and their Indian allies, he admired the martial culture and warlike methods of the Indians and adapted them to his own use. Like most successful frontier commanders, he included companies of Indians among his troops. While his battle success was mixed, his rangers were the invaluable eyes of the Anglo-American army in the Lake George–Lake Champlain region during the Seven Years War. In September 1759, Rogers led a force of rangers against the Catholic Abenaki Indian settlement at St Francis near Montreal. During the march overland from Lake Champlain, nearly a quarter of his force became disabled and had to be sent home. He successfully attacked the Indian settlement, burning the dwellings and killing or capturing a number of the inhabitants. Rogers claimed to have killed 200 Indians and to have captured 20, but some authorities accept the French figure of 30 dead. It is unclear how many Indian warriors were present at the time of the raid, but large numbers swiftly assembled in pursuit of the rangers whose retreat became a nightmare. They were reduced to eating roots and cannibalizing the corpses of comrades when supply boats failed to appear at their rendezvous on time. Rogers lost almost half of his command of 200 on this expedition.

Rogers proved that he could penetrate Canada and destroy the Abenakis' sanctuary. The Abenakis' sense of security was badly shaken by the raid, but it is not always clear who "won" engagements of this sort. Lieutenant Colonel John Armstrong's raid on the Delaware village at Kittanning on the Allegheny River on 8 September 1756 was celebrated as an Anglo-American victory at the time. Armstrong caught an unfortified village by surprise, killed a prominent Indian military leader, and rescued a few prisoners. After the attack, the Indians abandoned Kittanning and withdrew across the Ohio. Indian morale seems to have suffered from this blow, which in turn lifted sagging Anglo-American spirits. On the other hand, although Armstrong enjoyed the advantage of surprise and a numerical advantage of three to one, casualties were roughly equal on either side and the bulk of the prisoners remained in Indian hands. Armstrong's raid failed to end the Indian threat to Pennsylvania's white frontier settlements. Armstrong had achieved qualified success, but the Indian combatants, whose primary concern was to avoid loss of life, could also claim victory. As we will see, Europeans and Indians often defined victory by different standards.[2]

European "invasions" of America

During the seventeenth and eighteenth centuries, the period covered by this study, Indians in eastern North America conducted a protracted and often successful military resistance against what many historians now perceive to have been a series of European invasions of North America.[3] Armed resistance against English settlement began in Virginia in 1607 and ended in the "Old Northwest" only after the defeat of an allied British–Indian confederate army by United States General William Henry Harrison at the battle of the Thames

1. *Seventeenth-century eastern North America*

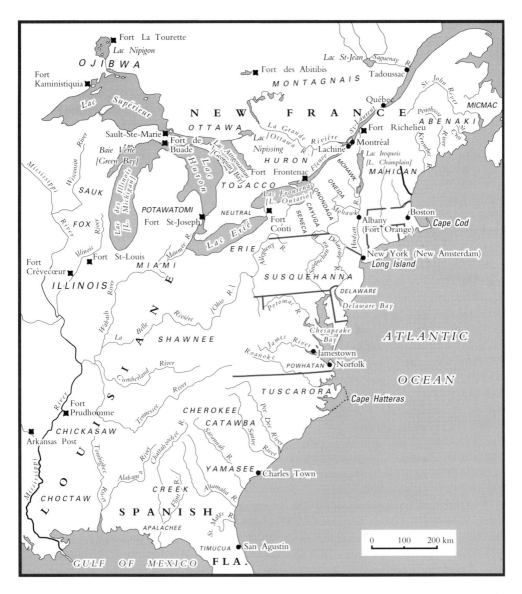

Fallen Timbers in 1813. During this time, Europeans fought Europeans for the control of an American "empire". Britons, French, Spaniards, Canadians, and Americans became involved in conflicts which increasingly resembled the conventional war practised in Europe. Indians fought on all sides of these conflicts for reasons of their own and played varying roles of central and marginal importance. However, when Europeans confronted Indians, it was usually within the context of frontier warfare, a kind of war in which the Indians were accomplished masters and in which the Europeans were frequently at a disadvantage. European officers found that if they were to be successful against Indian adversaries, it was best to have Indian allies. In retrospect, given the apparent European superiority in numbers, material and technology, it may seem surprising that Indian resistance lasted as long as it did. Europeans soon found that their apparent advantages did not guarantee success. They had a lot to learn about the ability of stateless native people to resist the advance of the most powerful, expansionist European empires.

Most successful in dealing with the Indians diplomatically and militarily were those who made an effort to understand them. But Europeans often avoided such an effort when they relegated the Indians to the status of "savages", a people without government, laws, social mores and cultural values. European conquest could thus be justified as a triumph of civilization over barbarism. Not surprisingly, Europeans tried to comprehend the Indians within a European context. New England Protestants' understanding of their Indian neighbours was inevitably influenced by the religious struggles of the seventeenth century. A "godless" people outside the law of European society was automatically suspect. Still worse from the point of view of these Protestants were those Indians who came under the influence of Jesuit missionaries. Their satanic nature was thus confirmed. This perspective was central to the development of Protestant Anglo-American historiography, which celebrated English conquest and settlement as the inevitable and benign march of progress. This tradition reached its apogee in the nineteenth century in the works of Francis Parkman and held sway among professional historians at least through the first half of the twentieth.[4] Indeed, despite the best efforts of revisionists, Parkman will probably influence the American popular historical tradition for some time to come.

Canadian writers have found Parkman's perspective rather less satisfactory. But they too have often defined the Indians from the standpoint of their own culture without dealing with the Indians on their own terms.[5] Historians of both societies have often written to advance their own agendas. Much of the history written by the heirs of a European conquest inevitably celebrates it and justifies it. The North American Indians, losers and lacking academic historians of their own, were denied a voice.

Recent scholarship on these issues has occurred within a changed context. Developments such as multiculturalism, the struggle for minority rights, the Native American movement, and the end of the era of European imperialism have challenged the old elites in North American society and the historical tradition that supports them. New scholarly methodologies applying anthropological techniques to historical studies have advanced understanding of and appreciation for the non-literate cultures of the past. Indian peoples have thus emerged as three-dimensional people to be understood within their own context and upon their own terms, free from the traditional stereotypes of noble or ignoble savage, images refracted through the lenses of European culture. Although the new context is hardly free from bias (the challenge to the old elites being central to the current "culture wars" in North America), the nature of the Indian resistance to the European conquest of North America is the subject of more informed and sympathetic investigation.[6]

This is a story that goes far beyond military history. Military conflict was only one aspect of a clash of cultures and the adaptation of one culture to another. Military institutions do not exist in a vacuum; European–Indian military conflict was but one element in a complex set of contacts and exchanges between the peoples of North America. Indeed, war may have been the least important vehicle of European conquest. Epidemic diseases killed far more native people than did muskets or cannon and undermined the resistance of many tribes. Estimates of the North American Indian population in 1492 range from 1 to 12 million. Most scholars despairing at incomplete demographic data seem to split the difference between the two figures. The prevailing view is that waves of European epidemic diseases devastated Indian communities to the extent that European soldiers engaged in something of a mopping-up action. Although the relationship between disease, the cataclysmic collapse of Indian population levels and European conquest has recently been questioned, individual cases seem to bear it out.[7] For example, estimates of the New England Indian population before European colonization range from 72,000 to 126,000–144,000. By 1670, on the eve of King Philip's War, according to one estimate that number had been reduced to 8,600. Europeans suffered from disease too, but by 1670 their number was over 50,000.[8] The populations of both the Hurons of modern Ontario and the Iroquois of northern New York were cut in half by epidemic diseases by 1640. Among the Great Lakes Indians in the late seventeenth and early eighteenth centuries there were population declines ranging from 25 to 90 per cent. A visitor to the Carolina Piedmont at the beginning of the eighteenth century found the remains of whole towns destroyed by smallpox. It was simply the most recent in a wave of epidemics which had beset the region from the earliest contacts with the Spanish in the sixteenth century.[9] As

7

will become evident, population disparities contributed to European–Indian conflict and to the ultimate success of white conquest.

Disease paved the way for non-military agents of conquest. The arrival of Jesuit missionaries in the Huron country in 1634 coincided with the outbreak of a series of epidemics that reduced the population by half in six years. Jesuit immunities appeared to demonstrate the power of their religious message when Indian rituals and medical practices proved helpless in the face of disease. Jesuit missionaries successfully capitalized on a people weakened and demoralized by these disasters. Puritan missionaries in New England found the majority of their converts among those Indians most stricken by epidemics. The Massachuset tribe, reduced from 24,000 to 750 by 1631, provided many "praying Indians", while the Narragansetts, unaffected by the epidemics, remained resistant to the appeal of Christianity and even experienced a revival of native religious belief.[10] Both Protestant and Catholic missionaries conducted campaigns to alter Indian cultural life to conform with European practices. The Jesuits were willing to go farther afield than their Protestant rivals and were more skilful in adapting their message to the native cultural context, but as one scholar has observed:

> The Jesuits' reputation for tolerance and willingness to adapt Christianity to the traditions of their converts is deserved, but only in comparison with other seventeenth century missionaries. At bottom, they and other Catholic priests followed in less extreme form the doctrine that English ministers called "civility before sanctity": only when Indians shed their native ways and adopted European customs could they truly become Christians.[11]

While missionaries transformed the lives of some Indian peoples, they created deep divisions in communities which were riven between converts and traditionalists. Consensus decision-making processes were undermined, elders lost influence, and the community lost the ability to respond to crises with unity. Factions among the Hurons in the wake of Jesuit missionary success sapped their ability to meet the Iroquois onslaught of the 1640s which destroyed their independence as a people.[12] For a variety of reasons French missionary activity among the Iroquois after 1667 was less successful in registering permanent gains, but their influence also resulted in divided communities. Conflicts between non-Christians and Christians in the late 1660s and the 1670s resulted in a large emigration of the latter to settle in the mission community of Caughnawaga in the St Lawrence River Valley.[13] Catholic Iroquois would prove valuable allies of the French in decades to come.

Jesuit missionaries possessed greater leverage with the Hurons than the Iroquois because they controlled the former's access to European trade goods and firearms. The Iroquois had alternative sources. During the seventeenth century, the eastern Indians of North America had become part of the worldwide economic system, a fact that transformed native economies, introduced material conveniences such as metal tools and woolen blankets, and rendered the Indians dependent upon European commercial policies and market forces. Indian rivalries and Indian–European relations became governed by the European demand for furs. One scholar argues that the fur trade was by its nature an unequal exchange which extracted wealth from the margins, the North American forests, to the benefit of the European centre.[14] This may have been true in macroeconomic terms, but clearly many Indians saw profit in the trade. While unscrupulous white traders sometimes used alcohol to take advantage of their Indian partners, other Indian traders showed that they had a shrewd idea of the value of their wares. Furthermore, the extent to which the trade disrupted the traditional Indian way of life seems to have varied. The leading expert on the Algonquian peoples of the Great Lakes Region finds that by the late seventeenth and early eighteenth centuries, the trade had caused little disruption of the native subsistence system. European items had more symbolic than material significance and the trade itself was conducted by the French more from diplomatic than commercial motives.[15] However, Indian economies which were deeply integrated into the fur trade were vulnerable to market changes. Demand for beaver pelts collapsed after 1660, causing a decline in the value of wampum, a fur-backed shell currency. As will be demonstrated in Chapter Four, southern New England Indians were pressured to sell land to pay their debts to English merchants. Tensions over land sales were a principal cause of the outbreak of King Philip's War in 1675. Indian peoples responded to the trade in ways which reflected their unique contexts. The Hurons, who had long traded with the hunting peoples of the north, were natural traders. The Iroquois, surrounded by peoples with similar economies, had little experience with trade and turned to war to increase their access to furs.[16]

The most baleful product of European commercial contact with North American Indians was alcoholism. Indeed, the Indian addiction to alcohol may be called America's first drug epidemic. All fair-minded contemporary observers lamented the unusual vulnerability of the Indian peoples to alcohol. The Swedish naturalist Peter Kalm believed that brandy had killed more Indians than war or smallpox: "A man can hardly have a greater desire of a thing than the Indians have for brandy. I have heard them say that by drinking brandy was a desirable and an honorable death; and indeed it was a very common thing to kill themselves by drinking this liquor to excess."[17] Within this context, the military dimension of the European "invasion" seems rather insignificant. Weakened as they were, Indian warriors fought their adversaries almost to a standstill in eastern North America nearly to the end of the eighteenth century.

This contest was never simply one of European versus Indian. North American Indians were not a monolithic block. While some tribes relied upon traditional religious practices as a bulwark against the European threat, others converted to Christianity and in varying degrees adopted a European way of life. Christian Indians often served as loyal soldiers in European forces and many non-Christian Indians entered into alliance with Europeans for reasons of their own. Lack of unity was a central weakness of Indian resistance to the expansion of white settlement.

The line between Indian and white settlement was never precise during the period of this study. European and Indian settlements were frequently in close proximity to one another and there was a great deal of peaceful interchange between the two peoples. Commerce and co-operation were as much parts of the European–Indian relationship as was war. Where ownership of land was not at issue, war was not inevitable. This was the case in Canada where Bruce Trigger concludes that "It is significant that not once was there a case of serious or prolonged conflict between Europeans and Indians living within the borders of Canada."[18] Viewed in this light, the traditional concept of the frontier as the advancing edge of civilization against savagery and darkness no longer has meaning. I use the term "frontier" in this work in two senses: first, as the zone in which the two cultures engaged one another in conflict and co-operation, and secondly and more importantly, as a form of warfare which was unconventional in the European sense, but which had its own inherent rules and methods. The Indians were the masters of this form of warfare. "The principles of their military action", observed the frontier veteran John Armstrong, "are rational, and therefore often successful. . . . In vain may we expect success against our adversaries without taking a few lessons from them".[19] Successful frontier soldiers did learn these lessons and, when they did, had indeed crossed a military frontier.

This book will also be concerned with the European soldiers who served as both opponents and allies of the Indians. They have been subject to caricature as often as have been the Indians. American nationalists have contrasted the image of the heroic frontier rifleman with that of the obstinate, inflexible, road-bound European regular. This is a stereotype as unconvincing as that of the "noble" or "ignoble savage". Professional European officers could and did learn to fight in the forest. Colonel Henry Bouquet, a Swiss officer in the British service recognized that his regulars were at a disadvantage in the woods:

without a certain Number of Woodsmen, I cannot think it Advisable to employ regulars in the Woods against Savages, as they cannot procure any Intelligence, and are open to Continual Surprises, nor can they Pursue at any distance their Enemy when they have Routed them, and should they have the Misfortune to be Defeated the whole would be destroyed if above one day's March from a Fort.[20]

Yet Bouquet proved himself to be an able frontier commander. His force, consisting mainly of regulars, defeated an Indian army in the bitter two-day battle of Bushy Run in August 1763. Similarly, the American General Anthony Wayne, who often expressed contempt for frontier riflemen, won the climactic battle of Fallen Timbers in 1794 by means of a bayonet attack.

When properly led, and used in the right combination with experienced woodland irregulars, European or Indian, the regulars were formidable troops. As in the case of Fort Bull, they could be counted upon to attack strongly defended positions and to follow orders unquestioningly. Troops recruited in the English colonies, referred to as Provincial by the British, usually possessed no special aptitude for forest warfare and experienced many of the same difficulties as their red-coated brothers in arms.

During the course of the seventeenth and eighteenth centuries, warfare in North America became increasingly Europeanized and, despite their formidable qualities as warriors, the role of the Indians became marginal to the outcome of the major conflicts. Seventeenth-century wars were small in scale compared to the great struggles of the eighteenth century: the War of the Spanish Succession (Queen Anne's War), the War of the Austrian Succession (King George's War), the Seven Years War (French and Indian War), and the War of American Independence. European settlers introduced muskets, cannon, and sophisticated fortification techniques into North America in the seventeenth century, but technology provided them with no special advantages over their Indian opponents in the conflicts of the era. During the eighteenth century, the scale of warfare dramatically expanded and European governments proportionally increased their commitment of military resources to the continent. The most important engagements of the climactic duel between Britain and France for North America in the Seven Years War involved operations against fortresses dominating strategic communications lines. Artillery, artillery fortification, siege warfare techniques, big gun warships on interior lakes, large armies of regulars dispatched directly from Europe, complex supply services, and sophisticated staff officers and engineers combined to transform North American warfare into something more closely resembling its European counterpart.[21] The War of American Independence only accelerated that transformation. This development did not guarantee that

Indian resistance to the expansion of European settlement would be over-come. The final defeat of resistance in 1813 was based upon a number of factors. First was the establishment of a unified United States and the reluc-tance of Great Britain to contest militarily American expansion into the Northwest. Second was divisions within the Indian confederacy itself and, third, was the emergence of able American commanders who understood and appreciated the strengths of Indian warriors and who developed the appro-priate combination of troops and tactics.[22]

"Civilization" versus "savagery"

Traditionally, the moral context of frontier warfare has been portrayed as a conflict between civilization and savagery.[23] Recent scholarship has rejected that stereotype and has sought to understand certain Indian practices such as scalping, torture and cannibalism, so repellent to Europeans, within the context of native American culture. One important conclusion is that not all Indian societies engaged in all of those practices and that Indian attitudes towards them were subject to change. Revisionists also point to frequent European violations of their own moral standards. Some traditional frontier heroes have lost their lustre and some villains their edge. Thus George Rogers Clark, the famous warrior of the Northwest frontier during the American War of Independence has emerged in recent historical writing as a coarse, brutal, ambitious figure whose violent acts were at least as reprehensible as those of his Indian opponents defending their homes and hunting grounds.[24] Clark adopted the Indian style of war as his own and did not hesitate to scalp Indian prisoners within sight of an enemy garrison to hasten its surrender. James T. Axtell has written that Clark's "exploits in the streets of Vincennes added a chilling new chapter in scalping's long and bloody history".[25]

The issue of moral responsibility in war is timeless and complex. Current guidelines rest largely upon historical precedent and thus the behavior of men such as Léry, Robert Rogers, and George Rogers Clark have contemporary relevance. Indeed Clark himself and his superior, Governor Thomas Jefferson of Virginia, accused Clark's opponent, the British commander Henry Hamilton, of war crimes in language suggestive of the Nuremberg charges. Moral issues present a special challenge for the historian. Throughout Western history one may point to certain moral traditions that have commanded respect in wartime, for example the belief that prisoners and non-combatants should not be harmed. Failure to observe such conventions, such as Henry V's order to kill the French prisoners at Agincourt, alarmed contemporaries as well as historians in succeeding generations. Perhaps these values transcend specific cultures and are common to all humanity. That is certainly implied by the Nuremberg principles. Nevertheless, historians must also be aware of context and the need to avoid anachronism. Recent scholars have been careful to evaluate Indian military behavior within the context of native American culture. This is a fair approach and one which I shall adopt. Unfortunately, some revisionists have rescued the Indians from traditional caricatures only to demonize their European opponents. It is perhaps easier to assume that, unlike native Americans, seventeenth- and eighteenth-century Europeans shared modern Western moral values and to judge them harshly when they departed from them. But I believe that the historian, if he renders moral judgement, should be sensitive to two levels: his own moral sensibility and that of the historical actors who inhabited very different moral universes. We cannot understand the actions of New England Puritans or southern slave owners until we attempt to see the world through their eyes. We must be aware of their moral standards and the extent to which they conformed to or departed from them.

The issue of moral responsibility in frontier warfare becomes even more complex when one considers that there was no clear line between European and Indian cultures. The story is as much one of cultural exchange as one of conflict. Thus, how is one to differentiate between the behaviour of Christian and non-Christian Indians? Presumably, conversion to Christianity meant that Indians had acquired Christian moral values. But many Indians may have accepted Christianity as an accommodation with a superior power while retaining the fundamental beliefs of their native culture which shaped their conduct in war. By what standard should they be held accountable? Similarly, successful European frontier warriors such as Clark adopted the Indian way of war without conceding their European identity. What is one to make of his practice of scalping opponents?[26] As Michael Walzer has pointed out, war defies the easy application of both moral and strategic judgements. All of the combatants in the frontier wars tried to win but often blundered. Most subscribed to some form of moral standard, but frequently fell short of the mark. These warriors were not saints; rather they were complex human beings, often operating under the extreme emotions of fear and anger. The historian's duty is to understand them before judging them.

Military historians have the luxury of enjoying the study of events which inflicted death and destruction on countless numbers of innocent people. Nevertheless war remains central to the human condition. It does settle things, in this case the control of eastern North America. Had European commanders in the second half of the eighteenth century studied the military history of American warfare in the preceding decades, perhaps they might have settled the issue sooner. Commanders' disregard of costly lessons is one of the disturbing features of the warfare of this period. It demonstrates the practical benefit of military study for military and civilian leaders. In addition, a study of European–Indian conflict suggests that war was not inevitable. European appetite for Indian land no doubt made war between the two peoples difficult to avoid. But European–Indian wars were also struggles between two cultures which often did not understand one another. Indeed, some Indian spiritual leaders at the end of the eighteenth century believed that whites and Indians were the products of two different creations. Often Indians did not recognize white enemies as fully human. Whites who attempted to impose "civilization" on "savage" peoples gave the latter something to fight about, whether or not land was at stake. Perhaps, if the two peoples had understood one another better, there would have been fewer innocent victims of the struggle for North America. This suggests, even to a very traditional military historian, the importance of multicultural studies as an agent of humanity in war.

This is a study of warfare between Europeans (principally Anglo-Americans and French-Canadians) and Native Americans for the mastery of northeastern North America in the period 1675–1815. Conflict between Europeans and North American Indians began before this time and continued afterwards. Spanish soldiers fought southern Indians, often with little success, in the sixteenth and seventeenth centuries. English settlers in Virginia engaged in a desperate struggle for survival with the Powhatan Indians during the early decades of the seventeenth century. In the same period, the French were drawn into the "beaver wars" between the Five Nations Iroquois and another Iroquoian people, the Hurons. It is unclear whether the latter suffered more from their Five Nations enemies or their French allies. By 1675, Europeans and Indians had great experience in fighting one another and in working together as military allies. This legacy is acknowledged in the course of my work, particularly in the thematic chapters.

My narrative begins with King Philip's War of 1675–6, not only because it was perhaps the most famous and decisive English–Indian war of the seventeenth century, but also because it was the first major war in which the Indians matched their European opponents in firearms. The Indian way of war had been evolving since the first encounters with Europeans equipped with firearms. Indian battlefield tactics had been transformed and the Indians had eagerly sought to provide themselves with firearms appropriate for forest warfare. This evolution was virtually complete by 1675; forms of frontier warfare were established that lasted until Indian resistance was crushed during the War of 1812. The two-year King Philip's War was thus a microcosm of a larger conflict pursued over 140 years. English advantages in population and material resources were temporarily nullified by superior Indian tactics and marksmanship. New Englanders' expectations of a quick and easy seizure of Indian lands were dashed as the Indians gained the military initiative. However, Indian societies lacked the material resources for prolonged war, and political divisions among Indian peoples undermined their resistance to European conquest. Without a European ally, Indians could be defeated by attrition. On the other hand, European allies in the wars of the eighteenth century provided Native American warriors with material aid and sanctuary, but exposed them to the uncertainties of European diplomacy. Europeans, however, found their military institutions sadly lacking when faced with the challenge of frontier warfare. In King Philip's War, as in subsequent conflicts, some European commanders incorporated Indian allies into their forces and adapted to the Indian way of war. More often European military institutions, the product of European culture and society, proved to be insufficiently flexible to meet the challenges of the frontier.

This study is organized in thematic and narrative chapters. Chapter Two will consider the "Indian way of war" and Chapter Three will deal with the European military experience as it was applied to North America in this period. A thematic approach requires generalization which may not always apply to particular circumstances. For that reason the study is limited to the period 1675–1815 and focused principally upon the northeast. Narrative chapters dealing with specific conflicts are intended to provide a balance to the general themes explored in Chapters Two and Three. Two of the narrative chapters focus on specific wars: King Philip's War and the Indian dimension of the American War of Independence which may be considered a parallel struggle for independence by Native Americans. A wider-angle lens opens chapters on the French and Indian wars and on the Indians' final battles for independence in the period 1783–1815, but the narrative is consistent throughout and illustrates the recurrent themes. The drama and tragedy of this "140 Years War" is as powerful as the Hundred Years War described by Froissart.

Chapter Two

The Indian way of war

Indian discipline

"I have often heard the British officers call the Indians undisciplined savages, which is a capital mistake – as they have all the essentials of discipline. . . . Could it be supposed that undisciplined troops could defeat Generals Braddock, Grant, etc.?"[1] This was the conclusion of James Smith (1737–1812), a man with great experience in the Indian way of war. Captured by the Indians while performing road work for General Edward Braddock's army, he was present at Fort Duquesne to witness the Indians torture the Anglo-American prisoners taken after their defeat at the Monongahela. Smith himself was roughly handled by his captors, but survived to be adopted into an Indian family. There his aversion was softened by the warmth and kindness extended by his new family and his growing admiration for the Indian way of life. He praised their "living in love, peace and friendship together, without disputes. In this respect, they shame those who profess Christianity."[2] Smith's account of Indian life in his captivity memoir evokes the ideal world of the "noble savage", one in which stealing and cheating were unknown unless introduced by white influence. The portrait is completed by his affectionate recollection of his adopted brother, the wise and benevolent Tecaughretanego, who resembles a woodland Socrates.[3]

Smith was not so taken with Indian life to pass up a chance to escape in 1759. He did not become a "white Indian", one of those captives who voluntarily remained with their new families and fully adopted their way of life. He returned to white society, gained prominence, and led military expeditions against the Indians. To a degree his account represents a critique of his own culture and his society's military conventions. He had a low opinion of British officers in the woods and believed that Americans had won

17

their freedom from Britain by adopting the Indian way of war. In Smith's memoir, the image of the Indian as a "noble savage" becomes a metaphor for American independence.[4]

Smith's discussion of Indian military discipline is shaped by a nationalistic bias, but is nevertheless informed and insightful. He portrays it as the reverse of British army tactics which might achieve victory on the fields of Flanders, but were hopeless in the woods. His description of Indian discipline manifests all of the qualities advocated by eighteenth-century British military reformers, particularly those interested in the development of light infantry.[5] "Is it not the best discipline that has the greatest tendency to annoy the enemy and save their own men?"[6] In contrast to European armies, Indian discipline was founded on individual honour rather than corporal punishment; leaders were chosen according to merit based on courage and experience instead of privilege or purchase. Commanders were concerned to save their men's lives and believed that victory did not justify unnecessary sacrifice. There was no disgrace in retreating to await a more favourable occasion for battle. Indian leaders taught their men to move in scattered order and take advantage of the ground, to surround the enemy or to avoid being surrounded. They practiced running and marksmanship and they became accustomed to endure hunger and hardship with patience and fortitude. While avoiding unnecessary casualties, the Indians were a martial people, ready to sell their lives dearly in defence of their homes. Smith believed that these were moral qualities which provided the Indians with the means to oppose European enemies who possessed seemingly overwhelming advantages in numbers, material and state power.[7]

The Indian warrior's moral advantage was enhanced by his physical endurance, which only the hardiest Europeans could equal. Captives who survived Indian raids often perished on the brutal marches to Indian villages sometimes as far away as Canada or Ohio. They were expected to maintain the pace of warriors who could march 30 to 50 miles in a day, frequently without food. One of the most famous captives, Mrs Mary Rowlandson, taken in a raid on Lancaster, Mass. on 16 February 1676, was forced to carry a wounded child through the snow. An Indian threatened to kill the child if she did not keep up. The only food available on this march was broth made from a horse's leg. She found that the Indians could exist on diets more demanding than those of modern military survival courses: acorns, ground nuts, horse guts and ears, skunks, tree bark, rattlesnakes, and extracts from old bones. Despite these hardships and the death of her child, Rowlandson survived and was reunited in captivity with a daughter and son. She was taken into an Indian family who did not treat her badly as long as she did her share of the work. Her comment on her experience perhaps says as much about Indian values as it does about her own religion: "*It is good for me that I have been afflicted.* The Lord has shown me the vanity of these outward things."[8]

Robert Rogers believed that the Indians

> have no stated rules of discipline, or fixed methods of prosecuting a war; they make attacks in as many different ways as there are occasions on which they make them, but generally in a very secret skulking, under-hand manner, in flying parties that are equipped for the purpose, with thin light dress, generally consisting of nothing more than a shirt, stockings and mogasins, and sometimes almost naked.[9]

Indians did not need "stated rules" such as those provided by eighteenth-century European military handbooks. The ability to exploit particular conditions was a hallmark of experienced warriors trained in the Indian way of war from as early as the age of 12 and kept honed by frequent participation in raiding parties. The rigid and inflexible discipline associated with the European armies of the era was a means by which inexperienced and unmartial peasants might be turned into soldiers. This was hardly necessary for Indian warriors who possessed the skills and discipline of modern commandos and special forces, and who were capable of adapting to whatever situation they encountered. They were masters of the "secret, skulking" war: the raid, the ambush, and the retreat. As their clothing indicates, they were practical. Many whites came to realize that Indian clothing was superior to European uniforms and shoes. General John Forbes, leader of the march on Fort Duquesne in 1758, ordered many of his men to dress in the Indian fashion: "I must confess in this country, wee must comply and learn the Art of Warr, from Ennemy Indians or anyone else who have seen the Country and Warr carried on in itt."[10]

Many frontier commanders such as George Rogers Clark adopted Indian dress and moccasins. The latter were especially prized because they could be dried more quickly than shoes. Europeans turned many Indian technologies to their own use in frontier warfare. Light birchbark canoes were excellent vessels for men moving quickly on inland waterways interrupted by frequent portages. The seventeenth-century Massachusetts Indian superintendent Daniel Gookin observed that one man could carry a five-passenger canoe on his back for several miles.[11] Snowshoes made feasible deep winter raids such as Léry's. Maize rations helped sustain troops on these operations.[12] Indians seem to have been able to turn any material to practical use in an emergency. Mary Rowlandson's captors eluded their English pursuers by crossing a river on rafts made from brush. Her would-be rescuers were forced to give up the chase. On the other hand, Indians quickly came to prize the products of European iron-working industries. These trade goods which transformed the lives of many Indians included tools such as knives, chisels, drills and hammers. Iron hatchets were employed as both tools and weapons. Indians with access to weapons such as metal arrowheads often gained military advantage over those who still relied on flint and stone.[13]

Firearms

Samuel de Champlain is generally credited with introducing the Mohawks to firearms in 1609; by the end of the century the eastern Indians of North America were well supplied with muskets. There is some debate about why the Indians came to prefer flintlock muskets to the native self-bow.[14] Early seventeenth-century matchlock guns, fired when the powder was ignited by a slow burning fuse or match, were unreliable, inaccurate, cumbersome and slow. In wet weather they were almost useless. Bruce Trigger has written "that the possession and use of guns conferred a military advantage on tribes has never been doubted. Yet the practical advantage of a cumbersome musket over a metal tipped arrow is doubtful. The real power of the gun in Indian warfare appears to have been psychological; its noise and mysterious operation added to the terrors of foes and to the confidence of those who used them."[15] However, Trigger's work concludes with 1660, a time at which self-igniting flintlocks began to replace the matchlock. The flintlock became the preferred weapon of many warriors. Nevertheless, a modern expert who has tested the flintlock against the bow has found the latter to be superior as a missile weapon in almost every respect.[16] Flintlock muskets were inaccurate single-shot weapons which were difficult to load in any position other than standing. While the musket's discharge made a frightening noise, this was hardly consistent with a skulking way of war, and the smoke emitted by black gunpowder exposed the musketeer's position. One reason that Europeans may have converted from bows to firearms was that it was easier to train a new recruit to become a musketeer than to become a skilled archer. But Indian boys were accustomed to the use of bows from an early age. Why then did Indian warriors convert?

The eighteenth-century military writer Comte de Guibert offered the example of the Indians as proof of the superiority of firearms to other missile weapons "such as slings, bows javelins lanced from the hand, etc. look with what eagerness the savages in America have, in spite of the inconvenience of noise, quitted these last to adopt our muskets; for men who exist by hunting and which exercise is alone their occupation, this is no fictitious inconvenience."[17] Patrick Malone believes that the New England Indians saw that bullets travelled faster than arrows and took a more direct route to the target, thus making the musket easier to aim. In addition, bullets were less likely to be deflected by brush and were more damaging on impact. Indians were skilled at dodging arrows, but this was almost impossible in the case of bullets. Muskets could also be loaded to fire several small bullets with one shot making it easier to strike the target.[18] During the eighteenth century lighter and more usable weapons became available for hunting and woodland warfare. European officers noted the Indian preference for the short-barrelled and lightweight fusil.[19] In the second half of the century, muskets with rifled barrels which enhanced accuracy and increased range became common on the frontier. European soldiers often dismissed rifles as being slower to fire and more fragile than standard smooth-bore muskets which could be fitted with bayonets. But rifles were marksmen's weapons especially suited for hunting and the Indian way of war. In the mid-1760s one frontier veteran became so concerned about the number of rifles acquired by the Ohio and Great Lakes Indians that he "submitted if it would not be a public benefit to stop making and vending any more of them in the colonies, nor suffer any to be imported".[20]

By the end of the seventeenth century Indian warriors had adopted firearms as their principal weapon. This did not mean that they entirely neglected the bow, for it retained its value as a stealth weapon. Nevertheless, its use in combat was sufficiently rare to prompt special mention. On 23 July 1757, a band of Indians attacked an Anglo-American woodcutting party near Fort Edward in upper New York with bows and arrows. "It is thought that the Indians Design was to fire upon the Guards of the Carpenters with their Arrows to prevent Noise, and so more easily carry off the workmen. . . ."[21] Nevertheless, major actions such as the destruction of General Braddock's army in 1755 were executed with firearms.

Furthermore, not only did Indians adopt these European weapons as their own, they soon demonstrated a superiority in their use. Indians drew no sharp distinction between hunting and warfare and therefore trained to achieve accurate marksmanship in both. From an early age, Indian men spent their lives in the acquisition of these skills so that they became second nature. In contrast, the European peasantry were disarmed by law in most countries. When recruited as soldiers, they were not trained to fire at marks, but rather in unaimed volley fire. Destructive enough at close quarters on European battlefields, this method of fire was of little use in the woods. European settlers in North America brought with them the European way of war. While they possessed firearms for self-defence, they remained for the most part an agrarian people with little skill in hunting or marksmanship. As Malone observes,

"Unfortunately, our popular image of sharp-shooting frontiersmen is questionable even for the early nineteenth-century settlers of Kentucky and is far removed from the reality of the seventeenth-century colonists of New England."[22] Ironically, North American Indians not only turned firearms to their own use, but became the most formidable marksmen in the seventeenth- and eighteenth-century world. The challenge that this presented to European soldiers cannot be overestimated.

The Indian commitment to firepower is even more striking in the context of the eighteenth-century European theoretical debate over shock versus fire. Many European officers believed that infantry firearms did relatively little damage and expressed a preference for attacks with cold steel. Generals such as Maurice de Saxe and, early in his career, Frederick the Great advocated advancing upon the enemy with shouldered weapons. The Sieur de Folard urged the reintroduction of the pike and the adoption of a military formation resembling the Macedonian phalanx. Folard had many disciples; his advocacy of the column in preference to the line (the natural formation for volley fire) and the *arme blanche* would influence French military thought and practice through the Napoleonic wars and beyond. These views may be considered an admission that French infantry lacked effective fire discipline (some believed it to be contrary to the national spirit). However, there were certainly concrete examples of battles won by shock over fire in the eighteenth century, most notably the exploits of Charles XII of Sweden and Prince Charles Edward Stuart. Within this context the Indian practice of aimed fire seems to represent a tactical advance over the best of European thought and technique.[23]

One scholar who has studied the battlefield tactics of late eighteenth-century northeastern Indians finds them more sophisticated than those of their European opponents. Indian warriors did not simply hide behind trees, but exploited available cover to conduct moving fire on the enemy. Indians were trained to outflank their opponents and usually quickly enveloped them in a horseshoe formation. On the other hand, they seldom completely surrounded the enemy, perhaps preferring to allow them to withdraw rather than to force a desperate struggle with high casualties on both sides. Indians also understood how to conduct orderly advances and retreats "blackbird fashion" in which warriors with loaded weapons covered those whose guns required recharging. They also were able to seize the psychological moment, charging from cover with war whoops that were likely in themselves to terrify all but the most seasoned soldiers. In short, eighteenth-century Indian tactics resembled those of modern infantry more than did those of their European adversaries.[24]

The Indians' conversion to firepower meant a dependence upon European suppliers for arms and ammunition. If Indian–European warfare had been a simple conflict between two monolithic blocks, this would have been a fatal dependency. Indeed, colonial governments often sought to prevent arms sales to Indians. But the situation was far too complex to render such regulations effective. Not only did French, Dutch, Spanish, and English colonial governments pursue different policies with regard to arms sales, but the English colonies themselves often did not co-operate effectively. Arms were an economic as well as a security issue, for they were an important commodity of the fur trade. The emergence of wampum as a means of exchange also facilitated the trade in arms. Furthermore, while it was clearly desirable to deprive hostile Indian warriors of firearms, it was equally desirable to arm one's allies. Indeed, failure to provide arms and ammunition could very well mean the loss of an Indian ally, thus creating a more serious threat. These complex economic and political conditions meant that the Indians of eastern North America were well supplied with firearms by the end of the seventeenth century.[25] Those who have followed modern attempts to regulate the international arms trade will no doubt find this story familiar.

Firearms require extensive maintenance and repair and thus presented the Indians with a new technological challenge. On the whole, native artisans adapted well. During the seventeenth century, New England Indians acquired the art of casting bullets and making gunflints. There is evidence that during King Philip's War Indian blacksmiths became proficient in the repair of muskets and in assembling them from parts.[26] On the other hand, gunpowder manufacture was an extremely difficult procedure in the seventeenth and eighteenth centuries, one which required considerable concentrations of capital and technological expertise. Indian craftsmen could become gunsmiths, but gunpowder was the product of an industry beyond the reach of Indian societies. While weapons could be repaired and re-used, gunpowder was an expendable and perishable commodity which only Europeans could supply. This was a key area of Indian military vulnerability. Tribes cut off from their ammunition supply could quickly experience a crisis. For example, during the spring of 1764 Colonel Bouquet received reports that the Ohio Indians were so short of ammunition that they were reduced to hunting with bows and arrows. These shortages coupled with a smallpox outbreak presaged the waning of the Indian uprising known as Pontiac's Rebellion.[27]

The Indian way of war was also influenced by the introduction of artillery to North America. Cannon generally remained a European monopoly, rendering traditional Indian palisaded fortifications vulnerable and frontal assaults on European forts suicidal. One Indian tribe did have access to cannon and demonstrated an ability to use them. In 1663 the Susquehannock Indians in the Delaware valley withstood a siege by a rival Five Nations army in a fort equipped with Swedish cannon served by Marylander gunners. In 1675 100

Susquehannock warriors defended their fort against 750 Virginia and Maryland militia. The militia declined an assault on a position equipped with cannon and fortified in the contemporary European style with earthen walls, bastions to provide crossfire, ditch, and strong external palisades. They chose to starve out the defenders instead, but the Indians escaped after seven weeks. "The Susquehannock had expertly used a European fort and weapons and defended themselves bravely by the martial standards of either civilization."[28]

Most Indian defences were not so well equipped. An Indian village surrounded by a large European force could become a death-trap, as was experienced by the Pequots of New England in 1637 and the neighboring Narragansetts in 1675. Some Indian peoples begin to modify their circular palisaded defences along European lines for greater security, but most abandoned their villages and scattered to the woods on the approach of a European army.[29] European commanders had to content themselves with burning the villages, which inflicted relatively little harm and with destroying crops and food reserves, which inflicted considerably more. Such hardships seldom impaired the Indians' ability to retaliate by means of ambushes and raids against white settlements. As we have seen, Indians would seldom risk a frontal assault on a fortified position. Settlers fortunate enough to gain the security of a blockhouse or stockade were relatively safe from raiders who lacked cannon. But conditions in these crowded and primitive defences were often appalling and those who ventured forth did so at great peril. Many settlers could not sit idly by and watch the destruction of their homes and farms and often sortied into disastrous ambushes, as did parties from neighbouring communities rushing to their relief. Regular soldiers with little at stake could sit out an Indian siege, but settlers could not always afford such patience. Even regulars were vulnerable to surprises and ruses, such as the seizure of the fort at Michilimackinac in 1763 by Indians pursuing a lacrosse ball. Indians also attacked forts with flaming arrows and carts loaded with combustibles. At Fort Presqu'Isle in 1763, they undermined the wall by tunnelling. But direct assault or prolonged siege warfare in the European style was not the Indian way of war. They were at a disadvantage whenever they were forced to fight in such conditions.

Firearms transformed the nature of Indian warfare in the seventeenth century. Previous Indian combat seems to have been distinguished by hand-to-hand encounters or exchanges of arrows between large contingents. Casualties seem to have been relatively lower than during succeeding decades. While Indian bows had a higher rate of fire than muskets and were at least equal in range and accuracy, it was possible for skilled warriors to dodge the arrows. Indian wooden armour provided better protection against arrows than against musket balls.[30] Both Europeans and Indians discarded armour in

America when their opponents acquired firearms. European musketeers had many deficiencies, but their volley fire against massed groups of men on open ground could be murderous. Seventeenth-century Indian peoples, faced with dwindling populations, could ill afford a form of warfare with a high butcher's bill. The "skulking way of war" was the logical response to the new conditions.[31] Firearms caused a significant shift in power relationships among Indian peoples. Those who had them were able to establish dominance over have-nots, though, given the widespread availability of guns, these were temporary advantages.[32] By the end of the eighteenth century most Indian peoples seem to have adjusted to the realities of firearms warfare.

Brutality in frontier war

Traditionally, historians have portrayed European–Indian warfare as more brutal than contemporary European conflicts. The Indians received the blame for this state of affairs because they were "savages" who did not recognize European codes of war which sought to maintain humane standards.[33] Thus during the Enlightenment, a period when European warfare was supposedly governed by moderation and restraint, American warfare was said to resemble the barbaric episodes of the Thirty Years War. European–Indian warfare was hard and frequently marred by atrocities against noncombatants. But the traditional picture is a distortion. Eighteenth-century European warfare when conducted against civilians in places such as Corsica or the Scottish highlands was hardly characterized by moderation. As revisionist historians have noted, it was the Europeans who introduced the practices of the Thirty Years War to North America; they needed no lessons from the Indians. Seventeenth-century English settlers also drew upon the recent colonial and military experience gained in Ireland with its legacy of "search and destroy" operations against the indigenous people. The European settlers may have been militarily inept in the new conditions of North American warfare, but they were not innocents. They came from a hard school and, if the conditions of frontier warfare resembled "total war", they were at least as much to blame as the Indians.

Indeed, there is evidence that the Indians were shocked by European violence. During the New England Pequot War of 1637, Connecticut troops and their Indian allies surrounded a palisaded Pequot village on the Mystic River. The Connecticut men unleashed a hail of fire upon the defenders and took the village by storm. Their commander ordered the houses burned and all of the survivors including women and children were put to the sword.

25

Many of the English Indian allies left the field rather than participate in such a slaughter.[34] Traditional Indian warfare practice appears to have avoided such excessive violence. As noted above, combats between Indian armies had resulted in relatively few fatalities. Many Indians seem to have preferred taking their enemies prisoner rather than killing them. The seventeenth-century Iroquois placed capture of prisoners above other war objectives as a means of maintaining population levels, which were under stress from disease and the new level of violence brought on by wars to control the fur trade. This concern with population shaped Iroquois military practice. Their warriors did not take unnecessary risks and were prepared to yield an apparent victory in the field if the cost in life was too high. The emphasis on "skulking war" was consistent with these concerns. Other Indian peoples observed the practice of "mourning war" by which captives were absorbed into the community of their captors.[35] Such unwillingness to accept high casualties differed from the European concept of bravery and discipline; it was one reason why many European officers believed that Indian allies were undependable and lacked staying power. Nevertheless, these attitudes were also inconsistent with the practice of total war.

Indian warfare has often been perceived as barbaric because Indians did not adhere to European military conventions that provided protection for the wounded, prisoners, and noncombatants. Much seventeenth- and eighteenth-century European warfare involved sieges of fortresses and fortified cities, which necessarily exposed civilians to the perils of war. Nevertheless, these sieges were usually prosecuted under widely accepted forms that often spared civilians from the ultimate peril of the sack and the massacre. A garrison that defended itself honourably and that did not impose unnecessary casualties on the besiegers by obstinately defending a hopeless cause was usually awarded generous terms in the capitulation agreement. They were allowed to depart safely and with the full honours of war with "matches lit and bullet in cheek", a phrase surviving the era of the matchlock. Many engagements between whites and Indians during our period involved forms of siege warfare, but as we shall see, Indians for reasons of their own did not accept European conventions. This gave rise to cries of Indian savagery and barbarism, but one should remember that European settlers, as in the case of the massacre of the Pequots, seldom extended the courtesies of war to the Indians.

Indian social and religious customs and the nature of Indian warfare itself determined the moral conduct of Indian warriors. The Indian warrior was primarily the equivalent of the modern commando or guerilla fighter. This is a form of warfare that even today cannot be easily waged according to the principles of international conventions and military codes. For example, commandos may find themselves in possession of prisoners whom they cannot safeguard and whose liberty would endanger them. Would they be justified in killing the prisoners in such circumstances? While lawyers usually respond decisively in the negative, some officers believe that military necessity would justify such an act.[36] Such tensions between principle and practice existed in the eighteenth century. For example, Robert Rogers' superiors issued specific orders for the protection of prisoners. However, when he captured prisoners on a scouting expedition near Ticonderoga in January 1757, he himself gave orders to kill them if attacked by the French garrison. Seven prisoners were "knocked in the head" in the subsequent engagement. William Eyre, Rogers' immediate superior was aware of this incident, but had only praise for Rogers' behaviour when he reported the action to General Abercromby.[37]

Indian warriors were not bound by European codes and conventions and it should not be surprising that they followed the imperatives of military necessity, which many soldiers believe to be the true law of war. Their "skulking way of war" involved many practices that Europeans thought were unfair or inhumane: ambushes, surprises, attacks on civilians and cruel treatment of prisoners. Aimed fire was a controversial issue in itself. Indian sharpshooters had no scruples about aiming at sentries and officers, a practice often frowned upon by European regulars, who regarded it as tantamount to murder. Western Europeans had yet to discard totally their concept of "true war" as manly hand-to-hand conflict. From the time of the *Iliad*, missile weapons had been associated with cowards (as in the case of Paris), barbarians, and the lower classes. By extension, it was one thing to stand up to the blasts of volley fire in battles such as Fontenoy in 1745 where 6,000 British and Hanoverian troops were killed and wounded in a single day; it was quite another when General Edward Braddock, his officers, and men were picked off by unseen marksmen in 1755. The former battle was considered a heroic failure replete with tales of chivalry; the latter was simply an unmitigated disaster, for European arms had been bested by an enemy who did not fight "fairly". Ironically the Indians' mastery of European firearms confirmed their barbarian status in the eyes of their opponents.[38]

For guerrilla fighters such as the Indians, the formal distinctions between soldier and civilian did not exist. Furthermore, the Indian way of war closely paralleled the male Indian's life as a hunter. More than one European observer concluded that the Indian warrior "uses the same stratagems and cruelty as against the wild beasts".[39] Some aspects of Indian cruelty towards captives which included torture, scalping, beheading and cannibalism may be explained by their close association of war with hunting. It appears that seventeenth- and eighteenth-century Indians did not perceive enemies or any non-member of their tribal group or community as fully human. Indeed Indian cosmologies did not award humans a position superior to other creatures. Indian hunters regarded wild animals as creatures deserving respect. They could be killed for food, but they possessed a spiritual nature that required ritual attention. The same attitude applied to human enemies. The Indian approach to war seems to have been deeply ritualistic, seeking support from supernatural powers and purification for the unnatural act of killing. The treatment of prisoners was rooted in these customs, though their sources are not fully understood today. As members of warlike cultures which prized bravery above all things, Indians seem to have had little sympathy for those who surrendered. The harsh treatment that they administered applied equally to the unfortunate Indian and European enemies who fell into their hands. Anger and revenge certainly played a part in some of the most gruesome episodes, but many of the practices which Europeans found shocking seem to have had some ritualistic purpose.[40]

Indians also did not draw the European distinction between war and murder. Richard White in his study of the Great Lakes Indians in this period demonstrates that the Algonquian peoples believed that there were two kinds of killings: those at the hands of enemies and those at the hands of allies. If the killer belonged to an allied group, his family and community expected that the dead would be "covered" with appropriate compensation and ceremony. If this did not occur, the killer became an enemy and a blood feud began. The Indians did not recognize the battlefield as a distinct cultural zone in which killing was sanctioned to the exclusion of other acts of killing which were defined as murder. Europeans believed that murder was a crime which required blood revenge; the Indians believed that killings by enemies demanded such revenge whether in or out of battle. These views obviously complicated each culture's understanding of the military values of the other.[41]

A striking example of the role of ritual in an Indian warrior's life was his relationship with women. As Mary Rowlandson's case suggests, women who fell into Indian hands could expect harsh treatment, but they were rarely sexually molested. Although Bruce Trigger provides a probable example of a public fornication ceremony among Huron warriors preparing to set out on a raid in 1641, most Indian warriors appear to have refrained from sexual intercourse with any woman whether wife or captive in order to avoid the unnatural mix of their warlike state with the woman's life force. They feared that the elaborate web of spiritual protection surrounding the purified warrior would dissolve if this taboo were violated.[42] This was a powerful sanction and apparently more successful than the laws against rape in European military codes. "A girl cannot step into the bushes to pluck a rose without the most imminent risk of being ravished, and they are so little accustomed to these vigorous methods, that they don't bear them with the proper resignation, and of consequence we have the most entertaining courts-martial every day", wrote the British officer Lord Rawdon from Staten Island in August 1776.[43] Many European officers regarded rape as a rather natural occurrence and were disposed to turn a blind eye. The hussar officer and military essayist Turpin de Crissé believed that many rapes were accomplished with voluntary compliance, and his fond recollections of a youthful exploit in a convent so shocked his editor that the latter deleted part of the account.[44] The historian Francis Jennings, a sharp critic of seventeenth- and eighteenth-century European military practices, has suggested an interesting parallel between the code of Indian warriors and medieval chivalry: "The sparing of women and children in Indian warfare fits snugly into the doctrines of chivalry avowed by feudal knights (and even practiced by them when the women and children were of their own religion). The practice was abandoned by the more rational or efficient killing machines organized by the nation-states; chivalry belonged to the knights, and the knights belonged to the Middle Ages."[45]

However, chivalry continued to influence seventeenth- and eighteenth-century officer values and the laws of war.[46] There were some officers, perhaps a minority, who remained true to the spirit of the medieval orders of monkish knights and advocated asceticism as the soldier's way of life. "If you wish to be a warrior", wrote one old soldier, "soyez chaste!"[47] Like the Indians, he believed that chastity was central to the warrior spirit. Furthermore, while Indians were seldom guilty of rape, they were prepared to kill or torture women and children captives who were not useful to them. In short, civilians could expect rough treatment at the hands of warriors of both races.

Ritual also governed other aspects of the Indians' treatment of prisoners. Many captives could expect only death or torture, but others passed through adoption rituals which gave them full membership in the tribal family. Thomas Gist was captured near Fort Duquesne in 1758 and was fortunate to be adopted into an Indian family as a replacement for a dead member. He recalled that:

> I was led into the house where I was to live, there strip'd by a female relation, and then led to the river. There she wash'd me from head to foot, leavin[g] none of the paint itself on me. We then returned to the house, where was gather[ed] all my relations and I believe few men has so many. Such hug[g]ing and kissing from the women and crying for joy, I never saw before. The men acted in a different manner; they looked very serious, shook my hand, and spake little. As soon as this ceremony was over I was clad from head to foot; then there was an interpreter brought to tell me which of my kin was nearest to me. I think they re[c]oned from brother to seventh cousins.[48]

29

The ceremonial bath and ritual greeting had transformed Gist into a full human being in the eyes of his new relatives.

The purpose of the most brutal episodes of torture and cannibalism is not always clear. In some cases torture was clearly revenge for a particular injury that the Indians suffered. For example, the brutal torture of Colonel William Crawford and his followers after their defeat by the Delawares at Sandusky in 1782 was a response to the massacre earlier in the year of a peaceful village of Moravian Indians by undisciplined frontiersmen.[49] Cannibalism may have been a means of acquiring control of a victim's spirit. But not all Indian tribes engaged in cannibalism and some cannibals gave up the practice. Trigger finds that cannibalism was in decline among the Hurons after 1550. The Delawares were never cannibals and expressed contempt for Mohawk "man-eaters". By the mid-eighteenth century many eastern tribes had begun to abandon the practice.[50] Why this change occurred is an interesting, but unanswered question.

Torture of prisoners was rooted in ritual. Among the Algonquian and Iroquoian Indians of the Great Lakes, women played a principal role in determining the fate of prisoners. The Shawnees possessed two sets of female "chiefs", one for war and one for peace. If women of the war society touched a prisoner first, he was burned and eaten.[51] Many Indian societies drew a distinction between male peace chiefs, usually older men of experience and wisdom dedicated to maintaining the harmony of the community, and younger war chiefs who had given themselves to the life of violence. The latter could be expected to act in a violent and brutal fashion. The Ottawa war leader Pontiac committed cruel acts in 1763–4, the most notorious being the drowning of a seven-year-old girl. But with a return to peace, he became known as one who acted humanely. A British officer who met him after the great uprising which bears his name complimented him on having "contrary to the Custom of most of the Indians" treated his prisoners "with the greatest lenity and gentleness".[52] Another formidable Indian leader, Tecumseh, was known for his anti-torture views.[53]

The most notorious Indian practice was, of course, the scalping of their opponents. While there have been allegations that scalping was actually introduced by Europeans, it now seems firmly established that it was a pre-Columbian custom widely spread among American Indians.[54] Scalps were a tangible token of a warrior's bravery. Indeed, women's scalps represented a special sign of prowess by demonstrating that a warrior had raided deep into enemy territory. While scalping itself was brutal and widespread, it was not as savage a practice as beheading and other atrocities committed by both Indians and Europeans. Some scalping victims survived to tell the tale of their experience. In the seventeenth century, European fighters also began to scalp their opponents and the practice continued throughout the period covered by this study. The most troubling aspect of European involvement in scalping was the offer of bounties for enemy scalps. Bounties transformed scalping into a financial transaction and encouraged its spread. Scalps were a way by which governments could be assured that they received a return on the money spent on raiding parties, but how was one to distinguish between friendly and enemy scalps? When Pennsylvania offered scalp bounties in 1756 as part of its war against the Delawares, the experienced Indian diplomat Conrad Weiser warned correctly that this was a menace to friendly Indians whose scalps were more easily procurable.[55] His predictions soon bore fruit and attacks on friendly Indians helped to further inflame an already violent frontier struggle. If Europeans did not begin scalping, they were guilty of taking it to another level of terrorist practice. Some leaders were worried about the moral or, at least, the public relations consequences of scalp bounties. This was especially true during the War of American Independence when each side accused the other of sponsoring scalping. Thus when the American commander at Fort Pitt, Colonel Daniel Brodhead wrote Pennsylvania President Joseph Reed about an offer of scalp bounties, Reed replied that General Washington and the Congress feared that it might become a matter of "national reproach". Nevertheless, Brodhead was given discretion to issue scalp bounties. In the following year, 1780, Pennsylvania formally announced rewards for scalps despite Brodhead's well founded fear that they would antagonize previously friendly Indians.[56] Europeans could turn scalping into an indiscriminate war by body count which played havoc with attempts to establish good Indian relations.

European and Native American allies

These good relations were crucial to any successful frontier military effort. European commanders found Indian allies to be indispensable in the wilderness. The most successful frontier leaders such as Benjamin Church and Robert Rogers included a large number of Indians in their commands, while generals such as Edward Braddock and John Forbes lamented their absence. Few Europeans could equal their woodcraft, scouting skills, and marksmanship. If anything, it was best to employ them as allies rather than to meet them as enemies. Indians were prepared to ally themselves with Europeans for a variety of reasons. Some sought protection against rival Indian nations, while Christian Indians allied themselves with European powers as a means of accommodation. The mission Indians of Canada associated themselves with the French cause through the influence of Jesuit priests who sometimes accompanied them on campaigns. In the late seventeenth century, New England authorities recruited Indian mercenaries whose pay and perquisites were an important source of income at a time when they were losing their lands.[57] Economic considerations sometimes dictated alliances. In the seventeenth century the French allied with the Hurons of modern Ontario against the Iroquois because of the former's strategic position in the fur trade. This ignited a prolonged period of war which devastated the Hurons, weakened the Canadian colony, and undermined Iroquois power and prestige. Indian economic dependence on European trade goods including arms and ammunition often formed the basis of political alliances.

The ability of European powers to deliver such goods was a key to successful relations. These considerations were important during the great wars for the control of the continent. Indians participated in these wars for motives of their own: to defend their families and land, to secure economic benefits from a European ally, to gain prisoners and booty, to gain revenge and the honour of martial prowess. They were not interested in lost causes. European military failure undermined Indian alliances; successful armies strengthened them. The Indians learned to be skeptical of European words. A British officer seeking Indian assistance against the colonists in 1778 asserted that "the Great King's Ships were as numerous as the sand on the sea shore and his Soldiers as numerous as the Leaves on the trees." To this an Indian tartly replied that, if this were so, "he did not imagine but they were sufficient to subdue the Americans without the help of the red people".[58] The Indians realized how dependent their European allies were upon their services in the woods and did not hesitate to remind them of the fact. For example, when one of a party of Delawares accompanying a company of British regulars to the Illinois country in 1764 decided to depart for home, the officers feared that all would desert. The remaining Delawares exploited the situation by threatening to leave if not indulged; "we were oblig'd henceforth to humour them, like so many children, in order to entice them to stay with us".[59] The Indians seem to have amused themselves by teasing the British soldiers in this way; no doubt they would have been surprised to learn that the British thought of *them* as children. Intelligent European leaders who recognized that the Indians only fought as allies as long as it served their own interests reaped the benefits of the skills of these remarkable warriors. Commanders who did not acknowledge these interests soon found themselves deserted.

The most successful European commanders were those who realized that the Indians had much to teach them about forest warfare and who adopted the Indian way of war as their own. These included ranger leaders such as Benjamin Church, Robert Rogers, George Rogers Clark and Canadian officers such as Léry. They did not ask the Indians to behave as European soldiers who unquestioningly obeyed the orders of their superiors. European officers who did not understand the Indians found them to be frustrating and unreliable allies. They complained that the Indians could not stand up to pitched battle, that they were greedy, and that they deserted after the first engagement. General Montcalm's aid, Captain Louis Antoine de Bougainville, was just such a critic. He admitted that the Indian allies possessed indispensable woodland skills, but regarded them not as soldiers, but as an undisciplined and parasitical mob. He was horrified by scenes of cannibalism: "What a scourge! Humanity shudders at being obliged to make use of such monsters. But without them the match would be too much against us."[60] He found the Indian violation of the capitulation terms at Fort William Henry to be an humiliation for French arms. But a recent study suggests that Montcalm's Indian allies saw the capitulation as a betrayal which threatened to deprive them of their rightful prisoners and booty. When the French intervened to protect the Anglo-Americans from an Indian "massacre", Montcalm's western Indian allies and many of the mission Indians concluded that their participation in the war was over.[61]

European–Indian alliances suggest that there was rarely such a thing as a simple European–Indian conflict. Divisions among the Indians facilitated European encroachment into native lands. But there was little in the way of European unity in this period as well. Britain, France, and Spain warred with one another for colonial advantage. English colonies quarrelled with one another and later with their mother country. Indians did not always know what to make of these disputes. The Catawbas of the Carolina Piedmont, accustomed to quarrels between South Carolina and Virginia, entered the Yamassee War of 1715 against South Carolina confident of the Virginians' neutrality and were shocked when the latter came to the aid of their fellow English.[62] As we will see, the Western Abenakis were puzzled by the war of British subjects against their king. Nevertheless, the Indians received a measure of protection from European disunity. Politically the establishment of the United States was a disaster for the Indians of eastern North America.

Because they lacked European political institutions, the Indians have sometimes been regarded as a "stateless" people. This was a convenient way of establishing their barbaric nature and could be used to justify the seizure of their lands by civilized Europeans. But Europeans negotiated alliances and land treaties with someone and in practice recognized that Indians had political institutions of their own. North American Indian political forms defy easy generalization for they varied according to custom and circumstance and over time. Iroquois unity, for example, as fostered by the "Great League of Peace and Power" originating in the fifteenth century, was rooted in efforts to maintain spiritual harmony among autonomous communities. The Iroquois confederacy appeared in response to the external challenges of the seventeenth century. League and confederacy served different purposes, had different leaders, and observed different processes. They seem to have embodied the distinction between "peace chiefs" and "war chiefs".[63] Indian communities are sometimes described as "kinship states", collectives of families and clans centered upon a sense of ethnic identity. Such an identity could be of recent creation. By the end of the seventeenth century many Iroquois were in fact adopted prisoners or the children of prisoners. Ohio Indian towns in the eighteenth century were often constituted from refugees from many tribes. The political characteristic that all communities seem to have shared was the politics of consensus and kinship. Chiefs seldom had power beyond persuasion. In war they often lost control to younger and more violent men. European alliances enhanced the role of some chiefs who could negotiate Indian support for trade goods, but chiefs who acted against the interests of the community were often repudiated. War could create internal crises which ruptured the consensus and harmony of Indian society. Leaders defending their people's interests could disagree upon means and pull their followers in different directions. Such conflict was not the least of the evils that the European "invasion" inflicted upon the Indians.[64]

Individuals had considerable freedom within their communities and could even go so far as to make "private" war upon an enemy. Young Indian men were encouraged to raid enemies to hone skills and achieve reputations. The absence of the European distinction between war and murder also facilitated "private" war. One scholar draws a distinction between private and "national" war among northeastern Indians. National war was conducted as the consequence of political consensus involving the entire community or groups of communities and with the guidance of the respected elders. National war could thus produce forces of considerably larger size than the small raiding parties associated with private war. The armies of hundreds of Iroquois warriors sent to fight the seventeenth-century "beaver wars" were apparently the result of "national" war decisions.[65]

Ethnic loyalty could also bind Indians divided by European alliances. French-Canadian authorities learned that their mission Indian friends often warned their Mohawk kindred, allies of the English, of impending raids. During the Seven Years War, many Indians seem to have recognized the futility of fighting one another for European gains. At the siege of Fort Niagara in 1759, the majority of Indians on both sides withdrew from battle rather than kill one another.[66]

Native religions provided another dimension of Indian unity against European "invasions". This was most evident in the famous "revitalization movement" in western Pennsylvania and Ohio in the early 1760s. Messianic prophets called upon the western Indians to renounce their dependency upon European goods and to return to the lives of their fathers. This message of spiritual purity and the recovery of a lost world had appeal across tribal lines and served as a stimulus to the rising of the Great Lakes Indians known as Pontiac's rebellion. The uprising was provoked by a number of factors, but it appears unlikely that the event would have inflamed such a vast area without the unifying message of the prophets.[67] Pontiac's Rebellion which will be discussed in a later chapter, demonstrates the ability of an Indian confederacy to wage war on a large scale and to fight a great European empire to a standstill.

Chapter Three

The European background to North American warfare

The modern art of war

The issue of European military development in the sixteenth and seventeenth centuries has recently been a matter of lively debate among historians. The historian Michael Roberts characterized the period as one of a "military revolution":

> By 1660 the modern art of war had come to birth. Mass armies, strict discipline, absolute submergence of the individual, had already arrived; the conjoint ascendancy of financial power and applied science was already established in all its malignity; the use of propaganda, psychological warfare and terrorism was already familiar to theorists, as well as to commanders in the field; and the last remaining qualms as to the religious and ethical legitimacy of war seems to have been stifled. The road lay open, broad and straight to the abyss of the twentieth century.[1]

Geoffrey Parker has expanded the Roberts thesis, emphasizing not only the significance of the military revolution for the foundation of the modern European state, but its central importance for European imperialism and "the rise of the West". The Roberts–Parker thesis has been challenged by Jeremy Black who disputes the significance of the dates 1560–1660, arguing that the dates 1470–1530, 1660–1720 and 1792–1815 were the true revolutionary periods of European military development. While recognizing that European naval powers achieved "global reach" in the seventeenth and eighteenth centuries, he suggests that European military force had only marginal impact upon the societies of Asia and Africa during this period. Black differs with Roberts and Parker on another important point by rejecting their suggestion

37

of a causal link between the military revolution and the concentration of power in the early modern state. Rather, he contends that the early modern state appeared as the result of co-operation between monarchs and the ruling elites. The military revolution was thus more likely to have been the result of rather than the cause of the development of state power.

This book focuses primarily on the period after 1660 and thus the "post-revolutionary" period as defined by Roberts and Parker. With the exception of Spanish expeditions in the southeast and southwest, military activity in North America was at the extreme margin of European warfare during 1560–1660; significant participation by the European powers occurred only during the period covered by Black. Before 1660, armed sailing ships allowed Europeans to reach North America, to penetrate its rivers and bays, and to establish secure settlements. These settlers brought with them the weapons and military institutions of their homelands, but for the most part they were expected to defend themselves. A discussion of North America will not in and of itself settle the larger issue of the military revolution in Europe, but certain facts do stand out. Although Spain first established a military base at St Augustine, Florida in 1565, construction of the massive stone Castillo de San Marcos commenced only in 1672. Its garrison of regulars scarcely resembled the adventurers who made up the sixteenth-century expeditions of Ponce de Leon and Hernando de Soto. The first significant detachment of European regular troops in the northeast, the French Carignan-Salières Regiment, arrived in Canada in 1665, four years after Louis XIV assumed personal rule. These regulars spearheaded two major campaigns against the Mohawk Indians, who were persuaded to make peace with New France. Nevertheless the regulars suffered horribly in frontier campaigning and by no means broke the power of the Mohawks. European military dominance in North America was not assured during this period. Furthermore, while New England colonists launched major efforts against Indian and French foes, substantial numbers of British regulars appeared on the frontier only with the introduction of Major General Edward Braddock's ill-fated army in 1755. Braddock's force was a projection of the power of the British "fiscal-military state", a post-1688 development which underwrote Britain's emergence as a world power.[2] By the mid-eighteenth century, European states had the means to transform the nature of North American warfare. Even at that late date, however, they had yet to develop tactics which would prove decisive in struggles with American Indians.

What does the North American perspective add to the debate over the military revolution? European ships and firearms were essential to the establishment and defence of European colonies in the seventeenth century, but they did not assure European primacy on the continent. Indians quickly mastered the use of firearms and excelled their European opponents in marksmanship and tactics. European success most often occurred when they adapted themselves to the Indian way of war. That adaptation may have been the most "revolutionary" military development in North America. Beyond the range of the big gunships, European ability to project power was limited. There was only small-scale intervention by regular forces until the latter half of the eighteenth century and their presence was not decisive. Material wealth, population density, and political decisiveness may have played more significant roles in the "invasion of America" than military means.

How well prepared were European soldiers for the challenges of frontier warfare in North America? American nationalist historians have long argued that European techniques were not applicable to American conditions and they have linked the colonial adoption of Indian tactics with the American victory in the War of Independence. This view does not withstand close examination. First, it is clear that the Americans won their independence with a regular army organized on European principles and employing European tactics. Frontier warfare contributed only marginally to the outcome of the American Revolution. Secondly, Europeans in the seventeenth and eighteenth centuries were no strangers to irregular war. Ireland, Scotland, and Hungary provided schools in which soldiers learned the lessons of unconventional warfare; in the eighteenth century it would become the subject of a large body of professional military literature. Many European officers would strive to adapt to frontier conditions and a number would succeed.[3]

Nevertheless, if we accept the fact that Europeans had experience in irregular warfare, the question remains of the validity of that experience. Was it the proper model for North American conditions? If soldiers were prepared, how extensive and appropriate was their training? Most of the burden of frontier war was born by colonial militias and volunteers rather than by professionals. Were they handicapped by inexpert reliance on European military technique or did they develop a new way of war which the regulars ignored at their peril?

The militia

During the seventeenth century the burden of European–Indian warfare was borne primarily by settlers with little in the way of direct aid from European military establishments. English colonists arriving in Virginia in 1607 based their defence on an ancient institution: the militia which had its roots in the

Anglo-Saxon fyrd. Despite the introduction of feudalism by William the Conqueror, all English freemen had retained the responsibility of participating in the defence of their country. As feudalism became militarily obsolete and politically suspect during the Tudor period, the militia acquired renewed significance for the defence of the realm. Elizabeth I's government gave increased attention to the training and equipment of the militia and established the elite trained bands which provided the militia with a well trained and well armed core. The trained bands were part-time soldiers and technically could not be drafted for service abroad, although they sometimes were. But they provided a solid foundation for the national defence.[4]

Special training was certainly required as firearms gradually replaced the hallowed longbow as the militia's missile weapon. Traditionalists among Elizabeth's soldiers lamented this conversion as a symbol of martial decay, and indeed the longbow retained many advantages over the slow and unreliable firearms of the day. Nevertheless, the majority of practical soldiers came to prefer the gun. In part this may have been due to the decline of archery as a sport, for good archers required lifetime practice. It was partly due as well to the improvements in firearms. Loading and firing a matchlock weapon was a complicated business as all military manuals of the time demonstrate. But one did not have to be an athlete to do so. The average man could become a proficient musketeer with the training provided by the trained bands.

This conversion from bow to musket was virtually complete by the end of Elizabeth's reign, only 75 years before the musket became the primary weapon of the New England Indians. English musketry training, however, differed markedly from that of the Indians. English militiamen were not part of a hunting culture. This was a sport reserved for the upper classes. Gentlemen sportsmen and poachers valued firearms as fowling pieces; a discharge of multiple shot was more effective against game than were arrows. But few militiamen had ever fired at a bird or any kind of mark. Musketeers were trained to co-ordinate with pikemen in the close-order fighting of European battlefields. Such conditions placed a premium on rapid and intense volley fire against infantry and cavalry who presented large compact targets. Such tactics would frequently prove useless in North American forest warfare where Indian marksmen had the advantage. Still, considering the decline in English standards of archery, it was fortunate for the settlers that European–Indian warfare was waged with firearms rather than bows. When Virginia settlers received an emergency shipment of obsolete weapons from the Tower of London in 1610, they left the bows and arrows untouched. Probably few knew how to use them.[5]

Militia organization and firearms were the two important elements of English military life that the first English settlers brought to Jamestown. They were crucial to the salvation of the colony when it confronted its first military crisis, the war with the Powhatan Indians which erupted in 1609. The situation was so perilous that the colony was almost abandoned before timely reinforcements and experienced soldiers arrived in 1610. The new governor and his officers imposed a strict military regime upon the inhabitants. Regulations borrowed from Elizabethan military practice required strict discipline and obedience to a well defined hierarchy of officers, sergeants, and corporals. The settlers' licentious behavior was constrained by strict penalties against the crimes of blasphemy, duelling, pillaging, and mutiny. Clean living and religious observance were required of all.[6] These regulations formed the basis of the fighting force that saved the colony.

Jamestown's new commanders included men who had served in Elizabeth's wars in the Low Countries and in Ireland. One expert concludes that "at present there is little evidence to permit an evaluation of the tenuous but indisputable relationship between English military experiences in Ireland and developments in Virginia".[7] The parallels are certainly clear. Cyril Falls, the historian of the Elizabethan Irish wars, points out that the Irish won most of their victories by ambush and that they were probably better shots than the English; he suggests that the Irish leader, the Earl of Tyrone, may have gone too far in copying the conventional tactics of continental armies instead of relying on guerrilla warfare. The English strategy to subdue the rebellion was fourfold: to seek out and destroy the enemy in open battle; to seek aid from among the Irish themselves; to hem in the enemy with fortifications; and, in the last resort, to devastate the countryside so that hostile forces could not live upon it. These methods are common to many counterinsurgency strategies and are extremely hard on the non-combatant population. Thus the Irish wars were conducted with great savagery by both sides.[8]

The English defeated the Powhatan confederacy by a similar strategy. The Powhatans lived in a region penetrated by numerous waterways. Their enemy exploited this geographical feature by hemming them in with lines of fortifications and sailing into their homelands on heavily armed ships. This enabled the English to burn villages and crops. When the Indians made a stand in the open fields to defend their food supplies, in battles referred to by contemporaries as food fights, they were no match for the English musketeers clad in arrow-proof armour.

This conflict revealed a central Indian weakness, which many European commanders would seek to exploit. Most Indians were settled agricultural people rather than nomadic hunters. Agriculture was considered woman's work and most Indian men were active hunters, but maize, beans and other plants were the staples of the Indian diet. If Europeans succeeded in penetrating the Indian agricultural districts, the latter were faced with the harsh choice between facing a heavily armed enemy who excelled in open battle or starvation. In Virginia, the English profited from a heavy advantage in firearms and by the use of armed ships which allowed them to launch their punitive campaigns in relative safety. Similarly, in 1637 New England troops exploited their ability to move by sea to carry out their devastating surprise attack on the Pequot village at Mystic. During the bitter war against the Wampanoag in 1675, known as King Philip's War, the strategy remained the same, but the English technical superiority was less overwhelming. English commanders learned that attacks on Indian villages, involving long marches through the forest, exposed their men to a form of war at which the Indians were masters. Furthermore, the militia were essentially local defence forces, not meant for long-distance campaigns. Such operations would require troops willing to serve beyond the usual constraints on militia service, new tactics to cope with "skulking" Indians equipped with firearms, and organizational and logistical efforts beyond the capabilities of the first settlers.

Both the Elizabethan and the colonial military experience suggest that the prerequisite to successful militia discipline was danger. Faced with a perceived external threat, communities were willing to make sacrifices. The termination of the first war with the Powhatan in 1614 meant the end of the strict military regime in Virginia. Renewals of that conflict and fear of the Indians, however, ensured that Virginia retained vigorous militia institutions during the first half of the seventeenth century. As the threat waned and social tensions increased in the second half of the century, the militia became smaller, excluding slaves and servants. The colony now relied upon imperial forces or diplomacy for external defence. The militia had become an agency of domestic order. By the second decade of the eighteenth century, the Virginia militia had atrophied to the point that it was virtually useless as a military force. John Shy has demonstrated that the histories of colonial militias varied according to circumstances.[9] The New England militias, recruited from towns governed by elected officials and faced with a long-term threat from hostile Indians and their French allies, remained a formidable force throughout most of the colonial period. The middle colonies, further removed from threats from Canada, and possessing different political institutions, allowed their militias to decay. South Carolina's militia remained active in the face of a threefold threat: Spanish and Indian enemies on the frontier and a large slave population within the colony's borders. However, South Carolina's unique circumstances made it difficult to assemble a large force. The white population was thinly spread across scattered plantations rather than concentrated in towns as in New England. Militiamen were reluctant to leave their homes unguarded against potentially rebellious slaves. The militia's military potential was neutralized by the demands of domestic order.

Canada

By the end of the seventeenth century, English–Indian conflicts merged with the great imperial struggle between England and France. These wars called for increased military effort on the part of the colonists including extensive campaigns against Canada. Militia service was necessarily part-time; few farmers could afford to desert their fields for an expedition to Canada. New sources of manpower and new institutions were required to meet the challenge. Colonial governments thus turned to the recruitment of volunteers who served for pay or the promise of loot. As we have seen in the previous chapter, the New England colonies hired numbers of Indian auxiliaries to protect their frontiers during the period 1675–1725. Volunteers frequently came from elements of the population not represented in the militia: Indians, free Blacks, white servants and apprentices, and others who lacked deep ties to white settler communities. During the dark days of King Philip's War New Englanders did not hesitate to employ convicted pirates as soldiers. By the eighteenth century, most frontier warfare was conducted by these soldiers while the militia constituted a part-time home guard with limited training. In some colonies the militias resembled social clubs more than military organizations.

The major exception to this picture was the Canadian militia, but this fragile, remote colony was seldom free of danger. During the seventeenth century, French Canada was drawn into the struggle of the Huron and Algonquian peoples against the Iroquois. The Canadian militia emerged from these wars as an effective fighting force, one which showed no hesitation in participating in long-distance raids. Unlike many of their English counterparts, the Canadians became well schooled in the Indian way of war. Only in Canada did the traditional stereotype of the superiority of the experienced frontier militiaman over the European regular hold true.[10] After the Carignan-Salières regiment returned to France in 1668, no *troupes de terre* were stationed in the colony until 1755. Experience proved that when they were present, they were best suited to garrison duty or conventional operations. Long-distance raids were best conducted by the militia and the *troupes de la marine*. These parties were usually accompanied by allied Indians of the Jesuit missions on the Saint Lawrence and often by Indians from the region of the Great Lakes. The latter were frequently joined by the *coureurs de bois*, Canadian traders who ventured far into the west in search of furs and who were at home with Indian customs, languages, and military practice. All of these soldiers were familiar with the Indian way of war. Although the *troupes de la marine* were regulars recruited in France, the fact that they were permanently stationed in the colony under Canadian officers meant that they were more seasoned to North American conditions than other regulars. Despite its small population, Canada possessed a frontier fighting force qualitatively superior to that which could be mounted by the English colonies.

Few English colonial officers, products of settled agricultural societies, could match the vast experience of frontier raiders such as La Corne Saint-Luc (1711–84), an officer of the *troupes de la marine*, who won a formidable reputation during the course of three major eighteenth-century wars. La Corne's career as a soldier was linked with his successful ventures in the fur trade, which he pursued in the far west on the route of the *coureurs de bois*. Fluent in "four or five" Indian languages, he became one of the richest men in Canada, an interpreter and diplomat, and a respected leader of both Canadian and Indian troops. He was chosen to "command" the Indians in Montcalm's army at the siege of Fort William Henry in 1757 and in 1777 led the Indians in the army of the British General John Burgoyne. La Corne was criticized for the behavior of the Indians on both occasions, but he realized that no European leader exercised absolute command over warriors who considered themselves allies rather than subordinates. In any event, he seems to have been more at home with the Indian rather than the European way of war. New Englanders referred to La Corne as "that archdevil incarnate". There is no doubt that he was a scourge of the frontier, but from another perspective he may be seen as a Canadian patriot and hero, a larger-than-life figure who was an extraordinary leader of irregular troops.[11]

Necessity and familiarity drew the Canadians to the Indian way of war, but Anglo-American militias and provincial troops remained rooted in the European military tradition. There were exceptions such as Benjamin Church, New England's most successful frontier commander in the last quarter of the seventeenth century, but they never became a model for English colonial organization and practice. As Ian Steele has pointed out, when war broke out with France in 1689, Massachusetts did not place Church in charge of an irregular frontier army capable of meeting French and Indian raiders on their own terms. Instead it launched amphibious expeditions under the inexperienced Sir William Phips in an attempt to capture Port Royal and Quebec.[12] Phips's unsuccessful assault on Quebec would set a pattern for Anglo-American strategy which culminated in Wolfe's capture of the city in 1759. Given overwhelming advantages in manpower, resources, and seapower, the knock-out blow strategy was a not unreasonable though technically difficult approach. But it did distract the English colonies from learning the lessons of frontier war and focused the attention of their officers on conventional matters. Because of fewer people guerrilla war was a necessity for the French-Canadians who made it into an art.

Military treatises

There were similarities between the best Anglo-American and Canadian colonial officers. Few had formal military training and most were successful planters, traders and entrepreneurs. They were practical men who could learn from experience. Virginia militia officers appear to have adopted loose order and to have acquired woodland skills in their war against the Powhatan, and Benjamin Church was an accomplished master of frontier warfare. But many English officers lacked sufficient woodland experience to equal their Canadian adversaries. Much of the training of the colonial militias consisted of drill and the rudiments of military behavior which remain part of the basic training of modern soldiers. The object of this drill was to instil discipline among troops and to train them to fire in volleys. Few commanders seem to have gone beyond that. Many did do professional reading to improve their skills as officers. Perhaps the most tangible evidence of something like a military revolution is the vast body of military literature available to aspiring officers in this period. The most popular military treatise among eighteenth-century colonial officers seems to have been *A Treatise of Military Discipline* by Humphrey Bland, a veteran of the Duke of Marlborough's European campaigns. Originally published in 1727, this work had run to nine editions by 1762. By reading Bland, a colonial officer could gain a good introduction to the mechanics of soldiering as practised in Western Europe in the first half of the eighteenth century. The treatise covers a variety of useful topics: infantry drill, firing, the formation of the battalion, defence of infantry against cavalry, rules for marching near the enemy, encampments, garrison duty, the conduct of sieges and the issuing of orders. Some, but not all, of these subjects were applicable to North American warfare. The emphasis is on a careful description of the detailed evolution of troops. Some orders require as many as 43 separate motions to execute; the order to prime and load a musket specifies 21 motions. There is little wonder that drill was at the heart of seventeenth- and eighteenth-century training.[13]

Officers charged with conducting the basic training of militia found Bland's treatise useful. It had some value as a basic primer for operations, but officers soon became aware of its limitations when they encountered the problems of forest warfare. The Virginian Robert Stobo had no formal military education before he was commissioned a Virginia provincial captain under George Washington in 1754, but he had carefully read Bland's treatise and carried it with him in his pack. In July of that year, he encountered the reality of frontier war when Washington was surrounded and forced to surrender to a combined French–Indian force. Stobo became a prisoner in Canada where he formed a business partnership with none other than La Corne Saint-Luc, who could have taught him more about frontier warfare than he could have learned from Bland. The Massachusetts provincial Colonel Ephraim Williams also depended on Bland for professional guidance. The treatise is listed in his library holdings and was included in the belongings in his military chest. On 8 September 1755, he lost his life leading a detachment into an Indian ambush near Lake George, New York, an incident known as the "Bloody Morning Scout".[14]

One may question how much any book could have prepared an officer to meet the uncertainties of forest warfare, but Bland's treatise was dated by 1755. European officers had been studying the problem of irregular warfare for 15 years since the appearance of large numbers of Hungarian light troops in the service of the Austrian army. Much professional writing was to be devoted to this subject, some of it applicable to North America. Bland, however, had found the issue to be irrelevant and distasteful. He admitted that armies sometimes had to lay waste the country, to levy contributions from inhabitants, and to disperse enemy foragers. But he thought it likely to do more harm than good by wearing out one's men and horses. "Formerly", he observed, "these sorts of exploits were much in vogue, particularly with the *French*, who call it *La Petite Guerre*; but of late they are very much left off, since they only serve to render the poor inhabitants more miserable, or particular officers, whose horses or baggage they take, uneasy in their affairs . . . which reason is sufficient in my opinion, to discontinue the practice, or at least not use it on particular occasions."[15] These sentiments embody what is sometimes described as the humane spirit of eighteenth-century war as contrasted with that of the preceding century. They certainly mark a departure from the attitudes of Elizabeth I's generals in Ireland. But they were irrelevant to the conditions confronting officers on the frontier and, for that matter, to European warfare in the mid–eighteenth century.

Irregular war

In a well known article, the historian Stanley Pargellis blamed Major General Edward Braddock's defeat near Fort Duquesne in 1755 on his failure to observe the elementary rules of warfare described in Bland's treatise.[16] Braddock's defeat is one of the most hotly debated events in American military history and will be discussed in a later chapter. However, the question of Braddock's preparation for forest warfare or lack thereof is central to the general question of the professional training of European officers arriving in increasing numbers in North America in the mid-eighteenth century. Braddock may have blundered in his march to the Monongahela, but he encountered a form of battle foreign to his experience and for which he had little in the way of theoretical guidance. Bland's treatise had little to say about guerrilla warfare. While many new treatises on irregular warfare began to be published in the 1750s, they appeared too late to have been of use to Braddock. These authors included Turpin de Crissé (1754), Hector de Grandmaison (1756) and Capitaine de Jeney (1759).[17] Their works were not a response to American conditions, but rather to the transformation of European warfare that began during the War of the Austrian Succession, 1740–8. Irregular troops played a greater role in this conflict than in previous eighteenth-century struggles. British and French officers' practical experience in *petite guerre* became the foundation for the theoretical treatises which appeared in the following decade. Indeed, some historians believe that the line between European and American warfare was less distinct after 1750 than formerly and that the officers arriving in America were better prepared to adapt to conditions than nationalist writers have maintained.[18]

What was the nature of irregular war in Europe *circa* 1750 and what models did it provide officers posted to North America? The term "irregular warfare" embraces many different kinds of conflict, each with their own unique problems and solutions. European officers had encountered three different types: (1) peasant insurrections, usually provoked by bad conduct on the part of the soldiers; (2) people in arms, including the Jacobite rebellions of 1715 and 1745 in Britain and the Corsican war of independence against France; and (3) irregular troops acting as auxiliaries to regular forces, such as the Pandours and Croats in the Austrian service. These conflicts were far removed from the stylized campaigns frequently associated with eighteenth-century armies, but they were a central part of the military experience of the age.

The leading historian of logistics, Martin Van Creveld, has dispelled the stereotype of road-bound eighteenth-century armies, tied to supply depots by vast chains of wagons and carts.[19] Armies lived off the countryside as they had always done, although they did so in a more orderly manner than during the Thirty Years War. Forces with effective supply services could impose contributions on peasants, which were no more than onerous taxes. But a poorly disciplined army was a plague to which the peasants responded with fury. The inhabitants of the countryside were never passive observers of military events. Frederick the Great was so frustrated by the hostility of peasants in the countries he invaded that he concluded that "if my sole object were glory, I would never wage war anywhere except in my own country because of all of the advantages".[20] While there is no complete record of serious peasant attacks on the military, there are enough major incidents to illustrate the scale of the problem. Comte de Merode Westerloo recalled that as the French army withdrew from Germany in 1704, a soldier blew upon a great brass alpenhorn that he had found. To the soldiers' delight many cattle emerged from the woods in response to the call. The troops "regarded this as manna from heaven, and in no time the camp resembled a slaughterhouse. However, this droll incident had one unfortunate repercussion; it encouraged the troops to scatter into the woods and hills – we could do nothing to stop them – and a few regrettable incidents resulted. The enraged peasantry eventually killed several thousand of our men before the army was clear of the Black Forest."[21] Similarly, French pillaging of the German countryside in 1761 provoked an uprising by 4,000 peasants who drove the army of Marshal Conflans from Emden.[22] Such incidents demonstrate that poorly disciplined troops, equipped with single-shot weapons, were extremely vulnerable to attacks by peasants who had few arms and little in the way of military training. Experienced commanders recognized that a campaign could founder upon peasant violence and that the only prevention was strict discipline and reasonable requisitions. Some American Indian uprisings contained the same elements of rage and despair that fuelled these peasant attacks on the troops. But the better armed, better trained and more warlike Indians presented a more formidable military challenge than these violent, but spasmodic *Jacqueries*.

The second type of irregular war experienced by European regulars was the "people in arms". Corsica and Scotland mounted popular resistance to government authority more substantial than peasant uprisings. In both cases irregular soldiers, sometimes using guerrilla tactics, tested the skills of regular officers.[23] A number of British officers who served in North America after 1754 had learned about irregular war during the Jacobite rebellion in Scotland in 1745. Prince Charles Edward Stuart's Highland troops were not professionals, but a warlike people who fought in a manner different from the linear volley-fire tactics of the British regulars. While they were well suited to a war of ambush and surprise, the Jacobite troops were formidable battlefield soldiers as well. Charles defeated the British regulars in two major battles and launched an invasion of England which shook the Hanoverian throne. Early Jacobite victories were achieved in favourable field conditions against poorly disciplined regulars. Shock prevailed against fire on these occasions. Typically, the highlanders advanced in loose order to within musket shot of the enemy. After firing a volley to create disorder among the enemy, they threw down their muskets, quickly formed compact groups and rushed upon their opponents with cold steel. Unnerved regulars gave way before such onslaughts. The Duke of Cumberland's victory over these warriors at the battle of Culloden was achieved in conditions that favoured the regulars, who now included veterans from Flanders. The barren Culloden moor provided an ideal setting for the Duke's field artillery and cavalry, and the Highlanders were exposed to a devastating flanking fire. Divisions within the Jacobite command may have contributed to the failure to launch a successful charge. Some commentators believe that Charles would have been wiser to avoid battle, disperse his men, and engage in guerrilla warfare. But this kind of war in itself could not have overturned the throne; the Highland charge was Charles's one true weapon. Victory depended on its success.

After Culloden, the government strategy to subdue the Highlands recalled that of Elizabeth I's commanders in Ireland. Europeans had employed these same strategies against the American Indians since the beginning of the seventeenth century. Tactically, however, Highland warfare was very different from that of the American frontier. Highlanders relied on the charge and hand-to-hand combat to decide the issue of the battlefield. Their musketry was but a cover and a prelude to the decisive encounter. By contrast, the Indians relied on marksmanship and usually retreated rather than face European bayonets. Thus, officers with Scottish experience had little, if any, exposure to anything like the Indian "skulking way of war".

During the Seven Years War, the British government recruited Highland troops for service in North America. Highlanders were often in the forefront of the major battles and suffered the highest casualty rates among the Anglo-American forces. Some commanders hoped that the Highlanders would prove an antidote to the menace the Indians posed to the regulars in the forest. Brigadier General John Forbes, who led the successful advance on Fort Duquesne in 1758, thought of his wild Highlanders as the Indians' "cousins" and was optimistic about their ability to screen his army's march through the woods. His Highlanders did drive the Indians away from the column and gained strength and experience from chasing them. On the other hand, they do not seem to have caught any.[24] Forbes's second in command, Colonel Henry Bouquet, did not share his chief's enthusiasm for Scottish soldiers. When marching to relieve Fort Pitt during the Indian rising of 1763, he lamented the absence of experienced woodsmen to serve as rangers, "having observed . . . that the Highlanders lose themselves in the Woods as soon as they go out of the Road, and cannot, on that acct., be employed as Flankers. . . . I cannot send a Highlander out of my sight without running the Risk of losing the man, which exposes me to a surprise from the Skulking Villains I have to deal with."[25] If one wished to launch a dangerous frontal assault on a fortified position, there were no troops like the Highlanders. The Indians, of course, had no use for that sort of war. While regular officers found Highland and Indian ways of war unconventional, they were not the same. Officers campaigning in the Scottish Highlands in the 1740s would have not learned many specific tactical lessons that could be applied to North America.

A third kind of irregular warfare, and one which was the focus of most of the professional literature on the subject, was conducted by light troops attached to the regular armies of the era. In 1810, the American Governor of the Indiana Territory, William Henry Harrison, observed that "If our Western militia should ever encounter a European army, they would be astonished to find themselves opposed by a body of men using the same arms with equal dexterity to themselves; making their attacks with the same unexpected velocity, and eluding their enemy with all the celerity and address, which distinguishes our backwoods riflemen."[26] Armies had always relied upon light infantry and cavalry for patrols, scouting, foraging, and so on, but the War of the Austrian Succession had transformed this dimension of European warfare. Maria Theresa's initial defeats at the hands of Frederick the Great prompted her famous appeal to her Hungarian subjects for rescue. In response, they raised large numbers of traditional Hungarian light cavalry, the hussars, and enlisted tough borderers from the Turkish frontier, the Croats and Pandours, whose wild, barbaric appearance and behaviour caused a sensation when they appeared in Western Europe. Despite the irregularities they committed, they added a formidable new element to Austrian arms. They were so effective in denying the enemy control of the countryside and access to food, forage and intelligence, that all armies soon found it prudent to increase their own light forces and to consider countermeasures against those of their enemies.

Service among the light troops always seemed to attract the most fiery spirits among the soldiers, but the Croats and Pandours became notorious for a new and higher level of brutality in warfare. Accounts of their atrocities match the most blood-tingling tales of the North American frontier. Particularly infamous were the Pandours commanded by Francis Baron von Trenck. These troops drew no distinction between war and robbery or between combatants and non-combatants. Trenck himself was known for cutting off the heads of his enemies and keeping them as trophies. His most successful coup was a raid on Frederick the Great's quarters which netted him the king's silver service. A reputation for ill-gotten wealth led to his removal as leader of the Pandours, but they continued their depredations under his successor, Colonel Baron Johann Daniel von Mentzel.[27] Allied British officers who encountered the Pandours portrayed them as a murderous mob who mocked the laws of war. "I should almost believe there would some judgement befall if we were to employ such in our service, unless the utmost necessity required it", wrote Lieutenant Colonel Charles Russell of the Coldstream Guards in 1743.[28]

These were the kind of soldiers likely to provoke the peasant uprisings dreaded by regular officers. Some questioned the military value of men whose primary motive was robbery. One such critic of the free companies, irregulars who lived off the country, was Clausewitz, who observed sarcastically that, while regular troops operated best in open country and militia in the mountains, the auxiliaries should be stationed "in prosperous areas where they will enjoy themselves."[29] Nevertheless, while the case of Trenck suggests that eighteenth-century European warfare was not as "civilized" as sometimes suggested, it would be unfair to tar all European light troops of the era with the same brush. Officers such as Johann Ewald and J. G. Simcoe, who commanded light troops in the British army during the War of American Independence, were serious professionals and respectable men who looked to the good conduct of their troops. Ewald's Hessian jagers, marksmen recruited from foresters and gamekeepers, were proper soldiers on the whole and should not be categorized with Trenck's Pandours.[30] They symbolize military authorities' recognition of the genuine value of light troops and the need to integrate them into the regular forces.

The second half of the century saw many attempts to create specialized light troops among the regulars. In this evolutionary period, the term "light infantry" lacks precision. Although the British Lieutenant Colonel Thomas Gage experimented with a detachment of regulars equipped and trained as rangers during the Seven Years War in America, the project had no lasting effect. In the British service, the term "light infantry" was usually applied to one of the elite "flank" companies of the regiments of the line. These companies were recruited from the most active and dependable men of the regiment and were used for special operations. In wartime, the companies were detached from their regiments and consolidated as *ad hoc* light infantry battalions. They were frequently assigned the most difficult tasks within the army and were, indeed, formidable troops. But they received no special training as rangers under frontier conditions. They were an evolutionary step to the creation of the true British light infantry at the end of the century.[31] Ultimately, the most significant development in European infantry training would be the integration of regular and light infantry tactics.

These developments prompted the publication of a flood of treatises on irregular warfare, often referred to as partisan warfare or *petite guerre*. Some European officers serving in America, such as Henry Bouquet, were serious students of the professional literature and, undoubtedly, this material provided food for thought. Theory does not have to be directly applicable; it has value if it simply opens the mind to new possibilities and new contingencies. On the other hand, the new literature was not particularly theoretical. Rather the emphasis was on practical advice for an officer in the field. It seems unlikely that an experienced commander such as Bouquet would have found much that was new in the treatises on partisan war.[32]

Bouquet was familiar with one of the best treatises on the subject, the *Essai Sur L'Art De La Guerre* by Turpin de Crissé, published in 1754. Turpin de Crissé was a very experienced hussar officer who had seen action at the major battles of Fontenoy (1745), Raucoux (1746), and Lawfeld (1747). The *Essai* had a wide circulation with translations in English, German, and Russian, and it was said to have been particularly valued by Frederick the Great. The light troops described by Crissé were professional soldiers, not the privateering brigands of Trenck. Crissé was consistent with the military reformers of his day in emphasizing the moral qualities central to successful soldiers: religion, patriotism, self-sacrifice, and a respect for the rights of humanity. In this respect, the *Essai* advocated increased professionalism among the light troops. However, in substance, the work was a practical handbook for troops involved in *petite guerre*. It described operations in mountainous and wooded country, the art of ambush and the means of avoiding one. There was good advice for soldiers in ambush: they should not smoke; horses should be carefully handled and kept silent, their tracks should be erased with tree branches; soldiers should be posted in trees to observe the country. There was a useful discussion on co-operation between light infantry and cavalry.

Crissé observed that, in the mountains and forest, a commander should always march as if expecting to be attacked. Heights and passages on the line of march should be occupied to deny them to the enemy; parties of infantry should guard the flanks while the vanguard should consist of the bravest and coolest soldiers who would be least likely to panic in case of surprise. Some cannon should be near the head of the column for use against enemy infantry in ambush. All of this was good advice, but Humphrey Bland had recommended the same thing and Braddock, with the exception of failing to occupy a fatal height, had followed it in 1755. Crissé's work was actually not very original, but a summary of what experienced European officers already knew. Thus, as it withdrew from Germany in 1743, Mercoyrol de Beaulieu's battalion was harassed by enemy Croats and Pandours as it passed through wooded country. The column marched in a hollow battalion square with officer and pack horses in the centre. Skirmishers armed with carbines were thrown out on the flanks and in the rear to keep at distance *"cette vermine"*, the hussars and light infantry of the enemy. The battalion made good its retreat without serious difficulty.[33] Braddock followed similar precautions with different results.

Braddock, however, faced a different tactical situation. This is reflected in Crissé's advice for an attack from ambush. He argued that the troops should not open fire; rather, they should fall upon the enemy with swords and bayonets. Such an attack, if pressed home vigorously, would be more surprising and overwhelming than a musket volley. Fire might also give away the ambush to other enemy troops who could thus avoid it or rush to the relief. Crissé's was a cavalryman's book and embodies the skepticism of many eighteenth-century soldiers about firepower. The light troops should consist of a mix of infantry and cavalry; in this mix cold steel was the offensive weapon, the musket a defensive one, in the hands of infantry whose primary role was to protect and support the cavalry.

Indian marksmen had no reservations about the value of firepower as an offensive weapon. This is one of the fundamental differences between eighteenth-century European military thought and the Indian way of war. While a European officer would find good advice in a treatise such as that of Turpin de Crissé, he would have profited more from a study of Indian practice. In this respect, the writings of Robert Rogers would have provided a better guide for forest warfare than those of his European contemporaries.[34] Rogers' biographer credits him with having "successfully compressed the shapeless mass of backwoods fighting experiences into a simple exposition of small unit tactics soundly based on timeless principles: mobility, security and surprise".[35] But he acknowledges that even Rogers failed to provide an understanding of how to survive the most dangerous enemy in the forest: nature itself. Hunger and exposure were greater threats to survival than any manmade weapon. Rogers' men endured expeditions in mid-winter conditions: snow, ice, freezing rain and sub-zero temperatures, and often without fires. Frontier commanders such as Rogers and Léry learned their lessons of survival from the Indians, but Rogers provides no guide in his writings. In addition, there were many details of frontier war that regulars could not know: "How did the rangers hide their own tracks or follow an enemy's trail? What were the signals in the woods? How were boats hidden? How were trees and bushes used for concealment? The rules have a deceiving simplicity; they actually could only be applied by expert woodsmen."[36]

To conclude, European military professionals had gained extensive experience in irregular warfare before 1755 and had begun to distill this experience in their literature. However, none of the three types of irregular warfare discussed provided an adequate model for the conditions of North American forest warfare. Furthermore, while European armies began to incorporate specialized light troops into their armies, they did not send them to North America to fight on the frontier. Indian allies and frontier militia perhaps appeared to make such troops an unnecessary addition to the forces despatched to North America. When European commanders sought to use the Highlanders as frontier light infantry, the experiment failed. Perhaps the best prepared woodland fighters from Europe were Ewald's Hessian jagers who, one assumes, would have adapted quickly to the Indian way of war, but they were never deployed on the frontier.

Professionalism

The only school of frontier war was the frontier itself. Nevertheless, it is clear that eighteenth-century officers did possess considerable experience in unconventional war and made a serious study of its problems. Their interest in this topic was part of the increased commitment to professionalism evident in the European officer corps. The term "professional" is in itself a relative one. The military organizations of the Old Regime appear quaintly anachronistic to the modern observer. Despite the establishment of military academies in most major European countries, few officers had formal military educations. In Britain, for example, artillery officers received training at the Royal Military Academy at Woolwich after 1741, but no comparable institution existed for the education of infantry and cavalry officers. Some studied abroad and others at private institutions such as that conducted by Lewis Lochée in Little Chelsea between 1770 and 1789. "The systematic grounding in military theory and practice provided by Lochée could only have benefitted those who paid attention to it while at the same time his pupils received a general education in subjects of particular value to future officers."[37] But Lochée's students never constituted as much as 10 per cent of the officer corps and few rose to the top of the service. Most officers seem to have learned their business "on the job" and by reading the professional literature. Many officers remained suspicious of formal study. "I have always been of the opinion that one ounce of Experience is better than a Tun of Theory", was the sentiment of one officer and he was not alone.[38]

By modern standards, advancement by merit was too often blocked by aristocratic privilege and favouritism, particularly at the senior levels. Nevertheless, there were clear trends towards increased professionalism. First was the increased power of the eighteenth-century state which transformed the mercenaries of the seventeenth century into national armies. Britain's Hanoverian rulers strove to limit the purchase of commissions and to assure the promotion of men of experience and merit. As officers looked to the state for advancement and retirement gratuities, they gained in professional commitment. Noteworthy also was a concern for honourable and humane conduct in war. While this attitude had its roots in medieval chivalry, the new emphasis was a symbol of a sense of professional responsibility.[39] Eighteenth-century officers are sometimes criticized for their harsh disciplinary policies. One writer argues that the punishments inflicted upon the troops were so harsh that "we should have to conclude that the British upper class officers conceived lower class enlisted men as enemies".[40] However, recent scholarship demonstrates that punishments meted out by courts martial were not out of line with those imposed by civil courts of the era and that the trend was to reduce their severity. Most British soldiers were not the impressed criminals of some stereotypes, but poor, respectable men. Severity of punishment usually depended upon the character and reputation of the individual soldier; all in all, the rank and file do not seem to have considered the system to be unjust. However, many military writers, inspired by trends in Enlightenment thought, argued for more sweeping reforms. A concern for the essential humanity of the troops is a principal theme in the professional literature of the second half of the century.[41]

Professionalism led some officers to become serious students of military matters. Much of this study, as in the literature on *petite guerre*, was of a purely practical nature. But the military writing of the century did not ignore more fundamental questions including strategy and moral conduct. French writers were more theoretical than their British counterparts. This was not simply a national trait. The basic concern of French and other continental writers, shock versus firepower, had been resolved in favour of the latter in the British army in the days of Marlborough.[42] Furthermore, the fact that British soldiers were usually on the winning side gave them less reason to examine the fundamentals than the French who found their military glory to be on the wane. Thus, the bulk of the new writing on *petite guerre* was French, but serious students in both armies read it.

This new critical study of the problems of war and the organization of armies is evidence of the influence of the Enlightenment spirit in the military thought of the era.[43] This suggests a break with tradition and a willingness to submit military problems to rational and objective analysis. A truly enlightened officer corps would thus have focused on the generic problems of frontier war and adapted accordingly. Of course, nothing like this ever happened. No officer can approach war as a blank sheet. Eighteenth-century military training relied upon tradition and the experience of European battlefields. The development of a professional ethos which, on the one hand, fostered the study of military principles, also sheltered the officer corps from new influences. Officers came to see war as a professional science, not a matter for amateurs. From the eighteenth century to the present, a hazard of military professionalism has been the officer corps' sense of itself as a closed society, bound by special rules, rituals and traditions. Institutional requirements rather than military realities have frequently dictated military professionals' attitudes towards war.[44]

French officers arriving in Canada during the Seven Years War found it difficult to adapt to frontier warfare as practised by colonial commanders such as Léry and La Corne. Montcalm thought Léry an excellent officer, but dismissed La Corne as a "braggart and a babbler".[45] The Marquis and his staff questioned whether the governor, the Marquis de Vaudreuil, and the colonials understood "real war". This was the sentiment expressed by Montcalm's *aide de camp*, Louis Antoine de Bougainville. The latter possessed a mind shaped by the Enlightenment and he would later establish a great reputation as a Pacific explorer. However, he arrived in Canada in 1756 as an inexperienced but opinionated young officer (in need of campaign seasoning thought Montcalm).[46] Bougainville concluded that "they never made war in Canada before 1755. They had never gone into camp. To leave Montreal with a party, to go through the woods, to take a few scalps, to return at full speed once the blow was struck, that is what they called war, a campaign, success, victory."[47] "Now", he continued, "war is established here on the European basis. Projects for the campaigns, for armies, for artillery, for sieges, for battles. . . . What a revolution!" This was a business for professionals rather than amateurs. Unfortunately, "townsmen, bankers, merchants, officers, bishops, parish priests, Jesuits, all plan this [war], speak of it, discuss it pronounce on it. Everyone is a Turenne or a Folard".[48] Ultimately, the great protagonists of the Seven Years War in North America – Montcalm, Amherst, and Wolfe – conducted a European style war. Out of necessity, some European professionals, such as Forbes and Bouquet, learned to adapt to the frontier. But this adaptation was not fostered by the European military culture.

Chapter Four

Total war in New England: King Philip's War, 1675–6 and its aftermath

King Philip's War

The end came for the New England colonists' most feared enemy on 12 August 1676. The Wampanoag sachem Metacom, better known among the English as King Philip, was at last brought to bay in a swamp near his home at Mount Hope (now Bristol, Rhode Island) bordering Plymouth colony. His relentless pursuer was one of the most notable frontier commanders in American history, Captain Benjamin Church (1639–1718), leader of a picked company of English and friendly Indians. While we know nothing of Philip's thoughts on this fateful day, he must have been exhausted and demoralized. The uprising which bears his name was in collapse and Church had already captured his wife and son. Philip's own followers were falling away and, indeed, it was a deserter who led Church to his camp on the swamp's edge.

It was still dark as Church's company advanced on the enemy position. One detachment was ordered to crawl on their stomachs as close to the camp as possible, taking care not to fire until first light to avoid hitting friends. Once discovered, they were to fire and fall on the enemy, each man shouting and making all the noise that he could. Church knew that, at the first sound of gunfire, Philip would flee into the swamp, a tactic that had often enabled him to avoid pursuit. Therefore he arranged an ambush placing Englishmen and Indians in pairs behind trees in the swamp, ordering them to kill anyone who should approach silently. Once he made this disposition, Church was confident that Philip was in his grasp. He took a brother officer by the hand and announced: "Sir, I have so placed them that 'tis scarce possible Philip should escape them."

Suddenly a shot whistled over their heads. Captain Golding, the officer leading the assault party, had feared discovery by an Indian who had risen to

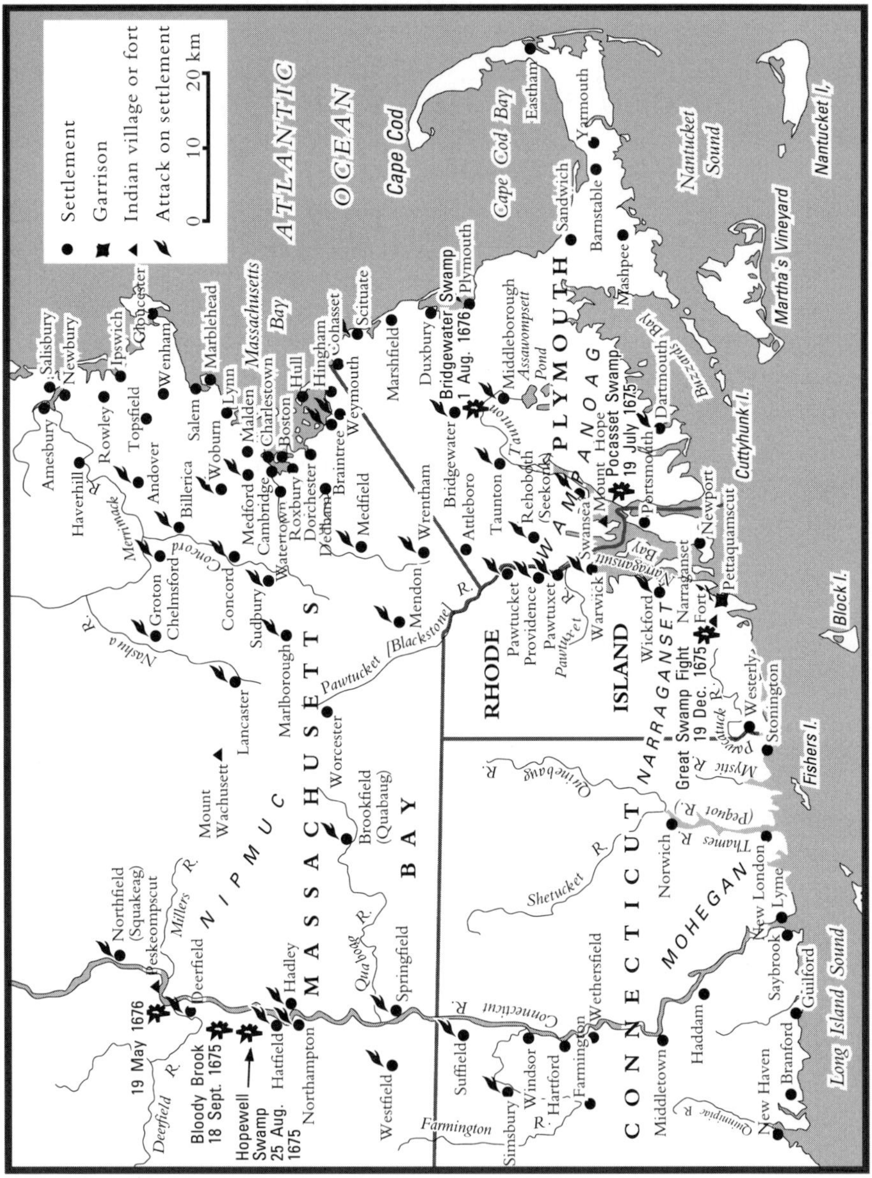

2. Southern New England at the time of King Philip's War, 1675–6

relieve himself. His shot provoked a volley by the entire party which overshot the enemy Indians, who had yet to rise from sleep. Almost immediately they fled into the swamp, Philip himself rushing upon one of the ambush positions. He was struck twice in the chest by musket bullets and collapsed in the mud. He had been killed by an Indian. Church awarded Philip no honours of war. Instead he called his "old Indian executioner" and ordered him to behead and quarter the body. "Philip, having one very remarkable hand, being much scarred, occasioned by the splitting of a pistol in it formerly, Captain Church gave the head and that hand to Alderman, the Indian who shot him, to show to such gentlemen as would bestow gratuities upon him. And accordingly, he got many a penny by it." It was thus that Philip, a symbol of fierce savagery and a name at which the world grew pale, was transformed into a curiosity.[1]

Philip had been hunted down by a commander versed in the Indian way of war. Church demonstrated the ability to carry the war to the enemy in the wilderness and into the swamps, which English colonists seldom penetrated. His men were trained to move in loose order, to take advantage of cover, to fire at specific targets, and to adapt themselves to the conditions of the frontier. Church achieved a high level of co-operation among his English and Indian soldiers. Indeed, it was his understanding and appreciation of Indian customs that made him such an effective leader. He often recruited enemy prisoners who served with astonishing loyalty and devotion against their own people. Such recruits brought with them a fund of intelligence about enemy movements and tactics and an intimate knowledge of the terrain. These were the very men who exposed Philip's hiding place and hunted him down.[2] No other New England commander achieved such a high reputation in the war. Church's fame rests partly upon his own account of the war, but it is supported by the admiration of his contemporaries. He was, wrote William Hubbard, one "whom God made an instrument of Signal Victories over the Indians".[3] In retrospect, it may be said that Church provided an example which should have been enshrined in all manuals dealing with frontier war. His experience stands out against the bitter lessons learned by most English commanders in King Philip's War. Unfortunately, they were lessons forgotten by most colonial miliary leaders.

The background

The war which erupted in 1675 shattered a half-century of peace between the Wampanoags of southeastern New England and their English neighbours. In comparison to Virginia, New England had been remarkably free of armed conflict between Indians and white settlers. Philip himself was the son of Massasoit, the able Wampanoag leader, whose assistance had proven vital to the early Plymouth settlers. The Wampanoags had never represented a military threat to the colony, for they had already been devastated by an epidemic disease during 1616–18. Nor did they appear to have found the fragile English settlement of 1620 particularly threatening. Relations between the two peoples had been managed with considerable skill by the first generation of Plymouth leaders and by Massasoit who died in 1660. The latter found the English useful as trading partners and as a counterweight to the powerful Narragansetts to the west and to dissidents among his own people. In turn the Wampanoags provided a buffer behind which the Plymouth colony could grow and develop. That development was enhanced by the decline in the Wampanoag population which made it possible for the settlers to purchase unused land from their Indian neighbours. Thus the history of Plymouth–Wampanoag relations was one of peace and mutual benefit. There was nothing to suggest that a war was inevitable.

This was generally true of the larger picture of white–Indian relations in New England despite frequent tensions rising from competing colonial claims to Indian lands. The most notable exception was the brief, violent Pequot War of 1637, which is sometimes seen as a prologue to King Philip's War.[4] The central incident of that conflict had been the massacre of a Pequot village near Mystic, Connecticut by an English force with an overwhelming superiority in firearms. The Pequot War introduced the New England Indians to the full fury of the European way of war and may have influenced the tactics they employed in 1675–6. It also exposed a critical weakness in any Indian attempt to oppose European settlement. Although the New England Indians were all members of the Algonquian language group and shared a common culture, they were deeply divided by political and commercial rivalries. The Pequot dominance over the fur trade in the Connecticut River valley was much resented by their neighbours and their appeals to form a common front against the Europeans fell on deaf ears. When the English military expedition marched into Pequot territory, it was accompanied by a large party of neighbouring Narragansetts. The Narragansetts' turn would come on 19 December 1675 when, in a battle known as the Great Swamp Fight, a fierce English assault devastated a fortified Narragansett village. Ironically, the Connecticut soldiers participating in this attack were accompanied by a detachment of Pequot warriors.

Peace and commerce, however, were characteristics of white–Indian relations during the first half-century of settlement. Indians supplied their English neighbours with food, furs and land in exchange for a variety of European goods including weapons. The integration of the Indian and colonial econo-mies in the decades before 1650, a period one writer refers to as the "golden age of trade", was symbolized by the appearance of wampum, strings of Indian-produced decorative shells as a fur-backed currency of exchange widely accepted by all of the peoples of New England. The subsequent decline in the demand for beaver pelts and the collapse in the value of wampum seems to have provided an economic context for increasingly strained white–Indian relations in the third quarter of the century.[5] Neverthe-less, one does not have to be a disciple of the classical economists to conclude that commerce had long exercised a peaceful influence in New England. On the other hand, the primary source of wealth in seventeenth-century New England was agriculture rather then commerce. Massachusetts' and Connecticut's designs upon the land occupied by Rhode Island dissenters and Narragansett Indians brought southern New England to the brink of war in the 1640s.[6]

A half century of peace suggests that King Philip's War was not the inevitable result of a clash of cultures. Puritan attitudes towards the Indians remain a matter of intense historical debate. Richard Slotkin, for example, in yet another analysis of the Puritan "mind" has offered a psychological inter-pretation which suggests that there was no alternative to violent conflict with the Indians. He concludes that the Puritans sensed in the Indians a dark threatening presence, a people outside civilization and without religion, whose very existence challenged those virtues among the Puritans themselves. The Indians were thus dismissed as agents of the devil and their religious practices relegated to the practice of magic and witchcraft.[7] One can under-stand that Puritan divines may have harboured such fears, but one may also wonder how many settlers, who, like Benjamin Church, actually had frequent contacts with the Indians, really believed all this. In any event, these myths produced no crusades aimed at extirpating the children of the devil. King Philip's War was no more a war of religion than it was a race war, though elements of each were present. Many Puritans supported the efforts of mis-sionaries such as John Eliot and Daniel Gookin to civilize and Christianize the Indians as part of the divinely ordained Puritan mission in the wilderness. In comparison with Jesuit missionary activity in Canada, these efforts had limited success. Nevertheless, according to one estimate, 20 per cent of New England's Indians had adopted Christianity by 1675.[8] These Christian Indians generally proved loyal to the English during King Philip's War, but many Indian allies such as Uncas, leader of the Mohegans, had proven resistant to the missionaries' appeals. After 1660 the Narragansetts seem to have under-gone a revival of their traditional religious practices.

The Puritans

Revisionist historians have not been kind to the Puritans. Francis Jennings has dismissed Puritan pieties as cant and he insists that King Philip's War should be properly named the "Second Puritan Conquest".[9] He believes that the English pursued a calculated policy of aggression towards the Indians of New England based upon their experience in sixteenth- and seventeenth-century Ireland: "1. a deliberate policy of inciting competition between natives in order, by division, to maintain control; 2. a disregard for pledges and promises to natives, no matter how solemnly made; 3. the introduction of total exterminatory war against some communities of natives in order to terrorize others; and 4. a highly developed propaganda of falsification to justify all acts of the conquerors whatsoever."[10] In this view, missionaries such as John Eliot have been reduced to devious hypocrites and confidence men. Indeed, Eliot's rather sanctified reputation as the "Apostle to the Indians" does not stand up under Jennings' critical analysis. The latter is not alone in portraying religion as a weapon in the European invasion.[11]

Missionaries were undoubtedly important agents of the European penetration and settlement of America. Eliot demanded that converted Indians surrender their cultural institutions and political independence and his missions served as agents of English land hunger. However, the view that the Puritans had adopted a calculating policy of extermination seems oversimplified given a record of almost 50 years of peace. That that peace was uneasy and often veiled underlying tensions cannot be denied, but that may be said of almost any period of peace in world history. The military practices of Puritan New Englanders in 1675–6 were not unique. Rather, they were consistent with those employed in Ireland and used in Virginia. The authors of such strategies were hardly Puritans. Rather, they adopted means which appeared to be the only effective tactics against guerrillas. It should not be surprising that, once war began, the New England clergy indulged in overheated rhetoric against the Indians or that contemporary historians such as William Hubbard or Increase Mather defended the justice of Puritan actions. Had it been otherwise, it would have been unique in the annals of warfare. John Eliot may have lost his heroic stature, but he and Daniel Gookin risked their reputations and perhaps more when they defended the Christian Indians from the anti-Indian hysteria unleashed in Massachusetts in 1675.[12]

Nevertheless, modern readers are unlikely to find very satisfactory Puritan explanations for the causes of the war. Increase Mather began his account of the war with a statement of self-evident truth; "That the Heathen People amongst whom we live, and whose Land the Lord God of our Fathers hath given to us for a rightfull Possession, have at sundry times been plotting mischievous devices against that part of the English Israel which is seated in these goings down of the Sun, no man that is an Inhabitant of any considerable standing can be ignorant".[13] William Hubbard admitted that many English settlers who traded with the Indians rejected the idea of an Indian conspiracy and believed that the "*Ruder sort* of the *English*, by their *imprudent and irregular acting*, had driven them into this *Rebellion . . .*". But Hubbard believed that the Indians had planned a general attack upon the English from New England to Virginia. He had no doubts about their motivation: "it is too evident, that the said *Indians* (who naturally delight in *bloody* and *deceitful actions*) did lay hold of any opportunity that might serve for a pretence to be put upon their *barbarous practices*".[14]

While it may be argued that the English settlers purchased their land from their Indian neighbours (fairly or unfairly being a matter of continuing debate), Mather's assertion of divine right is grist for the revisionists' mill. The revisionist case is further strengthened when Puritan claims are compared with the enlightened positions of dissenters such as Roger Williams, John Easton, and Samuel Gorton. Furthermore, the insistence that an Indian conspiracy was "common knowledge" or self-evident must give any historian pause. No one today is likely to attribute the cause of the war to the Indian's savage or barbarous nature. Nevertheless, our knowledge of the war is inevitably one-sided; the documentary record is almost entirely English and the historical debate is largely focused over interpretation of those documents. Did the leaders of the English colonists mean what they said? On the Indian side historians can only offer inferences based on sketchy evidence. Despite the efforts of ethno-historians, the Indian participants in the war remain shadowy figures, the creation of English fear, hatred, or prejudice. Of no one is this more true than Philip himself. Was he the calculating conspirator described in the early caricatures or a patriot defending a way of life? Did he play an active role in initiating hostilities or was his hand forced by others? What was his role as a military leader and as a diplomat? Why did he fail to unite the Indian peoples of New England? On these central questions, the record is silent.

Shifting power relationships

One fact stands out to explain altered English–Indian relations by 1675: an imbalance of power expressed in demographics. Estimates of population vary, but the European population was expanding and the Indian population, which had never recovered from the devastating epidemics of the second decade of the century, was static or in decline. Thus the pre-settlement Indian population of New England which may have numbered as many as 144,000 had probably declined to around 10,000.[15] This had great significance for the first settlers; the Massachusetts tribe, for example, had shrunk from 24,000 to 750 by 1631, thereby clearing the way for the Puritan immigration. It was among the survivors of such plagues that the missionaries often found their most willing converts. The immunities possessed by the English missionaries stood in sharp contrast to the failure of traditional religious leaders to protect their people from these catastrophes.[16]

Initially the fragile European settlements posed little in the way of a threat even to these decimated peoples. The former were too concerned with survival and were dependent upon Indian assistance. By 1675, however, there were about 52,000 Europeans living in the four colonies of New England: Plymouth, Massachusetts, Connecticut, and Rhode Island. The first three of these colonies were associated in the Confederation of New England, an organization founded for offensive and defensive war and for expansion at the expense of neighbouring Indians and Rhode Island. The Confederation was undermined from the beginning by conflicting interests and inequities in power. After 1655, when Massachusetts insisted on the right to veto the decisions of the Confederation commissioners, the organization lacked any real authority. Nevertheless, the colonists remained bound by language, culture and religion, all of which provided a common sense of place and purpose in the new world they inhabited. When threatened by war in 1675, these ties enabled them to revive the Confederation as an instrument by which war could be waged. It proved to be a blunt and fragile instrument, but, for all of its limitations, the Confederation provided the English with a unity that Indian opponents could not match.

The relative strength of the colonists appeared to provide substance for Increase Mather's claim of divine right to the land. And the growing English population needed more of it. This coincided with an economic crisis: the collapse of the fur trade and the decline in the value of wampum already discussed in this chapter. The Indian peoples in southern New England now possessed only one commodity which could be exchanged for European goods, their claims to the land itself. After 1660, increased tensions in English–Indian relations centred upon the issues of land sales and the subordination of Indian peoples to English political and legal authority. A new generation of English and Indian leaders was thus confronted with problems more complex than those of the first generation of the early years of settlement, problems rooted in a fundamental imbalance of power.

Such problems did not make war inevitable unless one falls back on such stereotypes as the conflict of civilization versus barbarism or assumes, as does Jennings, that the Puritans were bent on the conquest of their Indian neighbours by any means. Astute diplomacy is a way of peacefully overcoming such difficulties. Had Philip and the leaders of Plymouth been able to establish amicable day-to-day relations and an atmosphere of trust, war might have been avoided. Instead, the story is one of deterioration in the relations of two peoples who had once looked to one another for survival.

In the end both sides seem to have misunderstood the intentions of the other. Plymouth leaders demonstrated their misunderstanding of their neighbours when they referred to Philip as a king. In one respect this was a mocking reference to the pretensions of an Indian chief, but it also credited Philip with more authority than he possessed. It was true that he was the son of Massasoit, the most prominent of Wampanoag leaders who used his ties with the English settlers to increase his authority over his own people. But Philip was not a "king" and never wielded royal power over his followers. Philip was a sachem, a position of respect and authority, but he had to share this authority with the religious leaders, the powwows, and in wartime, with his tribe's military leaders. War frequently meant that experienced peacetime leaders, proven in diplomacy and committed to orderly and harmonious relations with neighbours, conceded power to younger and more aggressive warriors. There is some evidence that this may have been the case with Philip.[17] In any event Philip was the leader only of the Wampanoags inhabiting part of present-day Rhode Island, not of the entire alliance of villages which extended across southern New England from Narragansett Bay to Cape Cod or the islands. Philip never spoke for all of the Wampanoags; those on Cape Cod did not participate in the war. Philip himself never seems to have commanded more than 300 warriors. Therefore the initial Indian rising associated with his name was a limited affair. His escape from his peninsula home undoubtedly contributed to the widening of the war, but it remains unclear how he influenced its course.

Relations between the Wampanoags and Plymouth deteriorated after Massasoit's death in 1660. He was succeeded by Philip's elder brother Alexander (Wamsutta) who died in 1662 after rough handling by Plymouth authorities, who accused him of plotting against the colony. The real issue of Plymouth's concern was Wampanoag land sales to outsiders. A relatively weak colony without a secure charter, Plymouth depended upon its protectorate over the Wampanoag for protection against expansion by other colonies, particularly Rhode Island. Plymouth now exacted a new pact from Philip which confirmed previous agreements and gained Wampanoag acknowledgement that they were the subjects of the English crown. Philip agreed not to make war with other Indians or sell land to others without the colony's consent. Land sales were to prove a central issue of grievance between Philip and his English neighbours. The Wampanoags had land to sell to the expanding English population, but there were questions about Philip's legal rights to the land he sold and complaints that English buyers had not always acted fairly. Indians also found that their new English neighbours allowed their farm animals to run free, resulting in damage to Indian crops.[18]

Religion was also a source of tension. During the 1660s, the Reverend John Eliot sought unsuccessfully to convert the Wampanoags to Christianity. As one expert has pointed out, Eliot found few converts among cohesive native communities which possessed strong leadership.[19] The "praying Indians" were most frequently recruited from such people as the Massachusetts who had been so ravaged and demoralized by disease that they had few alternatives to conversion. Nevertheless, Eliot hoped that Philip might prove susceptible to the influence of the Indian missionary John Sassamon, who had been educated at the Indian school at Harvard. Sassamon lived among the Wampanoags in the 1660s and gained influence as Philip's secretary. However, Sassamon was expelled for crooked dealings at the end of the decade. The Wampanoags refused to turn their backs on their traditional religious practices. Philip would not have been the only sachem who concluded that living in a praying village would subvert his authority, undermine Indian land tenure, and challenge the cultural and social order of his people. Whatever his reasons, Philip rejected Christianity. The Wampanoags' hostility to Sassamon was made clear when three members of the tribe murdered him in 1675, the incident that provoked the war.

White–Indian relations were also complicated by recurring rumours of Indian plots to attack their English neighbours. While there does not appear to have been any substance to these rumours, they created an atmosphere of distrust that made it difficult to resolve concrete differences amicably. By 1671 Philip seems to have been forced by his powwows and younger, more aggressive followers to prepare for war. The issue seems to have been the new "frontier" town of Swansea, which extended Plymouth's presence deep into the territory traditionally claimed by Philip's people. Armed Wampanoags responded to this provocation by parading through Swansea. Philip does not seem to have had any real heart for war. He quickly backed down when confronted by a summons from the Plymouth General Court and agreed to surrender his firearms to the English authorities. He was also forced to pay a heavy fine. The severity of these terms prompted an appeal to the United Colonies who, nevertheless, confirmed Plymouth's conditions. This humiliation seems to have convinced the Wampanoags that no fair hearing was possible and could only make it difficult for Philip to maintain peace when tensions erupted anew in the wake of Sassamon's murder on 29 January 1675. The three murderers were tried and convicted by an English jury with six Indians seemingly participating in the decision. Their execution by the Plymouth authorities seems to have enraged the most warlike of Philip's followers.

Even a limited war between Philip's Wampanoags and Plymouth presented a threat to neighbouring Rhode Island, whose Quaker Lieutenant Governor John Easton urged the Indians to negotiate. His report of his discussions with the Indians provides a good summary of their grievances on the eve of the war. They said that the English missionaries threatened the authority of their leaders, that they had been cheated in land sales, and never received fair hearings in disputes with Englishmen. The English had made them drunk and their cattle and horses destroyed their crops. When Easton suggested arbitration, they replied that English arbitrators were always against them and they had lost much land thereby. Still Easton believed that war could be avoided. He proposed an arbitration panel consisting of an Indian "king" of their choice and the Governor of New York, Sir Edmund Andros. According to Easton, the Indians were well disposed to this novel approach. Plymouth, however, was determined to settle the dispute by military means. It seems doubtful that they would have accepted an arbitrator outside the framework of the United Colonies and it is unlikely that they would have been enthusiastic about Sir Edmund Andros becoming involved in what they considered the internal affairs of their colony, particularly considering that it was a colony without a secure charter. The war parties among both peoples now gained the upper hand. In June 1675, armed Wampanoags returned to Swansea and looted abandoned homes. The war began when a young Englishman shot and killed a looter.

A peace-maker such as Easton could only look on with foreboding: "now the English army is out to seeke after the indians, but it is most lickly that such most abell to do mischif will escape and women and children and impotent mai be destroyed and so the most abell will have les incumbrance to do mischif". There could have been no more accurate prediction of the course of events.[20]

Conflict

King Philip's War in southern New England consisted of five phases: (1) The initial skirmishes around Swansea and the mobilization of a body of Plymouth and Massachusetts troops who sought to trap Philip on the peninsula in which his home at Mount Hope was located. Had they succeeded the war might have been localized. Philip's escape along with that of the "squaw sachem"

Weetamoos, leader of the Pocassets, exposed New England to a wider conflict. (2) A rising by the Nipmucks, including converts of Eliot's mission, against the western Massachusetts towns in the upper Connecticut valley in which the colonists suffered a series of defeats and saw towns burned or abandoned. (3) The December 1675 campaign against the Narragansetts culminating in an assault on their fortified swamp village by a 1,000-man United Colonies army. Three hundred Indian warriors and as many women and children were killed in this attack by the colonists, who suffered dearly themselves. (4) An Indian offensive in February–May 1676, which struck a terrifying blow at eastern towns in Massachusetts, Plymouth, and Rhode Island. (5) A reversal of fortune in the summer of 1676 as the colonists adapted to the demands of frontier warfare and the Indian effort declined as a result of disunity and critical shortages of food and ammunition.

In retrospect, it seems unlikely that the Indians could have driven the colonists from New England even if that had been their common goal. The English had overwhelming advantages in numbers and material and possessed political and social institutions which allowed them ultimately to mobilize these resources to devastating effect. Nevertheless, when contemporaries surveyed the lists of English soldiers slain in ambush, of towns burned and their inhabitants killed or carried away into captivity, they could have not have been so sanguine. From the beginning the Indian warriors displayed a tactical superiority and an expert use of firearms that the colonists were slow to match. Indian proficiency with muskets came as a shock. Connecticut Deputy Governor William Leete concluded that they were "so accurate markes men above our own men, to doe execution, whereby more of ours are like to fall, rather than of theirs, vnlesse the Lord by speciall providence, doe deliuer them into our handes".[21] The New Englanders' training and militia institutions were quickly proven inadequate to the task of prosecuting a war against so formidable an enemy. Victory could be achieved not only by mobilization but by adaptation as well.

The military system of the United Colonies in 1675 was that of a mature militia based on the scattered self-governing farm towns. Militia companies elected their own officers and made and enforced their own rules. During the period of increased white–Indian tension after 1660, colonial governments such as Plymouth issued new military codes aimed at assuring a high and consistent state of readiness among the militia.[22] In addition, the United colonies provided a structure for military co-operation and allocation of responsibility which was the basis of the armies raised to fight King Philip's War. But little thought seems to have been given to how an Indian war should be fought. Training remained rooted in the European technique introduced by Plymouth's first professional, Miles Standish. The overwhelming victory achieved by the colonists in the Pequot War gave them no reason to doubt that European tactics would prevail in future conflicts. The Pequot defeat, however, provided food for thought for Indian military leaders and may have been the catalyst for the Indian commitment to firearms and the skulking tactics that they would use with such success.

Furthermore, the militia were not an army, but a partially trained home guard best suited to local defence. Events were to prove that isolated communities were vulnerable to determined Indian attacks despite the presence of their militiamen. The forces raised to meet the challenge of 1675 were *ad hoc* creations, a mix of volunteers and conscripts raised from the New England towns under quotas established by the United Colonies. The men had never served together before and their officers had little experience on commands of this sort. It is little wonder that the officers fell back upon textbook formulas for the direction of these forces, but the limits of their training soon became apparent.

The troops who participated in the first phase of the conflict, the relief of Swansea and the advance on Mount Hope in June–July 1675, illustrate the mixed nature of the colonial forces. Massachusetts Bay dispatched three companies to Swansea. The first consisted of 100 militiamen drawn by quota from 11 different towns. A second consisted of mounted troops; while cavalry were seldom employed in North American warfare, mounted infantry often were. Indeed they were an extremely valuable asset in warfare that demanded rapid movement over long distances. The third company stood outside the New England social order. They were volunteers under the command of Captain Samuel Moseley, a former privateer, whose men included servants, apprentices, seamen, and convicted pirates. They were a different lot from the farmers who made up the first company and the more affluent citizens in the second who could afford mounts.

Moseley was not a militia officer, but had recently won fame by the capture of "Dutch pirates" who had been preying on New England shipping, some of whom now joined his company. He was a fiery spirit, at home in war. His men were in the forefront of many of the major engagements and he became a hero for many who despaired of good news. Thus he was praised as: "an excellent Souldier, and an undaunted Spirit, one whose Memory will be Honorable for his many eminent Services he hath done the Publick".[23] But Moseley represented the dark side of the colonial war effort. He was an Indian-hater and treated friendly and enemy Indians alike with indiscriminate brutality. His attacks on friendly Indian settlements threatened to turn them into enemies and he was censured by the Massachusetts General Court. Whatever hardships Mary Rowlandson may have experienced, she was fortunate not to have fallen into the hands of someone like Moseley.

On 16 October 1675, he added a postscript to a letter referring to a captured Indian woman: "This aforesaid Indian was ordered to be torn in peeces by Doggs and she was soe dealt with."[24]

Moseley embodied the anti-Indian hysteria which gripped Massachusetts in the first year of the war. One cannot escape a sense of increasing racial tension between whites and Indians before the outbreak of the war and now it found full voice in the fears of the inhabitants of Massachusetts Bay, who believed that their Christian Indian neighbours could not be trusted. Ironically, this attitude undermined the colony's military potential. Daniel Gookin, the Massachusetts Bay Indian superintendent, believed that the eastern praying Indian towns might form a defensive wall around the greater part of the colony. Were these towns, which were located 12 to 14 miles apart, provided with a garrison, one-third of whom would be English, a formidable barrier would be created and the fidelity of the praying Indians assured. Gookin realized that the militia were not properly trained to oppose the Indians in the woods. Massachusetts security, he believed, required praying Indian patrols in the gaps between the fortified villages.[25]

The majority of the Massachusetts population, however, seems to have regarded the praying Indians not as allies, but as an internal security problem. Since it was difficult to distinguish between a friendly and an unfriendly Indian, they concluded that no Indian could be trusted. The praying Indians were disarmed and confined to their place of dwelling. They were not allowed to travel unless in the company of an Englishman and could be shot on sight if alone. As terrifying reports of Indian military success poured in, the colonists became increasingly angry at the Indians in their midst and at those such as Gookin and Eliot who tried to defend them. Eliot warned that these actions which were "worse yn death" would only prolong the war.[26] But popular opinion was better reflected by another writer who referred to the Christian Indians as the "preying" Indians: "they have made preys of much English Blood but now they are all much reduced to their Several Confinements; which is much to a general Satisfaction in that respect".[27] Eventually some 500 praying Indians were confined to Deer Island in Boston harbour in conditions of great distress.[28] As a result the colony dispensed with a valuable military asset at the time of its greatest need.

Among the troops initially dispatched to Swansea by Massachusetts Bay was a company of 52 praying Indians. But these soldiers had little opportunity to prove themselves. They were met with distrust by many of the officers and soldiers who claimed that "they were cowards and skulked behind trees in a fight, and that they shot over the enemies head".[29] Half of the company was released after only 25 days' service, the rest remaining until Philip made good his escape. Their critics within the army had yet to learn the central tactical lesson of the war: that skulking was not cowardice, but the only way to defeat the Indians at their own game. Had the praying Indian company been properly used it is conceivable that Philip might have been taken at Mount Hope and the war stifled.

Connecticut authorities also distrusted the Indians in their midst and passed regulations restricting their movement similar to those of Massachusetts.[30] Nevertheless, they did not hesitate to employ non-Christian Pequot and Mohegan Indians in their forces. One hundred were in the colony's pay in October 1675 and they were offered bounties of "foure coates of tradeing cloathe" for every prisoner or head they brought in. Deputy Governor Leete so despaired at the prospects for victory that he proposed recruiting the neutral Indians by offering to "purchase so many foreskins of these Philistines now in hostility." After the Great Swamp fight in December, it was concluded that "they proved very faithful in our service and were very well treated by us".[31] Connecticut troops suffered less from Indian ambushes during the course of the war because of the assistance of these Indians.

Not until April 1676 did Massachusetts Bay again recruit Indian troops. Captain Samuel Hunting was authorized to raise a company of 40 praying Indians from those confined to Deer Island. Eventually this company increased to 80 men as sufficient firearms arrived from England, the praying Indians having been deprived of their own. Thus the praying Indians only took the field as life was ebbing from the Indian uprising. Gookin credited the change in fortune to their participation in the conflict. Certainly they made an important contribution, proving themselves invaluable as scouts and, according to Hunting, killing or capturing some 400 of the enemy with the loss of but one man.[32] The success of Hunting's company undoubtedly contributed to the Massachusetts practice of recruiting Indian troops to protect its frontier during the next 25 years.

Styles of war

The colonists' initial rejection of the praying Indians reflected a confidence in their overwhelming military power. It was a confidence that was rapidly shaken, for they were confronted with a war beyond their experience. King Philip's War was the first in which the Indians were well equipped with modern flintlock firearms. One militia officer concluded that the combination of firearms with bows and arrows actually gave the enemy a decided advantage in weapons and, no doubt inspired by the example of Gustavus Adolphus, he advocated matching them with leather field pieces mounted on carts.[33] The

Indians may have had a superiority in flintlock weapons, since some militia continued to be equipped with matchlocks and pikes. Furthermore, as Patrick Malone has demonstrated, the Indians were superior marksmen and their skulking tactics, disparaged as cowardly by the colonists, were clearly superior to those of the enemy. Malone also observes that for the first time the New England Indians abandoned traditional restraints on war. They appear to have learned well the lessons of the Pequot War and were now prepared to wage total war on all of the colonists, making no distinction between combatant and non-combatant. The New England tradition of the captivity narrative begins with King Philip's War.

The colonial military leadership was caught unprepared for this entirely new and formidable challenge. Their troops consisted for the most part of partially trained militiamen who could not long be spared from the farm. These men were certainly brave and were formidable in local defence. Despite attacks with flaming arrows and other combustibles, Indian assault parties seldom could capture a determinedly defended garrison house. Colonial authorities gave detailed attention to the construction of town defences, specifying flanking blockhouses for crossfire. Careful orders enforcable by fines provided for sentry duty, for protection of field workers, and for scouting nearby woods. Because Indian raiders usually struck at dawn, Connecticut ordered that the inhabitants of each garrison should stand to arms an hour before sunrise until half an hour after it had risen.[34] Local defence improved with these measures. But experience proved that road-bound soldiers, trained in close order and volley fire, were badly outclassed in the wooded countryside. From August 1675, New Englanders were bombarded with terrifying reports of ambushes and massacres. Contemporary observers noted that the Indians were masters of concealment and movement in the swampy thickets of southern New England. These swamps provided the Indians with natural fortresses, one being described as "so full of trees that a parcel of Indians may be within the length of a Pike of a Man, and he cannot discover them; and besides, this as well as all other swamps, is so soft Ground, that an Englishman can neither go nor stand thereon, and yet these bloody Savages will run along over it, holding their Guns cross their arms (and if occasion be) discharge in that position."[35] The religious dissenter Samuel Gorton warned John Winthrop, Jr of the perils of warfare in the swamps and bogs which were

> more pernicious to valiant souldiers then are bullwarkes, towers, castles, and walled cities. I remember the time of the warres in Ireland, (when I was young, in Queene Elizabeth's dayes of famous memory) where much English blood was spilt by a people much like vnto these, the

Earle of Terrone being their leader, where many valiant souldiers lost their liues, both horse and foot, by meanes of woods, bushes, boggs, and quagmires. . . .[36]

Daniel Gookin recalled that the English expected no difficulty in chastising the Indians:

But it was found another manner of thing than expected; for our men could see no enemy to shoot at, but yet felt their bullets out of the thick bushes where they lay in ambushments. The enemy also used this strategem, to apparel themselves from the waist upwards with green boughs, that our Englishmen could not readily discern them from the natural bushes; this manner of fighting our men had little experience of, and hence were under great disadvantage.[37]

William Hubbard also believed that inexperience was the cause of English defeats, but contended that the Indians frequently outnumbered the colonists by six or seven to one.[38] Indeed, small parties of English soldiers did blunder into ambushes in which they were overwhelmed.

Initially the colonial military leadership had no solution to the dilemma of Indian warfare. Militiamen lacked the discipline of the Indians, who moved silently through the woods. Gookin observed that the English talked too much and made such noise that they frequently gave themselves away to an ambush. He related the story of a Mohegan warrior who, accompanying a party of Connecticut soldiers in the woods, made one of them take off his squeaking shoes and exchange them for moccasins and another wet down his leather breeches to prevent them from rustling.[39] Indeed, it is likely that the democratic nature of the New England militia contributed to generally lax discipline. One of the first major colonial defeats occurred on 18 September 1675 when Captain Thomas Lathrop and 80 men were ambushed while convoying supply carts near Deerfield, Massachusetts. The Indians struck from the cover of a swamp and fewer than ten of the colonists survived. Hubbard blamed Lathrop for having dispersed his men among the trees in the Indian style, thereby allowing them to be overwhelmed by superior numbers. Even after the war, Hubbard continued to maintain that Lathrop should have kept his men in close order, for the Indians would never have challenged the English face-to-face on the open field. But it may have been that there was no order at all. Increase Mather attributed this defeat to poor discipline. He wrote that Lathrop's men had stopped to gather grapes and had carelessly stacked their arms in the carts.[40] In any event, Lathrop's defeat offered the colonists an important lesson: "Our People, since the Loss of Captain Lathrop . . . are grown not less valorous, but more cautious: Experience is the Mother of

Prudence, and little Good comes of despising an Enemy." This writer went on to observe that Lathrop "in the Pequot Wars, had done Exploits".[41] Lathrop's defeat illustrates how far things had changed since 1637.

The Narragansetts

By November 1675 the first two phases of the war had gone badly for the colonies. Philip had eluded capture and the Nipmucks of western Massachusetts, including some of the praying Indians in that area, had risen and devastated the towns of the upper Connecticut valley. In response to this deteriorating situation, the Commissioners of the United Colonies arrived at the most controversial decision of the war: a campaign against the powerful and neutral Narragansett tribe. Ostensibly, the Commissioners acted from fear that the Narragansetts were in secret league with the enemy, harbouring their fugitives contrary to commitments given in July and supplying them with food. They told one colonial official that they feared to surrender refugees to whom they were related lest they be put to death or sold into captivity.[42] There were good reasons for such fears. All modern authorities view the Commissioners' justification skeptically.[43] There was no firm basis for the assertion that the Narragansetts were hostile. Ninigret, sachem of the Niantics or southern Narragansetts, had cultivated good relations with the English and emissaries from the tribe had professed their intention to abide by previous treaties. Rhode Islander Richard Smith reported to Massachusetts Secretary Edward Rawson in October that he had spoken with the sachem Canonicus. He found that "they have quick intilligence, and seem to be somewhat transported with the newes they have of the slauter of oure men up in the Cuntrey, yt I know Cononcos inclyns nott to mak warr."[44]

Frustration in pursuit of a skulking enemy may have prompted a pre-emptive strike against the Narragansetts. But interest as well as fear motivated this campaign: hunger for the Narragansetts' land and for the captives and plunder which would be reaped. These were the stakes which seemed to justify the risks of a winter campaign and the hazard of driving a formidable neutral people into the camp of the enemy. To achieve their goal, the United Colonies raised the largest army to be deployed in the war: over 1,000 men (about 2 per cent of the white population of New England) under Plymouth Governor Josiah Winslow.

Even in good conditions, supplies for 1,000 men would have strained colonial resources. In September one officer had stated that his men as an "absolute necessity" required "powder, shott, biscake, cheese or raisins, large and warm waistcoats and drawers, tobaco, some hatchets and a Chirurgion [surgeon]."[45] A winter campaign confronted the colonies with formidable organizational and logistical problems. Travel overland was difficult in the best of times, but snow-blocked roads and paths could bring operations to a standstill. Transportation difficulties would exacerbate a difficult supply situation. The army and its horses would have to be fed from the colonies' food surpluses in a time in which war had interfered with the normal course of agriculture. Sufficient winter clothing had to be provided if the army were to survive the conditions of wet and cold. Earlier mobilizations such as the concentration at Swansea during the summer had been *ad hoc* responses to emergencies. The Narragansett campaign required a new level of planning and co-operation by the United Colonies commissioners. This was, observes Douglas Leach, "the first campaign in New England history that was really supposed to be carefully planned before it was set in motion".[46]

Each colony contributed troops in proportion to its population (Massachusetts, 567; Plymouth, 158; Connecticut, 315) and each town in turn was assigned a quota which it filled by volunteers or, if necessary, by conscription. Recruiters encountered a lack of enthusiasm for winter service, and in Massachusetts draft dodging became a concern. To encourage recruitment, the authorities offered the prospect of the reward of Indian lands in addition to pay. In February 1676, Massachusetts began to solicit loans secured by lands to be conquered. However, the war would not pay for itself. Even those New England families whose lives were not disrupted by military service would feel the bite of the war's financial burden. The town of Dorchester, Massachusetts found its colony tax bill explode from £28 in 1671 to £408 in 1675.[47] The colonists' material resources and their taxation powers gave them a decided advantage over their Indian opponents, but the war would exhaust an economy that in fact was modest in scale.

Winslow had never commanded so large a force and, indeed, no New England commander, including his adviser Benjamin Church, had experience beyond small unit actions. Winslow was confronted not only by unusual supply problems, but by the challenge of holding together a large confederate army. Indeed, Winslow, as leader of the smallest contingent, was probably chosen for diplomatic rather than military considerations. Certainly his diplomatic skills would be taxed, for there were tensions between the Massachusetts and Connecticut forces over the conduct of the war and its spoils. One issue was the role of friendly Indians. The Pequot–Mohegan detachment which accompanied the Connecticut troops on the Narragansett campaign outraged Indian-haters such as Moseley, who considered them traitors. These conflicts would contribute to the demise of the United Colonies as a viable confederation even before it was terminated by the crown.

The strategic objective of the campaign was unclear. Ostensibly, the army's purpose was to threaten the Narragansetts with force if they did not abide by previous commitments. But little in the way of negotiation occurred. Moseley's company was transported to the Narragansett country by sea and arrived ahead of the main army. His men made it clear that, whatever the announced purpose of the campaign, their goal was slaves and loot. The United Colonies planned to support the army in the Narragansett country for two months. If it withdrew at the end of that time without disarming the Narragansetts, nothing would have been accomplished. But in European–Indian warfare, blows delivered by large armies frequently missed their mark, for Indian peoples often dispersed before a superior force. Thus European campaigns would often be delivered at the stored food supply of the Indians rather than the enemy themselves. Destruction of food was a serious blow and might sometimes bring the Indians to seek peace. But it was not a definitive military solution.

On this occasion the colonial army profited from the winter conditions. The bare trees deprived the Indians of their usual cover and the frozen pathways opened the way into the Great Swamp which they had deemed impenetrable by Europeans. Within the swamp the Narragansetts were completing a large palisaded village, which was crowded with dwellings of their families. This sense of security was fatal to them when an Indian deserter led the colonial army through the swamp to the site of the fortified town on 19 December. The Indian position was fortified with a strong palisade and blockhouses for flanking fire. It was a formidable objective for a force without artillery and without any experience in sieges or assaults on forts. Nor does the army appear to have approached the village with any predetermined plan. The leading troops under Moseley were fortunate to arrive before an uncompleted gate, where they launched an attack. Other troops were simply fed in as they arrived. There seems to have been no attempt to surround the enemy. The Great Swamp fight was a furious encounter battle in which the English were driven back on at least one occasion. It is not clear why the English seem to have prevailed. No one knows how many Indian warriors actually opposed them. English estimates were that they had killed 200 to 300 warriors, but that may have been an exaggeration. The Narragansetts fielded more women and children than warriors, which may account for the English success. The battle for the village was resolved only when the order was given to burn the wigwams. The fire claimed many Indian victims and drove the rest into the swamp. It left the English in the midst of a smouldering ruin, themselves deprived of shelter and encumbered with scores of wounded as the bitter winter night closed in.

The English lost 20 dead and 200 wounded including many of the officers. They were without food and adequate medical treatment and could not be sure that the enemy would not renew the battle. Their retreat to their supply base at Wickford was as costly as the battle. Eventually more than 80 English died from wounds suffered in the Great Swamp fight. The expedition was a failure. It insured that the Narragansetts would enter the war on the side of the Wampanoags and Nipmucks, and while the battle may have weakened the Narragansetts, it did not destroy them. The Indians were exposed to great hardship, but as we have seen, they were capable of enormous endurance. After the battle, Winslow seems to have had no strategy for bringing the war to the enemy. In what became known as the "hungry march", the army undertook a futile pursuit of the Narragansetts until it was disbanded in early February. The United Colonies' offensive had ended and would not be renewed.[48] On 10 February, the Indians struck at Lancaster, Massachusetts in the raid that carried off Mary Rowlandson. The next phase of the war had begun as the Indians began their offensive against the Massachusetts towns.

The Indian spring offensive

The Indian attack on the Massachusetts frontier towns was the most memorable phase of the war. The goal of the Indian offensive is unclear, but since the raiders did not distinguish between combatant and non-combatant, it was a campaign of terror. Fortified garrison houses offered the inhabitants of the frontier towns refuge, but residents caught outside or in undefended dwellings were in peril. Surprise was the key Indian advantage and lack of intelligence the great English weakness. Massachusetts' failure to employ the praying Indians as scouts was a critical mistake. In fact, two praying Indians sent as spies to determine Narragansett strength after the Great Swamp fight provided warning of the Lancaster raid, but they were recommitted to Deer Island where they languished until April.[49] Thereafter, the first news of Indian movements was usually that of a town in flames.

Columns of troops hastening to the relief of these beleaguered towns were tempting targets for ambush. Even detachments accompanied by friendly Indians were vulnerable: on 26 March Captain Michael Pierce of Scituate in Plymouth Colony and his company of 63 English and 20 Cape Indians were surrounded and destroyed by a Narragansett war party.[50] Colonial troops appeared helpless in the face of this offensive. The desperation of the authorities was evident on 23 March when a council at Boston ordered the construction of a stockade between the Charles and Merrimack rivers, leaving the frontier towns exposed. Even the towns to be protected by the fortification were unenthusiastic. Marblehead's response to the project seems to have been typical. It replied on 28 March that it was too poor, that the stockade offered no security for towns cut off, that the Merrimack was fordable in many places, and that the expense of maintaining fortifications was too great. It announced that it was even too poor to send a representative to discuss the matter.[51] Bad morale and war exhaustion were evident throughout the colony. There were many petitions for exemptions from service from men who needed to attend to families and farms. In April an entire company which had been in service since August asked to be allowed to return to their homes and be replaced by others.[52]

The climactic event of this phase of the war occurred at Sudbury, Massachusetts on 21 April. Indian raiders surrounded the town during the night and struck at first light. The defenders of Sudbury, however, were well organized in their fortified houses and the Indians had to content themselves with burning unoccupied buildings. Sudbury's would-be rescuers were less fortunate than its inhabitants. First a small party from Concord was wiped out. Next a company from Marlborough, led by the experienced Captain Samuel Wadsworth, was lured by a few Indians into a classic ambush and forced to make a desperate stand on a nearby hill. The battle raged for an entire afternoon despite efforts of other detachments to come to Wadsworth's aid. At the end of the day Wadsworth and over 30 of his company of 50 to 60 men were dead. This was the last major Indian assault. Sudbury appears to mark declining Indian strength in a population that was not large to begin with. The captive Mary Rowlandson recalled that when the Indians returned from their victory at Sudbury, "they came home without that rejoicing and triumphing over their victory, which they were wont to shew at other times, but rather like Dogs (as they say) which have lost their ears".[53]

Although they arrived too late to participate in the fighting, the Sudbury battle also marked the first appearance of Captain Hunting's company of praying Indians. On the following morning, they scouted across the river and reported that the English could safely gather and bury their dead. Gookin observed that "after the attack of Sudbury (at which time our Indians first went forth) the Indians went down wind amain".[54] For the first time the Massachusetts forces had acquired the ability to pursue effectively the Indians in the woods. The success of the praying Indians dampened the fires of the anti-Indian hysteria and may explain what appears to be a decline in Moseley's popularity.

There are ironic parallels between the Narragansett campaign of December–January and the Indian offensive of February–April. Ultimately, both culminated in raids against towns which probably contained more non-combatants than combatants. Both carried out their assaults indiscriminately and with great brutality. Neither campaign had a clear objective or strategy for achieving success. Neither resulted in the defeat of the enemy. The prime feature of each was terror, but in neither case did terror convince the enemy to sue for peace. Indeed, the principal result of both efforts was the exhaustion of the raiding forces. Neither side had the means to achieve a decisive victory.

Ultimately, Indian tactical superiority could not mask the imbalance against them in population and resources. By the spring of 1676 they were facing war exhaustion resulting from battle casualties, disease, and shortages of food and ammunition. On 18 May a mounted party of Massachusetts men struck an Indian fishing camp on the Connecticut river, killing many non-combatants, destroying two forges and dealing a blow to slender food supplies. The troopers barely escaped total disaster when the Indians rallied and almost cut off their retreat. A quarter of the 150-man force including its commander were slain as the withdrawal turned into a rout. Nevertheless, the loss of family members must have been a demoralizing blow to the warriors who now could see no end to the war. The Indian cause had never commanded unified support. Not only had the Christian Indians allied themselves with the English, but so had the non-Christian Pequots and Mohegans. During the winter Philip seems to have gone as far as New York seeking allies, only to be attacked by the Mohawks who were no friends of the Algonquians of New England. Jennings believes that Philip's defeat at the hands of the Mohawks was the decisive turning point of the war.[55] Indeed, the Wampanoags and Narragansetts found members of their own tribes arrayed against them in the war. By the summer of 1676, many of the hostile Indians were looking for an end to the fighting. On 10 August, Captain Hunting reported that Indian captives revealed that the enemy were in want of food and had lost the will to fight.[56]

This occurred as the colonies seized the tactical initiative by adapting to the Indian way of war. Hunting's praying Indian company, the English–Indian task force of Connecticut Captains George Denison and James Avery, and Church's mixed company began operations as the Indian war effort was in decline and disarray. This perhaps explains Church's extraordinary success in recruiting Indian prisoners to serve against their former comrades. Had Indian morale been higher, his achievement might have been less. Indians no doubt preferred surrender to Church to the fate that awaited them at the hands of other captains: death or enslavement, practices of which Church disapproved. Church was equally effective as a mediator and a warrior. His personal knowledge of Indian leaders served him well when he negotiated the surrender of Philip's war-weary ally Awashonks, the "squaw sachem" of the

Sakonnets and 80 or 90 of her people (who were sold into slavery despite Church's protests). It was a victory as significant as any he won by force of arms.[57] In the end Philip's death commemorated a war that was already sputtering to a close.

Total war

Was this a total war? In one sense it was not. The war began as a limited conflict between Philip's Wampanoags over issues that might have been settled peacefully. Had the colonial forces captured Philip in the summer of 1675 with an overwhelming show of force, the matter might have been quickly resolved. Even after the war widened and despite the racial hatred expressed by combatants on both sides, there is no evidence that either side sought the extermination of the other's "civilization" or "race". Indeed, there is no evidence that either side had a well defined strategy. Both sides in the war were hampered by disunity. The Indians' problem in this regard has been noted above. As for the colonies, the war was fought without the active participation of one New England colony, Rhode Island, and co-operation between the United Colonies collapsed after the Narragansett campaign. Afterwards each colony looked to its own defence and its own interest.

Nevertheless, whatever the initial limits in the summer of 1675, the war became total in effect. All authorities agree that King Philip's War was the costliest American war in terms of relative population. For the Indians, the defeat was total. James Axtell has concluded that of 11,600 Indians in southern New England in 1675, the war claimed 7,900 or 68 per cent of the belligerent population. These include almost 2,000 dead as a result of battle or wounds, 3,000 dead of disease or exposure, 1,000 sold as slaves and transported, and 2,000 permanent refugees.[58] Native Americans in southern New England would never again be able to withstand English claims to the land and to sovereignty.

One contemporary estimated that 800 English men, women, and children died in the war, but the loss of life was probably higher.[59] The agricultural economy and the financial stability of the colonies had been dealt a blow from which it would take years to recover. Large numbers of homeless people and demanding war veterans placed new burdens on treasuries already exhausted by the burden of conducting the war. The physical and psychological impact of the war on this town-centred society can be measured by this statistic: of 90 New England towns, 52 had been attacked, with 25 pillaged and 17 destroyed.[60] "All in all", writes Francis Jennings, "the second Puritan Conquest was a fiasco for its victors. Instead of easy plunder, the Puritans netted massive debts and smoking ruins, to say nothing of heavy casualties."[61] The unity of the colonies had been shattered by the war; it would be imposed again by imperial authority in the form of the Dominion of New England.

King Philip's War may also be considered a total war in the manner of its conduct. It was a war of attrition. Despite tactical superiority, the Indians had no strategy by which they could reverse the consequences of their inferiority in manpower and resources. Although the English and Indians initially employed different tactics, neither observed traditional European military conventions. Both sides waged war against the other's total population and, without well defined military objectives, relied upon terror to overcome the enemy. The captivity narrative tradition demonstrates that Indian terror became a permanent part of white New England memory.

The Indian way of war meted out harsh punishments for opponents, although some contemporary charges of Indian atrocities, rape of white women for example, seem inconsistent with Indian practice.[62] The English also waged a war of terror. Their religious leaders assured them that their cause was just. Even a non-Puritan such as Roger Williams was convinced that the war was a just war and he referred to the enemy as "barbarous men of Bloud who are as justly to be repelled and subdued as Wolves that assault the sheepe." But Williams urged that captives should be spared.[63] John Easton was "so perswaided of new England prists thay ar so blinded by thr spiret of persecution . . . that thay have bine the Case that the law of nations and the law of arems have bine voiolated in this war".[64] Had the English observed the traditional laws of war in the Narragansett campaign, they would have given the enemy an opportunity to surrender before storming the town at the cost of so many non-combatant lives. Their assault was consistent with the destruction of the Pequot village in 1637, Virginia's campaigns against the Powhatan confederacy, and England's Irish wars. Terror was the English way of war against an elusive, skulking enemy who would not fight on traditional European terms. The English might invoke necessity as a justification for throwing out the rule book, but in doing so they abdicated their claim to moral superiority.[65]

New England respect for the Indian way of war is evident in the tactics employed by Church and Hunting in the summer of 1676. The loyal and successful service of the praying Indians did much to relieve the hostility of Massachusetts whites. For the remainder of the century, whites would look to Indian mercenaries to protect their frontiers. Those frontiers remained vulnerable. Although the English settlers had destroyed their Indian neighbours, many refugees were assimilated into northern Algonquian tribes such as the Abenakis and continued decades of hostilities against remote English settlements such as the coastal communities of Maine. After 1689 they found a powerful new ally in French Canada which supported and encouraged raids against the New England frontier. Accounts of this warfare demonstrate that the colonists had yet to cope successfully with Indian tactics.[66] Church remained a respected commander and participated in a series of campaigns against the Indians and the French in Maine from 1689 to 1704.[67] Once again he led volunteer companies of English and Indian troops, but he did not enjoy the same success. For some reason his troops do not seem to have been particularly well disciplined, lighting fires against his instructions and ignoring the warnings of sentries.[68] He was also operating on unfamiliar ground against enemies unknown to him. His Abenaki opponents were under the influence of an alien European power which he abhorred and held accountable for the attacks on the New England frontier. He was particularly angered by the French and Indian devastation of Deerfield, Massachusetts in 1704 and seems to have wanted a war of vengeance against the French. He sent a message to the Governor of Canada threatening him with Indian terror if attacks on the frontier did not cease.[69]

New England did not adopt Church's strategy for dealing with wars directed from Canada. Instead it responded with the first of a series of joint military and naval expeditions aimed at the capture of Quebec. Such expeditions were better suited to the kind of military training which remained the rule among the New England militia. Why had not New Englanders adapted their training to the lessons learned in King Philip's War? The answer seems to be that the Indian way of war was an integral part of the Indian way of life; it was learned in childhood and was constantly practised. For farmers and part-time soldiers who knew little of the woods, traditional militia drill was the most compatible form of training. It was adequate for local defence and formed the basis for the armies that would march towards Quebec. But frontier war required hard, disciplined soldiers experienced in skulking tactics and for whom war was a full-time commitment. In New England colonial society such men were to be found only upon the margins. They were expensive in wartime, but expendable and soon forgotten. The continued colonial commitment to a military system that was socially acceptable, but militarily inadequate, offers a revealing insight into the relationship between war and society.

Chapter Five

Indians and the wars for empire, 1689–1763

Imperial wars

We now turn from a two-year period of war in New England involving settlers and natives to the protracted imperial struggle for the control of North America. Conflict between France and Britain now determined issues of peace and war in northeastern North America. King William's War (1689–97), Queen Anne's War (1702–13), King George's War (1744–8) and the Seven Years War (1756–63) had their roots in Europe rather than America. Peaceful relations between frontier neighbours could be ruptured arbitrarily as the result of diplomatic breakdowns between London and Paris. Years of warfare might also end abruptly with peace treaties restoring the *status quo ante bellum* without regard for the sacrifices and interests of North American combatants. A prolonged period of peace and co-operation between Britain and France between 1713 and 1740 also meant diminished conflict on the frontier. From the European perspective, North American conflict was initially a sideshow, but by the Seven Years War, European armies and fleets would intervene on a large scale, transforming the nature of warfare and achieving decisive results.

Nevertheless, European–Indian conflict in North America was also governed by motives independent of the policies of European cabinets. Expanding English settler populations pressed on Indian lands, reaching the Ohio River by 1760. Indians sometimes resisted this expansion by diplomatic means, invoking the protection of imperial powers, or retreated to more remote and secure regions. But they were also prepared to use force to protect their autonomy, security and rights to the land. Indian motives for war were no different from those voiced at the time of King Philip's War. Now, however, Indian tribes could look to one or the other of the European powers

3. *The French and Indian War*

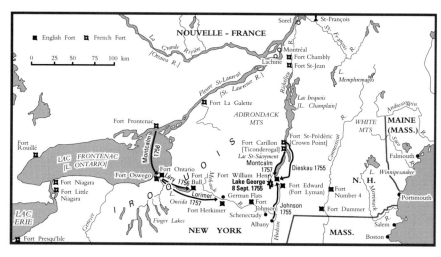

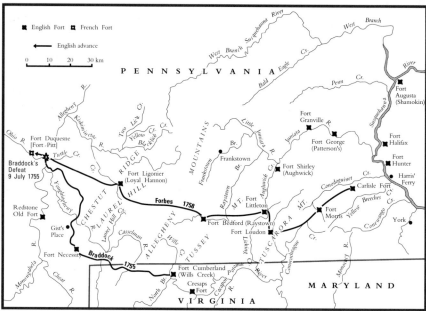

as allies in their wars of resistance. Indians participated in the imperial wars of the era for motives of their own. Although they were a powerful military asset, Indian allies were reliable friends only as long as their allies recognized their interests. Thus, when the Iroquois found that an English alliance did not protect them from disastrous defeats at the hands of the French, they concluded a peace with the French in 1701 and pursued a policy of neutrality in the imperial wars until the Seven Years War. Indians also made war in times of imperial peace. The western Abenaki chief Grey Lock carried out a successful guerrilla war in 1723–7 which barred much of Vermont from settlement. He does not appear to have had any regard for imperial interests, but fought to protect his people's independence.[1]

Despite the vast theatre of operations embraced by the imperial wars, eventually ranging from Newfoundland to Detroit and along the southern frontier, the nature of warfare remained consistent with that which emerged in King Philip's War. The Indians remained the masters of frontier warfare and frequently defeated European militia and regulars in large-scale and small-scale actions. In all of the wars Indian raiders were able to strike frontier settlements almost at will, killing or abducting inhabitants found outside their forts and eluding or destroying their pursuers. Details of these raids are familiar to those who have studied the Indian offensive against New England in the spring of 1676. While the French suffered enormous disadvantages in manpower and resources in the imperial wars, they possessed a clear advantage in frontier warfare because of their Indian alliances and the adoption of the Indian way of war by colonial officers and militia. This was a formidable combination. Although some English colonial officers such as Robert Rogers would follow the example of Benjamin Church and create detachments of specialized Anglo-Indian frontier fighters, the majority of English soldiers remained at a tactical disadvantage in the forest. The English strategy against New France would remain a solidly conventional one: armies and fleets directed at Quebec itself or its outlying defences such as Port Royal or Louisbourg. Unsuccessful expeditions were launched against Quebec in 1690 and 1711 before it fell in 1759. Port Royal was captured in 1710 and Louisbourg twice in 1745 and 1758. The Seven Years War was a decisive British success because they were able to transform it into a conventional European war in which they had the advantage. For the first time Britain was able to dictate the terms on which the war was fought. French Canada was thus ceded to Britain in 1763. Britain had defeated France, but not her Indian allies. Military and diplomatic success represented by the Treaty of Paris was soon clouded by diplomatic and military failure on the western frontiers. During 1763 triumphant British regulars would be chastened by native foes who continued to possess tactical superiority in forest warfare.

French–Indian relations

The names of the wars discussed in this chapter reflect the imperial dimension of North American conflict. "King William's War", "Queen Anne's War", "King George's War" recall these events from an English perspective. So too does "French and Indian War", the name commonly applied to the North American aspect of the Seven Years War when conflict actually began in 1754. But "French and Indian War" within the Anglo-American historical memory recalls not only the imperial struggle for the possession of a continent, but also a certain kind of war: the war of the frontiers, a war in which the French and their Indian allies excelled and which terrorized the inhabitants of the English border settlements. The ferocity of those raiders still conjures up nightmares, as the present author can testify, having been thoroughly terrified as a boy by the warrior Magua in *The Last of the Mohicans*. The Indians always seem to have been on *their* side, placing Americans' hapless frontier ancestors at a distinct disadvantage. Of course that was not always the case, but it was sufficiently true to have given the French the military initiative until 1758. Indian alliances were the most important military asset possessed by the French Empire in North America.

French success in forming such alliances is attributable to many factors, intelligent leadership not being the least. The very nature of French imperialism in North America made France the more desirable partner for many native peoples. It was an empire of commerce rather than settlement, one whose reach, thanks to the exploitation of excellent interior water communications, was extensive but light. French traders brought prized European goods including firearms to distant peoples in Illinois and on the Great Lakes, but did not threaten their autonomy. The small French settlements which followed the trade were as much assimilated into Indian society and culture as the reverse. Jesuit missionaries have been criticized for bringing disease and dissension among the Hurons and other Indian peoples, but they were relatively more successful than Protestant rivals in winning converts and allies. Their success created a satanic alliance in the eyes of New England Puritans, who saw Jesuits such as Father Rales, missionary to the eastern Abenakis, as their most dangerous enemy. The French were successful when they treated the Indians as allies rather than subjects. Thus the Indians of the midwest gave the French governor the name "Onontio" or "Great Mountain" to describe him as the leader of an alliance of Algonquian peoples. It was a term of respect for a powerful figure who could intervene to protect the harmony and security of the peoples of the region. But Onontio was an alliance chief, not a sovereign. When Céleron de Blainville marched through the Ohio valley in

1749 burying leaden plates claiming the region for Louis XV, he received a hostile reception from the inhabitants who regarded the land as theirs.[2]

When the French established their settlements in the St Lawrence River valley in the seventeenth century, they encountered a great Indian enemy: the Iroquois or Five Nations. This confederacy of Mohawks, Oneidas, Onondagas, Cayugas, and Senecas located in northern New York between Albany and Lake Ontario was France's most significant military opponent in the seventeenth century. Hostilities began when Samuel de Champlain allied himself with a force of Huron and Montagnais Indians in a battle against the Mohawks in 1609, a battle that introduced the Iroquois to firearms. Champlain participated in other campaigns against the Iroquois as an ally of the Hurons, a large confederacy whose strategic location between Lake Ontario and Lake Huron made them the middlemen in the fur trade between the French and the western Indians of the Great Lakes or *pays d'en haut*. Control of the fur trade was the central issue in the "beaver wars", the French–Iroquois wars of the seventeenth century.

These intermittent conflicts began in 1635 and their first victims were the Hurons. French friendship was perhaps more dangerous to the Hurons than Iroquois enmity. Between 1634 and 1640 Jesuit missionaries introduced epidemic diseases which decimated the Huron population, while controversies between Christian converts and religious traditionalists undermined the unity of the confederacy. During the 1640s the Iroquois gained access to ample supplies of firearms and ammunition from Dutch traders at Albany, while the Jesuits insisted on limiting firearm sales to Christian converts among the Hurons, excluding the unconverted. These factors shifted the balance decisively in favor of the Iroquois, who drove the Hurons from their homeland in 1649.[3] During the second half of the century, the French and Iroquois struggled for control of the western fur trade which the Mohawks sought to redirect to Albany. The threat posed by the Iroquois confederacy to the weak French settlement was so serious that Louis XIV placed the colony under royal control in 1663 and despatched a regiment of regular troops to deal decisively with the enemy. The ensuing campaigns demonstrated the ability of a European state to assert "global reach" in the age of the "military revolution" and the limits to such power when applied on the frontier.[4]

The new royal governor constructed forts along the Mohawks' Richelieu River–Lake Champlain invasion route which convinced all of the Five Nations except the Mohawks to agree to a peace. Governor Courcelle and his military commander, Marquis de Tracy, then launched a winter expedition to smash the recalcitrant Mohawks. Despite the failure of their Indian scouts to appear at the appointed time, 300 regulars of the Regiment Carignan Salières and 200 Canadian volunteers set forth from Montreal in January, 1666. It was a recipe for disaster. The troops faced a march of 300 leagues through snow and across frozen rivers. None had experience with snowshoes and all were burdened by 25 to 30 pounds of biscuit, made even more necessary by the absence of Indian hunters. Temperatures were so severe that most of the men suffered from frost-bite by the third day. Without guides, they frequently lost their way. In the end they encountered only Mohawk snipers and empty villages. Courcelle was fortunate to blunder his way to the Dutch village of Schenectady, New York whose inhabitants saved his men from starvation. Canada's military leadership had thus gained a lesson in what not to do.[5]

After unsatisfactory negotiations, the French launched a second invasion of the Mohawk country in September 1666 with 1,300 men, including 100 Indians, 300 light bateaux and canoes, and two pieces of artillery. The weather was certainly better, but the boats and cannon required gruelling labour at the portages. The Mohawks were not prepared to make a stand against so formidable a host and once again abandoned their fortified villages. The French burned the villages and the provision stores: "those who are acquainted with the mode of living of these barbarians doubt not but famine will cause as many to perish as would have been destroyed by the arms of our soldiery".[6] Destruction of Mohawk villages and food supplies rendered psychological blows and created hardship sufficient to convince the Mohawks to make peace, but the power of the Iroquois confederacy remained undiminished. These campaigns proved that regulars from France could not force a decisive battle on the frontier. Campaigns against Indian villages conducted by heavily burdened regulars were seldom conclusive and as likely to do the assault force more damage than it inflicted. A French missionary at Onondaga warned Governor La Barre not to attack the Senecas in 1684 lest the united Iroquois destroy the French colony: "he will never fight by rule against us and will not shut himself up in any fort in which he might be stormed. They are under the impression that, no person daring to come unknown into the forests to pursue them, they can neither be destroyed or captured, having a vast hunting ground in their rear".[7] La Barre's imposing army fell apart from disease and hunger and he was forced to sign a peace in which he abandoned his western Indian allies and with them the French commercial position in the west.

The French government responded to La Barre's humiliation by despatching the able Marquis de Denonville to humble the pride of the Iroquois and to restore French power in the west. Denonville constructed a fort at Niagara and invaded Seneca territory. He succeeded in beating off a Seneca attack and ravaged their country. His force of *troupes de marine* and militia was accompanied by Christian Indians of the Jesuit missions on the St Lawrence, many of

whom were themselves Iroquois, and western Indians such as th/
who, now equipped with firearms, were a match for the Senecas. T..
of the western tribes would prove fatal to Iroquois ambitions in the wesь.
Denonville did not defeat the Senecas, but his expedition did result in another
truce with the Five Nations, a truce soon broken when the latter entered King
William's War on the English side. This was a serious error on their part. The
French, now thoroughly trained in frontier warfare and possessing powerful
Indian allies, inflicted a series of stinging defeats upon the Iroquois in the
1690s. By 1701, the Five Nations had enough. They signed a peace agreement with the French and adopted a policy of neutrality between the con-
tending empires which was to last until the Seven Years War.[8]

Much has been made of the power of the Five Nations. Francis Jennings
has demonstrated that they were no more formidable than their Indian
opponents when the latter were also equipped with firearms. The English
colonies had good reason to exaggerate Iroquois predominance over other
tribes, for they were bound to the Five Nations by an alliance known as the
Covenant Chain. Although the Iroquois were allies and not subjects, the
Treaty of Utrecht of 1713 acknowledged English suzerainty over the Five
Nations. Iroquois claims to supremacy over western Indian tribes were thus a
vehicle by which English land claims could be advanced. However, after
1701, the Iroquois might claim the respect of Indians in the Ohio valley, but
could not compel obedience. The retreat of the Iroquois "empire" in the west
was accompanied by the expansion of the French with forts constructed at
Michilimackinac (1700), Detroit (1701) and Niagara (1720).[9] But this was an
empire that rested upon the consent of the native inhabitants and required
astute diplomacy and material reward rather than force. French attitudes
towards a western empire were ambivalent. Colbert and subsequent ministers
discouraged French settlements in the west which dispersed the small Canadian population and proved independent of imperial control. On the other
hand, French policy beginning with Louis XIV envisaged a chain of French
posts from Quebec to New Orleans which would bar the English from the
western commerce. Despite conflicting signals from Versailles, colonial officials, merchants, and traders pursued the fur riches of the interior and gave the
French empire a momentum of its own.

Denonville would not be the last commander despatched from France to
find Indian allies indispensable, but "disobedient" and unreliable. The success
of the French empire depended upon leaders who understood the Indian way
of life and the Indian way of war. By the 1690s the French had learned the
lessons of frontier war in the hard school conducted by the Iroquois. Canadian
officers and militiamen, veterans of western fur-trading expeditions, became
expert frontier warriors. They ambushed Iroquois war parties, raided their

villages and disrupted their fishing and hunting. Denonville's replacement, Louis Buade, Comte de Frontenac, was not always fortunate in his conduct of Indian affairs, but he did wage war in the Indian style, even to the extent of roasting Iroquois prisoners over slow fires. This was a form of war that earned Iroquois respect and led to the 1701 peace. The French had also concluded that regulars such as the *troupes de marine* were of little use in the woods without long seasoning. They were relegated to garrison duty and work details.[10]

The English

This was the military force turned against the English colonies during over half a century of imperial wars. King William's War was distinct in that it coincided with the final round of conflict between the Iroquois and the French. English failure to assist their allies resulted in the 1701 peace between the Five Nations and the French. The neutral Iroquois remained a buffer between Canada and New York and the latter was thus relatively insulated from war during the next half century. The New England frontier would not be so fortunate: Canadian militia and Abenaki warriors would terrorize the frontier settlements and rouse New Englanders to massive assaults on New France. The Indians fought to check the expansion of English settlement, the French as part of a larger imperial conflict. W. J. Eccles has observed that if the French had not attacked the frontier so aggressively, New Englanders would not have committed themselves to the conquest of Canada. Nevertheless, the English record of border war was dismal. With the exception of Benjamin Church's attacks against the eastern Abenakis and the destruction of the eastern Abenaki settlement at Norridgewock in 1724, the English lacked the ability to strike deep into the enemy's country or to prevent his raids upon their settlements.

The Deerfield raid of 1704 which aroused Church's anger, demonstrates French Canadian prowess. Hertel de Rouville led a force of 48 militia and 200 Abenaki, Caughnawagas (Iroquois mission Indians), and Hurons nearly 300 miles across the Green Mountains in the dead of winter to surprise Deerfield, Massachusetts on 29 February. They killed 40 to 50 inhabitants, burned the town and carried off 109 prisoners. Twenty prisoners died from exposure or were killed on the raiders' demanding return march. The family of the Reverend John Williams suffered grievously in the Deerfield raid. The attack claimed two of his children and his Negro servant. Williams and the surviving members of his family were captured and subjected to the brutal return march through deep snow. His wife was killed apparently because she could not keep up. On the other hand, their captors provided them with Indian snowshoes and constructed sleds to carry the children and the wounded. Williams' Indian master carried his pack when he became lame and saved the family from starvation by shooting five moose along the way. Arriving at Chambly near Montreal, he was treated kindly and experienced no worse torture than argumentative Jesuits. Finally he and two children were redeemed from the Indians by Governor Vaudreuil and allowed to return home. But much to his consternation, one son converted to Catholicism and his daughter Eunice chose to remain in Canada and married an Indian. While she later visited her family at Deerfield, Canada became her home.[11]

The Deerfield raid is illustrative of the frontier campaigns of the first half of the century. The French militia had thoroughly adapted to the Indian way of war. Their successful round-trip march of 500 to 600 miles in severe winter weather stands out in sharp contrast to Tracy's disastrous winter campaign against the Mohawks in 1666. There seems to have been little to distinguish between Indians and Europeans on this raid. The Canadians do not seem to have had any scruple about attacking unarmed civilians or disposing of prisoners if they did not keep up. Indeed Williams appears to make it clear that it was his Indian captors who made his survival possible. Only in Canada did the French begin to extend kindness to captured civilians. And this came at a cost, for if the raiders had killed Williams' wife and two children, the Jesuits claimed the soul of his son. This conversion and Eunice Williams' voluntary adoption of the Indian way of life are perhaps the most curious aspects of this extraordinary episode.

In contrast, English punitive expeditions rarely located their enemy in the remote Vermont countryside. Unlike the English settlements, which seldom had early warning of a raid, Indian villages were deserted when English militiamen did find them. Things were no better on the New England frontier as late as King George's War. By 1749 every English settler was driven from Vermont while one English observer complained that the only English-men to have sighted a French settlement during the course of the war had been captives or bearers of flags of truce. The English experience in this war closely resembles that of King Philip's War. Militia patrols returned empty-handed or decimated by ambush. Colonial authorities squabbled among themselves about how to fight the war, who should do it and how to pay for it. Once again there were experiments with dog patrols and attempts to enlist Indian soldiers to do the fighting. Massachusetts offered large bounties to Indians who would raid Canada and even larger payments for prisoners and scalps. All of this was to no avail. The New England colonies were forced to remain on the defensive. As long as the Abenaki and other warriors in the field had secure access to French ammunition and supplies and safe havens for their families at St Francis, they possessed advantages which the New England Indians of 1675–6 lacked. In addition, Iroquois neutrality meant that few Mohawks would take up bounty offers. There would be no repetition of the Mohawk attack on Philip's party, an event that may have been fatal to the Indian war effort in 1676. Indeed, the Iroquois in the field during King George's War were more likely to have been Catholic converts of the Caughnawaga mission.[12]

For the imperial powers the War of the Austrian Succession was a drawn match with a return to the *status quo ante*, the principal feature of the peace agreement. However, King George's War on the New England frontier was a French and Indian victory. Vermont had been barred to English settlement and the English colonies' military system had proven helpless in the face of the Indian way of war. The strategic solution to this dilemma was to strike directly at the Abenaki sanctuaries and sources of supply. Previous efforts by the colonists demonstrated that this could be accomplished only by a massive commitment of British naval and military might. In 1755 the commitment was made.

The Seven Years War

The Seven Years War (1757–63) was preceded by hostilities in North America when representatives of the two empires clashed over the control of the upper Ohio Valley. Here the ambitions of Virginia and Pennsylvania land speculators and settlers came into conflict with the strategic plans of the French government, which sought to secure the Ohio and the western trade by a chain of forts which would exclude the English from the region. The Ohio Indians thus found themselves in the midst of imperial rivalry over land that they considered to be their own. For the next half century the native peoples struggled to maintain their independence by diplomacy and by force of arms. Although they were ultimately driven from the region, their superior way of war allowed them to mount decades of successful defensive war against seemingly overwhelming odds.

The Ohio Indians of the mid-eighteenth century were relative newcomers to the region. The seventeenth-century Iroquois "beaver wars" had rendered the area virtually uninhabitable and Ohio began to be resettled only after 1724 by refugees from the prior conflicts and by Indians moving west before the tide of English settlement. Shawnees, Delawares and Senecas were the primary tribal groups in this new wave of settlement, but as one of the leading experts demonstrates, tribal denominations meant little in this amalgam of settlers who formed autonomous towns of mixed tribal heritage and created new ties through marriage and kinship.[13] The Ohio peoples stood outside traditional French alliances in the *pays d'en haut*. French diplomacy during the 1740s and early 1750s did little to entice the Ohioans into the alliance network. Economies imposed by the French government meant fewer presents for the "alliance chiefs", leaders whose ability to funnel material benefits gave them local prominence and bound them to the alliance. Instead of diplomacy, the French used force. Although Celeron de Blainville's parade through the Ohio country made little impression, a 1752 raid led by the *metis* Charles Langlade killed the pro-English leader La Demoiselle (who was eaten by Langlade's Ottawa and Chippewa followers) and forced the independent Indians into the French alliance. The French were now committed to a policy of holding the west by forts and settlements rather than a true league of Algonquian children under the protection of Onontio. This was a dangerous policy for the French, whose forts and garrisons were thinly spread over a vast region and dependent on the local Indian peoples for supplies and co-operation. Indeed when Paul Marin de la Malgue proceeded to the Ohio country in 1753 to begin the construction of the fortress system, the Ohio Indians looked to the English colonies for aid. The inability of Virginia and Pennsylvania, rivals for western lands, to co-operate and George Washington's unsuccessful attempt to expel the French in 1754 undermined chances for an Anglo–Indian alliance in the Ohio valley. Had such an alliance been forged the French position would have become immediately untenable.

The defeat of Washington's small force in 1754 set the stage for imperial intervention in 1755 with the despatch of Major General Edward Braddock to assume command of all British forces in North America. Braddock was to co-ordinate a vast and complex operation against Canada with offensives aimed at Fort Beauséjour in Acadia, Crown Point on Lake Champlain, Fort Niagara and the new Fort Duquesne at the forks of the Ohio. In the summer of 1755 he personally led a force of some 2,000 regulars, Virginia militia, seamen and Indian scouts on a gruelling march from Fort Cumberland in Virginia through the forest to one of the most famous disasters in British military history. Seldom has a battle been more closely dissected or hotly debated. American nationalist historians and British imperialists have fired broadsides at one another almost from the time the news of Braddock's defeat became public. Many political agendas have been served in this debate, but in retrospect Braddock's defeat is hardly surprising.

By 1755 one might have thought twice about sending a force of recently recruited regulars fresh from Europe into the woods against a formidable combination of experienced Franco-Indian fighters. Braddock's fate may have been sealed before he set forth when he rejected an offer of support from the Delaware leader Shingas in exchange for a pledge that the Ohio country should remain in the hands of its inhabitants.[14] Braddock thus made it clear that the Indians had less to fear from the French than from the British. Had he acted otherwise the French position in the west might have collapsed without a fight. But frontier war in 1755 seems to have been a blank sheet for Braddock and other British commanders. Seventeenth-century military expeditions had taught the French valuable lessons about the wisdom of despatching large numbers of inexperienced regulars into the woods. Too few survived to make it worthwhile. Now the British were to study in the same school.

As demonstrated in a previous chapter, there was little in the European military experience to prepare regular troops for the task ahead. Braddock had no light infantry and few Indian scouts. Some American writers have believed that the Virginia militia were superior to the regulars in woodland tactics, but there is little in colonial American military history to justify such a claim. The Virginia militia, which had gained considerable experience in fighting Indians in the first half of the seventeeth century, was a decayed institution by 1755. The Virginians in Braddock's army had little frontier experience; most of the so-called rangers who were expected to screen the army on the march were recruited from the tidewater settlements and many had never seen an Indian.[15] Braddock never recruited more than 50 Indian scouts and only eight remained with him on the day of the battle. Squabbles between the governors of Virginia and South Carolina deprived Braddock of the expected assistance of Cherokee and Catawba warriors. Others may have been discouraged by Washington's presence on Braddock's staff, for the Virginian had done little to inspire their confidence during the preceding summer.[16] Braddock thus began his campaign with no experienced frontier troops. In 1755 the British empire did not possess a force capable of executing the mission assigned to Braddock's army. Those who have debated whether the defeat was the fault of the officers or of the men have missed the point. The British were defeated by a numerically inferior, but qualitatively superior enemy fighting in a style with which it was familiar.

Braddock departed from Fort Cumberland on his march to Fort Duquesne on 30 May 1755, cutting a road as he went in order to bring up his artillery and supplies. While the weather was better than that encountered by the French in their winter campaigns, the men were unsuitably clothed in their heavy uniforms for their burdensome labour. Transportation was a problem and Braddock complained that the colonists had failed to supply sufficient carts and provisions. On 18 June he divided his force and attempted to move forward more quickly with two-thirds of his most able-bodied men. Since this detachment still had to carry ten pieces of artillery with them, it was hardly a flying column. Nevertheless, Braddock succeeded in approaching within eight miles of his objective. It is unlikely that the French garrison at Fort Duquesne would have risked a siege by an enemy with an artillery train; certainly their Indian allies would have abandoned them if that had been their plan. In 1758 the French would abandon and burn the fort before Forbes could invest it. The French commander Pierre de Contrecoeur therefore sought more favourable battle conditions and despatched a mixed force of 208 regulars, 146 militia and 600 Indians, who intercepted Braddock shortly after the British had safely forded the Monongahela river. Captain Beaujeu, the leader of the detachment, is said to have roused the reluctant Indians to action by inspiring oratory.[17] Perhaps the latter were cautious about attacking so large an army, but the Ohio Indians present at Fort Duquesne were not passive followers. They had their own reasons for wishing to prevent the British from reaching the Ohio, nor is it likely they would have agreed to a fight for which they were unsuited. The result was an encounter battle in which the French and Indians quickly exploited the advantages of the terrain. Concealed by trees and ravines, they aimed a devastating fire upon the hapless British, who offered a clear and compact target. One participant in the action reported that "Scarce an officer or soldier Can say they ever saw at one time six of the Enemy and the greatest part never saw a Single man of the Enemy." He also recalled the sound of the enemy fire "like Poping shots, with little explosion, only a kind of Whizzing noise; (which is a proof that the Enemys Arms were riffle Barrels)".[18] Braddock was mortally wounded while trying to rally his men, who broke and fled after two and a half hours.

Stanley Pargellis's argument that Braddock was defeated because he did not obey contemporary military principles as articulated by Humphrey Bland is not persuasive. As we have seen, Bland had little to say about this kind of fighting and Braddock did take precautions similar to those used against light troops in Europe. He has been criticized for not occupying the high ground to the right of his line of march and for moving forward too quickly to support his vanguard when firing commenced, but mistakes such as these commonly occur in battles and need not be fatal.[19] What seems clear is that neither he nor his officers knew what to do when they encountered the enemy who, in turn, knew exactly what to do. No doubt the British troops were tired, frightened and confused, but that is what officers are for. Those who blame the defeat on the soldiers' panic seem to miss the point.[20] In the final analysis, regulars and militia trained in conventional European tactics were no match for the masters of forest war. L. H. Gipson and D. S. Freeman were correct in identifying the absence of Indian allies as central to Braddock's defeat. The most surprising thing would have been if Braddock had actually won this battle.[21]

> This is, and always will be the consequence of Old England Officers and Soldiers being sent to America; they have neither Skill nor Courage for this Method of Fighting, for the Indians will kill them as fast as Pigeons, and they stand no Chance, either offensive or defensive: 300 New England Men would have routed this Party of Indians. . . . This is our Country Fighting.[22]

This is an important contemporary statement of a growing American national consciousness, but it is a myth. Ironically many Americans by the middle of the eighteenth century seem to have believed that they had evolved a way of war similar to that practised by the Indians at a time when all militia training remained traditionally European. Militia officers of the Seven Years War still marched to war with copies of Humphrey Bland in their knapsacks. The writer quoted above reported that George Washington, a member of Braddock's staff, had begged the general for permission to scour the woods with 300 men when the battle began. Washington blamed the regulars for not allowing the provincials to save the day.[23] On the other hand, at least one British officer reported that the "American troops though without any orders run up immediately some behind trees and others into ye ranks and put the whole in confusion."[24] It is unlikely that either Washington or the Virginia militia could have turned things around. This was the same Washington who had been surrounded and trapped at Great Meadows the preceding year and who, during the American War of Independence, rejected calls for guerrilla war and created an army of which Bland would have been proud. Great soldier and great man that he was, Washington was no frontier warrior. To the extent that he shaped the American military tradition, it remained untouched by the Indian way of war.

Braddock's defeat cast a cloud over the campaign of 1755. French reinforcements prevented the attack on Niagara, but Fort Beausejour was taken on 19 June. On 8 September Provincial Colonel Ephraim Williams led colonial militia into an Indian ambush near Lake George, demonstrating once again that these troops were outclassed in the woods. This success was thrown away by the French General Baron Dieskau who, against the advice of the victorious Indians, threw his regulars against William Johnson and the remaining English assembled behind breastworks. The French were routed and Dieskau wounded and captured. It was not a good year for the professionals.[25]

Britain declared war on France the following year. As a result, war in North America became increasingly Europeanized as commanders and regular troops despatched from Britain and France began to play decisive roles. Now the British and their American colonies were able to realize their strategy of striking at the heart of Canada. With the fall of Montreal in 1760, French power in North America was broken. This goal was achieved in spite of a brilliant French defence which initially seemed capable of overturning the odds. The first phase of the war was crowned with French victories. In August 1756, Montcalm captured Oswego and in August of the following year he took Fort William Henry. In July 1758, he routed the army of General Abercromby before Ticonderoga

By 1758, however, Britain had mustered the men, resources and leadership to produce one of her greatest imperial triumphs. The fortress of Louisbourg was captured in July 1758. Fort Frontenac was taken in August of that year and General John Forbes arrived at an abandoned Fort Duquesne. In 1759, the *annus mirabilus*, Niagara was captured and Wolfe triumphed over Montcalm at Quebec. That fall also saw Robert Rogers' raid against the Canadian Indian mission at St Francis.

Europeanization of the war

This brief chronology of the war reveals some of its characteristics and obscures others. The British succeeded in forcing the French to fight the war on their own terms. While Canadian governor Vaudreuil and his Canadian militia and Indian allies continued to prosecute the war in the traditional frontier manner, the defence of Canada was ultimately placed in the hands of an experienced professional who conducted a war of posts familiar to any European commander. Montcalm and his advisors treated the Canadians scornfully as amateurs and dismissed the Indians as unreliable savages. There remains a debate about the French strategy. Some Canadian writers find Montcalm to have been excessively defensive and pessimistic, concerned more with his professional reputation than the fate of Canada. He has been criticized for awaiting a superior enemy behind his defensive lines.[26] Rather, it is suggested, vigorous Canadian–Indian offensives in the frontier style offered the best chance of disrupting British plans and seizing the initiative. Some critics see him as an unscrupulous intriguer and a brutal bumbler.[27] His record, however, remains impressive. He commanded four major sieges or engagements and won three of them. Most generals would be content with such a record. When he had freedom to manoeuvre during 1756 and 1757, Montcalm acted aggressively. Afterwards he could but react to the British strategy of a massive three-pronged offensive against the heart of Canada.

Given the scale of the British commitment, it is doubtful that any French strategy could have prevailed. Delay was the best a commander could hope for. French defeats in Europe guaranteed that delay would not be enough to save Canada for the French, for their diplomats came to the peace table empty-handed. The loss of the French empire was limited only by the size of the British appetite.

The Europeanization of the war, featuring armies of unprecedented size, siege warfare and combined military–naval operations over a theatre of vast extent, overshadows the continued significance of frontier warfare. In the midst of the clash of empires the Indian peoples of the region were confronted with new threats to their independence. They responded by seeking neutrality or by alliances with those who could best secure their interests. Often Indian communities were divided on how best to meet these challenges. The Iroquois found that their neutrality was compromised by a war that was fought in the midst of their homeland and their confederacy was rent by how best to respond. Some under the leadership of Sir William Johnson allied themselves with the British. Others, notably the Iroquois mission Indians, fought on the French side. European commanders on both sides complained when Iroquois warriors proved reluctant to fight their kinsmen.

The French were able to recruit from traditional allies such as the Great Lakes Indians and the Abenakis of Vermont. These warriors participated for reasons of their own and in no way considered themselves French soldiers. For the Abenakis the issue remained the protection of their homeland from English settlement. They indicated that they viewed the war as their own and would fight the English whether the French governor wanted them to or not.[28] Their independence caused the French commanders to complain of their undiscipline and insubordination. The Great Lakes Indians participated as the traditional allies of Onontio, but also for the rewards of war: plunder, prisoners and proofs of manhood. As Ian Steele has pointed out, their participation could terminate quickly once those objectives were satisfied or denied. The Great Lakes tribes were of course far removed from any immediate threat of English settlement. Not so were the Ohio native peoples, who supported the French reluctantly as a shield against Indian expansion into the Ohio valley. They fought a parallel war, one which was not resolved by the British conquest of Quebec. The war also seems to have forged a growing sense of ethnic unity among the Indian peoples in the face of European expansion. Indian warriors appear to have become increasingly reluctant to fight Indians on the other side, and the movements of the warriors and the debates on what to do fostered the beginnings of movements for pan-Indian unity.[29]

Frontier war also continued to operate parallel with conventional European practices. Vaudreuil organized raids against the frontiers of New England, Pennsylvania and Virginia that created havoc in settler communities. These attacks were the only way that the French could seize the initiative. It was a time-proven formula which the Indians had exploited successfully as early as the spring campaign of King Philip's War. Terror campaigns could demoralize the enemy and throw him on the defensive. Vaudreuil showed no scruple in launching raids which could be justified on grounds of military necessity (a standard French justification for atrocities committed by Indian allies whom they could not control) and as a way of hastening the war's end. French regulars sometimes felt compelled to voice misgivings about such tactics, but Montcalm expressed satisfaction at their success. Montcalm and Vaudreuil had many differences about how to conduct the war, but the morality of a terror campaign was not one of them.[30]

The problems inherent in European–Indian warfare did not vanish with the Europeanization of the war. Frontier defence remained an unsolved problem for the British colonies. Regulars moving in the forest were aware that Braddock's debacle might be repeated. Brigadier General John Forbes took Braddock's example to heart when he marched to Fort Duquesne in 1758. He chose a shorter and easier approach through Pennsylvania and used great caution in moving from one fortified post to another. By this means he foiled an enemy attack on his advanced force, who retreated behind breast-works and were supported by mortars and cannon. Forbes noted sourly that this was not much of a victory since his men gave no pursuit; their self-congratulations surprised their Indian allies, who by this time had decided to return home. Forbes found the problem of acquiring Indian support continu-ally vexing. He reported that Cherokee and Catawba warriors recruited for the expedition arrived before the appointed time and grew impatient while waiting for the army to assemble. News of Abercromby's defeat at Ticonderoga made them skeptical of Forbes's enterprise and he found that they could not be satisfied with promises and presents. Like Braddock, he was forced to set out with insufficient Indian scouts. Forbes was no arrogant European martinet. He realized that his men must learn the Indian way of war, at least enough of it to survive in the forest. He did his best to recruit experienced woodsmen and experimented with Highlander scouting parties (with indifferent success). He advocated dressing troops in frontier fashion to allow them to operate more easily in the woods. Few of these experiments were successful and not all of his inferior officers shared his respect for the enemy. Thus Colonel James Grant recklessly led an advanced party into a disastrous encounter with the Indians near the fort. Forbes's success was owing to his awareness of the enemy's tactical superiority, which caused him to advance cautiously from one fortified post to another, protecting his line of supply. His arrival at Fort Duquesne ensured his success. The French abandoned and destroyed the fort and peace advocates among the Ohio Indians found their hand strengthened. Forbes was a quick learner about frontier conditions and his death in 1759 deprived the British of their most able commander in this respect.[31]

The Lake Champlain–Lake George army also saw experiments in frontier tactics. Most notable was the formation of the legendary Rogers Rangers, which like Church's frontier company contained a mix of white frontiersmen and Indians. The Rangers have had mixed reviews from the beginning. Some regular officers complained that the independent-minded Rangers were poorly disciplined and set a bad example to the other men.[32] General Jeffrey Amherst relied upon Rogers for scouting, but expressed contempt for the Stockbridge Indians who, he thought, lacked discipline. "I had the Provincial Battalions teach them how to form, and to enforce silence among the men and obedience to their officers, etc."[33] It was unlikely, however, that the Provincials could have instructed them in their main task. Nevertheless, the example of the Rangers inspired Colonel Thomas Gage to begin an experiment of forming specialized light infantry from among the regulars.[34] Gage hoped to relieve the army of its dependence on the Rangers by this force of 500 brown-clad regulars. His provisions for sensible clothes and light equipment were reasonable, but the new regiment, the 80th foot, were not woodsmen and could not replace the Rangers. The experiment was ephemeral and the regiment disbanded in 1764. Regular officers also accompanied Rogers' scouting expeditions to learn their way in the woods. Lord Howe of the 55th was especially interested in Rogers' techniques, but his death at Ticonderoga on 8 July 1758 brought his career to an untimely end.

The Rangers' combat record against a formidable adversary was mixed, but that is as one should expect considering their opponents. Rogers' force provided Amherst with a vital asset, one which could penetrate deep into enemy territory, provide intelligence, harass communications and deprive the foe of a sense of sanctuary. Rogers overstated his achievements and the Anglo-American public, thirsty for frontier heroes, accepted his accounts. But these were the best forest fighters available to the British during the war and they seem to have been more competent woodsmen than has been suggested by Francis Jennings, their harshest critic.[35]

As indicated in Chapter One, Rogers exaggerated the success of his raid on the St Francis mission in 1759. When compared to Léry's destruction of Fort Bull, the expedition appears to be something of a fiasco. Colin Calloway, the expert on the western Abenakis, agrees that Rogers, at great cost to his own men, failed to deliver a decisive blow. Abenaki military effectiveness was unimpaired. Nevertheless, Calloway finds that the raid was a psychological disaster for a people accustomed to minimal battle casualties and who kept their families at a safe distance from the war zone. By penetrating deeply into the Abenakis' Canadian sanctuary, Rogers demonstrated a new capacity for bringing the war to the Indian peoples.[36]

Few regular officers achieved Rogers' understanding of frontier war. Thus despite certain limitations, Rogers' writings on the subject provide the best available guide. There were many reasons that regulars could not adapt easily to Rogers' practices. For one thing Rogers' officers were not gentlemen; one, Captain Jacobs, was a Mohegan Indian. A rude spirit of equality among the Rangers threatened officer notions of subordination and obedience. Camp discipline was indeed lax. Although the Rangers were under the Articles of War, Rogers' authority over the men seems to have been the result of the force of his personality. It did not always extend beyond his presence. The Rangers' discipline more closely resembled that of the self-reliant Indian warrior taught to react immediately to surprising circumstances in the woods. It was a form of discipline that veterans such as Amherst could neither recognize or understand.

Differing military cultures

Indian participation in the great campaigns highlighted the two cultures' differing attitudes towards war. As independent allies, the Indians would not accept subordination to European officers. The latter, both French and English, thus complained of Indian unreliability, avarice and poor discipline. The Indians no doubt considered officers such as Baron Dieskau suicidal blockheads. Indian warrior training and spirit grew naturally from their culture. European soldiers, servants of an impersonal state, were artificial creations shaped by ceaseless drill and an elaborate system of punishments and rewards. The European military code drew a distinction between war and murder, between combatant and non-combatant, a conception non-existent in Indian cultures. Europeans regarded prisoners as temporary captives to be exchanged or released when peace was achieved. Indians often looked to adopt prisoners into their communities and were horrified when told that they must yield up new family members. Although European military practice allowed for many cruelties, Indian war rituals such as cannibalism shocked many European soldiers.

Commanders who professed dismay at Indian practices nevertheless eagerly sought their assistance. This raises the interesting moral question of the responsibility of officers who knowingly employed warriors who they knew would violate European standards. Indian warriors accompanied the Marquis de Montcalm on his sieges of Forts Oswego and William Henry. The warriors were useful in cutting off the forts' communications, but were not the troops for an assault on a fortified position. That was the regulars' business. Nevertheless, the Indians added a new menacing dimension to siege warfare. Montcalm threatened besieged garrisons with Indian terror if they did not surrender. When they did surrender on terms, the Indians took matters into their own hands and plundered, captured or killed prisoners in violation of the capitulation agreement.

These incidents caused a sensation at the time. Bougainville, who was not present at the "massacre" at Fort William Henry, found the violation of the capitulation to be a national disgrace.[37] Lord Loudon, the British commander-in-chief, denounced the barbarity of the French who "in this country . . . have kept no faith and have committed every Cruelty in their Power".[38] In his protest to Vaudreuil, Loudon observed that a general who cannot control his troops is in no position to negotiate a capitulation. "I chuse to carry on the War with strict Faith between the Nations and the greatest Humanity to the Particulars, – Whatever Troops you bring into the Field are to me French, therefore if any Part of them break through the Rules of War, will immediately lay me under the disagreeable necessity to Treat the whole of your People in the same manner." Loudon concluded by reiterating his desire to place "the War in America on a European footing".[39]

British commanders could afford to combine morality and practicality. After all, they hoped to win by conventional means. (On the other hand, General James Wolfe did not hesitate to employ terror against the civilian population of Canada when it served his interests.[40]) Loudon ignored a central fact: the Indians in Montcalm's army were not French and no one should have expected them to act like Europeans or to be forced to do so. There is some debate about Montcalm's motives in these incidents. Francis Jennings argues that Montcalm knew very well that the Indians would violate the agreements. He believes that at Fort William Henry he made an agreement with the Indians "that they could pillage at will and seize prisoners whom he would subsequently ransom as he did . . . in the pattern of Oswego".[41] In this view Jennings differs sharply from Ian Steele, who concludes that the Indians regarded the capitulation negotiated between the European commanders as a betrayal of the Franco–Indian alliance, depriving them as it did of their rightful booty and captives. The idea of a capitulation was foreign to the Indian warriors. When the French confiscated their prisoners, many concluded that their participation in the war was over.[42]

Montcalm was not an experienced leader of Indians. He seems to have been genuinely embarrassed by what occurred and Jennings offers no evidence of his foreknowledge beyond inferring "he must have known." Francis Parkman blamed the Canadian commander of the Indians, La Corne St Luc, for the breakdown, offering the testimony of Miles Whitworth, a regimental surgeon, who said that La Corne and the other Canadians did nothing to help the wounded men.[43] Since La Corne had adopted the Indian way of war as his own, he may have simply considered their conduct to have been normal. Some French officers blamed the British who had retained their arms for not standing up to the Indians. This was the attitude of Captain Pierre Pouchot, who ordered his men to stay together and resist any attempt by the Indians to seize their weapons when they surrendered Fort Niagara in July 1759.[44] But the British appear to have been too disorganized and demoralized at Fort William Henry to protect themselves.

Indians also accompanied the British in their expeditions against French forts. Commanders such as James Bradstreet and Sir William Johnson were perhaps better suited to understand Indian expectations than were the French regular officers. At the surrenders of Fort Frontenac (August 1758) and Fort Niagara, the British commanders recognized that the Indians would plunder the fort without regard for the terms of the agreement. They gave their allies free rein and concentrated on protecting the prisoners. This seems to have satisfied the Indians and drew praise from French officers.[45]

Sir Jeffrey Amherst, however, never seems to have understood or appreciated his Indian allies. His journal is peppered with complaints about their conduct. At the surrender of Fort Levis in 1760 he ordered his grenadiers to bar the Indians from entering the fort. Within days large numbers of the Indians appropriated the army's whale boats and abandoned the campaign.[46] Amherst's record in America was mixed. Although he won no spectacular victories himself, he presided over the reduction of Canada. He succeeded in Europeanizing the war and thus came to regard the Indians as having only marginal military value. This was an attitude that he shared with most regular officers, but it was a dangerous misconception. The French cause was in ruins by the end of 1760 and the remaining French regulars would go home. The Indians remained in their homelands. They were a formidable military force who could not be defeated by war on European terms. Historians who conclude their discussion of Amherst's career in America with the fall of New France regard him as one of the most successful British commanders of the century.[47] Unfortunately for Amherst, his American service extended beyond the Treaty of Paris. The Indians of the midwest would see to it that he left for England with his reputation considerably diminished.

Pontiac's Rebellion

France's defeat rendered her Indian allies vulnerable but unconquered. They now faced new imperial policies and the challenge of increased settlement. The western Abenaki homeland was exposed as never before, as New Hampshire militiamen cut a road through the Green Mountains. Down it came a surge of white settlement with the population of northern New England exploding from 60,000 to 150,000 in only 15 years.[48] Ohio Indians would also find their autonomy threatened by English settlement. Despite imperial attempts to regulate immigration, 50,000 white settlers would live west of the Appalachians by 1774.[49] As in New England in 1675, these population figures in themselves represented the greatest threat to the Indian way of life. In 1763, however, British imperial policies provoked renewed frontier warfare with the Indian peoples.

The French cession of their Canadian empire came as a rude shock to the native inhabitants, who did not consider that their land was France's to give away. France's western empire had rested upon commerce, missionary effort and shrewd diplomacy. Onontio was not a master, but a father, a keeper of peace and harmony among the varied peoples of the western world. When the French had begun to maintain their presence in the Ohio country by constructing forts and making claims to sovereignty, they drew a hostile response. The Ohio Indians had only supported the French against a greater evil during the war. Now the French regime was replaced by an imperial regime which claimed the region by right of conquest.

The continuation of the British garrison at Fort Pitt demonstrated that the British would not abide by promises to withdraw from the Ohio country at the end of the war. Failing to take the Indians seriously, Amherst pursued the worst combination of policies. On the one hand he occupied a vast network of military posts ranging from Fort Pitt along the lower Great Lakes to Detroit and Michilimackinac. At the same time he cut back on the presents which represented the symbolic bonds of alliance and thus undermined the influence of Indian leaders who wished for peaceful accommodation with the British. British insistence on receiving the market price for trade goods transformed traditional understandings about the nature of commerce in the west. For the French, commerce had been an adjunct to diplomacy and prices had been regulated with that object in mind. Since Britain laid its claim on force rather than diplomacy, the justification for price regulation disappeared. Ironically, the British decision to rely on force came at a time when their army in North America had been reduced to but a handful of the 20,000 regulars and provincials under arms in 1760. Tiny detachments of regulars under junior officers with little frontier experience were now thinly spread across the western empire. The obvious contempt that Amherst and other officers displayed towards the Indians exacerbated the situation. It was one thing for Major Henry Gladwin at Detroit to cut back on presents and ammunition as a result of orders, but as one Detroit resident observed, the General did not order him to call the Indians "Dogs, Hogs, and bid them go out of his house."[50] Experts on Indian affairs such as Sir William Johnson were well aware of the perils of these policies, but Amherst would not understand until too late that the British position in the west was founded upon sand.[51]

This is the background to the conflict often known as "Pontiac's Rebellion" after the Ottawa chief who led the Indian siege of Detroit. Recent scholars have renamed it the "Western Indians' Defensive War".[52] Once again the title reflects one's perspective. Is one looking east or west? Discussion of this event is included in this chapter as the final phase of Indian involvement in the conflict between the French and British empires. Not for the first time, the French and British had concluded a peace without consulting all of the interested parties. The war which lasted from 1763 to 1765 demonstrated that the British would have to make peace with the western Indians as well. Amherst's Indian policies made this difficult. The British had little understanding of western Indian military and diplomatic issues and lacked the means to impose their will by force. Indeed Pontiac's significance may lie less in his abilities as a war leader, which were considerable, than in the British need to find a recognizable figure with whom to negotiate. The "Emperor Pontiac" was a British creation.

The Treaty of Paris was signed on 10 February 1763 and the British garrison at Detroit was attacked by Pontiac and his followers on 7 May. Detroit was tied to the east by a slender thread of tiny British posts surrounded by militarily superior Indian peoples. These small forts were quickly overwhelmed by their Indian neighbours.[53] The Indians, who were on familiar terms with the small garrisons, experienced little difficulty in using ruses to capture or kill the soldiers. Only at Fort Presqu'Isle did the Indians find it necessary to launch a major attack by shooting fire arrows at the blockhouse and digging to undermine its foundation. Detroit and Fort Pitt, defended by large garrisons with artillery, were more formidable objectives. These the Indians placed under siege and urged the garrisons to go home.[54] The rising reflected widespread Indian dissatisfaction with British imperial pretensions and policies. While Pontiac played a significant role in the siege of Detroit, he was no more the leader of a unified Indian war effort than had been Philip. Great Lakes Indians and Ohio Indians had different motives in going to war and there were divisions and mistrust among Indian communities over the decision to fight. As was often the case, young war leaders prevailed over the advice of older chiefs. Great Lakes Indians, far removed from the pressure of trans-Appalachian white settlement, seem to have envisaged the restoration of the benign French alliance. While they received encouragement in this hope from French traders and settlers, French garrisons in the west did not intervene. Letters from the French commander in Illinois urging the Indians to make peace disheartened the besiegers of Detroit.[55] Ohio Indians had held aloof from both the French and British alliances. Their goal was the autonomy of their communities. In this regard they responded to the appeal of the nativist religious leader, the Delaware prophet Neolin, who called upon the Indians to reject white materialism and culture and to return to native traditions and religious practices. Neolin offered his followers a pan-Indian sense of identity around which unified resistance to white imperialism and settlement could rally. Gregory Evans Dowd has concluded that Neolin played an important role in the development of Pontiac's ideas for resistance.

It took General Amherst some time to understand the dimensions of the crisis he had done so much to create. His contempt for Native Americans blinded him to their military potential, and his disgust at what he believed to be their savage nature provoked him to fury. On 4 May, he responded to reports of Indian disaffection with one of the most extraordinary suggestions ever made by a British officer: "You will Do well", he wrote to Colonel Henry Bouquet, "to try to Inoculate the *Indians* [with smallpox], by means of Blankets, as well as to Try Every other Method, that can serve to Extirpate this Execrable Race".[56] Bouquet was equally bloodthirsty in his rhetoric; he agreed to distribute infected blankets and "as it is a pity to expose good men against them I wish we would make use of the Spanish Method to hunt them with English Dogs supported by Rangers and Some Light Horse, who would I think extirpate or remove that Vermin".[57] Thus regular European officers were prepared to cast aside the rules of war in combatting a non-conventional enemy. Biological warfare was not addressed in eighteenth-century treatises on the law of war, but poisoned weapons were condemned specifically.[58] But the law of war frequently becomes silent when different cultures and ways of war collide. In this regard the regulars were no more scrupulous in waging a war of extermination against the native peoples than were frontier militiamen and Puritan divines.

In the end the Indians could not drive the British army from the midwest or stem the tide of settlement. Nor could the British claim to have conquered the western Indians. The British succeeded in relieving Detroit and Fort Pitt and in 1764 Bouquet threatened the Ohio Indian towns in the Muskingum valley, an expedition that led to a peace agreement. The Indians had compiled an impressive series of military victories during the war, but could not convert them into a conclusive victory. Nevertheless they were much more successful in their struggle against Europeans than were the New England Indians of King Philip's War. In 1765 the Indians had retained control over their lands. There are discernable parallels between Pontiac's War and King Philip's. The Indians could capture small posts and ambush European troops in the woods. But Indian societies lacked resources for a long war. They were unwilling to sustain the casualties that such conflicts produced. Their food supplies were vulnerable, particularly when warriors were diverted from hunting. Ammunition supplies were always precarious. Some French traders provided powder during the conflict, as did some English traders, much to Bouquet's fury, but there was never enough. In 1764 Bouquet received a report from an escaped prisoner that the Delawares were so short of ammunition that they were hunting with bows. Finally, Amherst's hopes were realized. Although it is not clear whether the germ warfare plan was executed, smallpox ravaged the Indian towns.[59] These conditions produced exhaustion among Indian peoples that created desire for peace despite a record of military success.

On the other hand, Pontiac's war demonstrates that Europeans had not solved the tactical problems of forest warfare. Captain James Dalyell relieved Detroit in July 1763 only to lead a disastrous march into an Indian ambush which cost him his life and 150 casualties out of a force of about 250. The Indians also understood the vital significance of the key land portage at Niagara. On 14 September 1763 they ambushed and annihilated a supply convoy escorted by 30 men. Two infantry companies rushing to the rescue were destroyed as well. Five officers and 67 men were killed. The Indians returned again on 20 October to attack a relief force setting out to Detroit.[60] Bouquet, who marched to relieve Fort Pitt with a force of about 500 regulars in July 1763, had no illusions about the challenge confronting him. He found his Highlanders to be useless in the woods and sought experienced woodsmen to screen the column in the forest. At Bushy Run, 26 miles from the fort, he encountered an Indian force which engaged him in a furious two-day battle. Although his Highlanders and Royal Americans were no woodsmen, these veterans were clearly superior soldiers to Braddock's green troops and their officers were steadier. The Indians quickly deployed on the high ground in their horseshoe formation, firing on the advanced guard and the Black Watch who came up to their support. On this occasion, however, the British troops did not stand around in confusion, but drove the enemy from the heights with a bayonet attack. This bought but a scant breathing space as the agile warriors quickly returned, surrounded the column, and recommenced their fire. The first day's battle lasted until dark, with 60 British casualties. Bouquet faced a renewed attack on the second day, burdened by numerous wounded, terrified civilian drivers, piles of supplies and dead horses. The Indians now pressed home their attack, seeking to penetrate the camp. The British commander saved the day by a ruse of his own. He feinted a retreat after concealing two companies behind a hill. These fell upon the pursuing Indians and routed them. Despite continued sniping, Bouquet was able to proceed and relieve the fort.[61]

Bushy Run demonstrated that experienced and steady officers with veteran troops could escort a supply column through woods infested by formidable Indian warriors. Bouquet had reason to be proud of his achievement. Nevertheless, his victory was far from decisive. His detachment was so far reduced by casualties and exhaustion that it could undertake no further operations that year. The Indians were far from conquered. Bouquet's correspondence contains numerous references to Indian threats to Fort Pitt's communications with other eastern forts. Michael McConnell concludes that the Indians did not regard Bushy Run as a British victory, for they had sought to delay the regulars rather than destroy them. No more than 200 Indian warriors may have been present and they measured their success more by their lack of casualties than those they inflicted.[62]

Even so experienced a frontier veteran as Bouquet failed to introduce new tactical measures. He was constrained by the material with which he had to work. He recognized that European regulars could not successfully act offensively against Indian warriors. Such combat required experienced and hardy woodsmen who were in short supply. European troops continually risked ambush and could not catch the enemy when they fled. He continued to recommend that colonial authorities rely on dogs to detect and pursue the Indians; he suggested that hounds and experienced handlers be imported from England for that purpose. They would deter the Indians "more effectively from a War with us than all of the Troops we could raise".[63] Nevertheless, he also recognized that success with the regulars depended upon close order and the use of the bayonet. His notes outlining his order of march to the Muskingum in 1764 reveal a cautious, but conventional approach. The column was to be organized thus:

A detachment of volunteers.
A company of light infantry with axes.
A party of light horsemen accompanying Bouquet.
The cattle and sheep protected by light horse.
The front division of the column protected by flank guards.
The reserve marching in a hollow square with powder and baggage
in the centre.

The rear division of the column.
The rear guard of light infantry and light horse.

In event of attack, the troops were to halt immediately and form a square, the front and rear divisions becoming the front and rear faces and the reserve the sides. The cattle and light horse were to be brought into the square with the powder placed in the centre. The pack horses were to unload behind the faces of the square with the horses posted behind their loads. All this was to be done without hurry or noise to avoid confusion. The troops on the faces of the square were to be posted with one knee on the ground, resting on their arms, and were not to fire until ordered. Under an able and seasoned commander such as Bouquet, such measures offered a good degree of protection. It should be noted that there is nothing here of loose order, taking cover behind trees, and independent aimed fire. The precautions were those that any commander would take against irregular troops in Europe.[64]

Bouquet's objective was to bring his troops safely to the Indian towns and to destroy the enemy's capacity to make war. It was, he thought, the only way to defeat the Indians. In the end his march convinced them to make peace rather than see their towns destroyed. Bouquet thus pursued an old but successful strategy in fighting the Indians. His tactics were traditional, but, by ensuring march security, they were successful. On the other hand, had Bouquet made this attempt in 1763, before the Indians had been weakened by disease and ammunition shortages, his march dispositions would have been put to a serious test.

Pontiac's war ended as a standoff between the British empire and the Indian peoples of the midwest. Rather than fight Bouquet on the Muskingum, the Indians agreed to a truce and met the central British demand of the return of all prisoners, even those who had been adopted into Indian families. But the British made no demands for land cessions. Amherst's Indian policy had been proven bankrupt; his successor General Gage recognized that the western empire could better be secured by diplomacy than force. Military presence was reduced to a few large posts. The way was open to the return of the old French imperial policy of commerce and diplomacy, but this prospect soon vanished in the wave of Anglo-American settlement that swept across the Allegheny Mountains in the wake of the French defeat in the Seven Years War. This movement defeated all imperial policies which sought peaceful relations with the Indians. The settlers brought with them a disdain for imperial regulation and a hatred for Indians. Such hatred had manifested itself in Pennsylvania in 1763 when the "Paxton Boys" murdered peaceful and defenceless Indians. This incident outraged Bouquet who wrote "will they

109

not say that they have found it easier to kill Indians in a Goal than to fight them fairly in the woods?"[65] The spirit manifested by the Paxton Boys augured a dark new chapter on the frontier. New forces would be unleashed which would sweep away the old empire and force the Indians to fight yet another war of independence.

Chapter Six

Wars of independence: the revolutionary frontier, 1774–83

Jane McCrea

Jane McCrea was murdered by Indians near Glens Falls, New York on 27 July 1777. The unfortunate young woman was travelling to meet her fiancé David Jones, a loyalist officer in the British army of Major General John Burgoyne then advancing on New York from Canada. In one of those not uncommon quirks of history, Jane McCrea was soon transformed in the public imagination into a heroine of the American Revolution. The murder of this virginal maiden by the King's "savage" allies appeared to confirm the charge in the Declaration of Independence that George III had encouraged ferocious tribes to take up the hatchet against his defenseless subjects. It could be claimed that a government which resorted to such barbaric practices had ceded legitimate authority. McCrea's murder was a priceless gift to propagandists for the American cause and for British critics of government policy. The country-side was said to be roused against the invaders by news of this bloody act: "Thus an army poured forth by the woods, mountains and marshes. . . . The Americans recalled their courage; and when their regular army seemed to be entirely wasted, the spirit of the country produced a much greater and more formidable force."[1] In what became the legend of Jane McCrea, her death at the hands of her Indian escort fired a torch which incinerated Burgoyne's army and the forces of Lieutenant Colonel Barry St Leger operating in the Mohawk Valley. Burgoyne's defeat at Saratoga was of course the turning point of the war and the catalyst for the Franco–American alliance. Although she herself seems to have been a loyalist, McCrea's sacrifice was the salvation of the American cause.

The facts of the McCrea murder are not as clear as tradition would have it. It is uncertain who may have killed her or whether she was murdered at all.

It has been suggested that she met her death at the hands of Christian Indians of the St Francis mission or that she was killed by the fire of pursuing Americans. American farmers did not require news of her death to take up arms against invading armies of redcoats, Hessians, and Tories, not to mention Indian warriors. One scholar who has studied the mobilization of the American militia who defeated Burgoyne's German troops at Bennington has concluded that there was no connection between McCrea's murder and the muster of the Vermonters.[2] Nevertheless, Jane McCrea retains symbolic importance in American history, embodying white Americans' fear of the dark "other" of the wilderness as described by Richard Slotkin and as evidence of the illegitimacy of British authority. British critics of their government's American policy pounced upon Burgoyne's Indians as proof of the war's injustice: "We claimed a right of binding our dear brethren *in all cases whatsoever.* This was unjust. We set their cities on fire; we scalped their women and children; and we butchered whole legions of their husbands and fathers for not submitting to this impious claim. This was more unjust still."[3] Defenders' of the government's employment of Indians squirmed under this sort of rhetoric. They could, of course, invoke the ultimate sanction for all acts of war: military necessity, but they knew that, in a war for the "hearts and minds" of the Americans, this was a weak argument. Even Lord George Germain, a statesman with little regard for public opinion, believed that reports of atrocities committed by Indian allies should be censored.[4] The image of the Indian as a murderous savage was a powerful weapon in the hands of Britain's enemies.

However, this image was a two-edged weapon. British soldiers were quick to equate the crime of rebellion with Indian savagery. They were outraged by the minutemen's Indian style sniping at the battle of Lexington and Concord and accused the enemy of tomahawking and scalping wounded men. The presence in Washington's army before Boston of Pennsylvania riflemen in frontier dress confirmed for British officers the lawless and villainous nature of the rebellion. It required no great leap of imagination for these officers to associate the rebel-savages with the wild Highlanders of the 1745 Jacobite rising and to call for the same kind of brutal repression.[5] Throughout the war both sides would attempt to apply Indian warpaint to the face of the enemy.

The historian Bernard Sheehan has concluded that the Indians' significance in the American War of Independence was more symbolic than substantial. For all of the violence which the war unleashed upon the frontier, the Indian contribution to the outcome of the war was marginal.[6] Other writers have concluded that even though the Indians represented great military potential, they were in fact a liability to the British:

For all of the terror that they spread among the Americans, it is by no means clear that the Indians really helped the British in the war. They were a distraction. They diffused and dissipated British energies. They exacerbated opinion back home and turned many a neutral frontiersman into an implacable enemy. They were not reliable on a long campaign or in a battle. Properly used they might have changed the fortunes of the war; actually all they did was to change the nature of the war and for the worse.[7]

Another student of the war credits the northern and southern Indians on the frontier with possessing 26,000 warriors, but concludes that "the British were to find the unstable and unreliable Indians unsatisfactory as combatants".[8]

No doubt the British would have been delighted by the arrival of 26,000 Indian troops under British officers to join their army on the eastern battlefields, but these comments ignore the realities of Indian life and the Indian way of war. As has been seen in previous chapters, Native Americans were not passive clay which might have been "properly used". Nor were they mercenaries: "They were not Sepoys after all", a remark as true in 1776 as in 1755. These observers fail to consider the Indians as independent peoples whose participation in the war was guided by their own interests, which remained the security of their families, their land, their culture and way of life. They also assume that the Indian peoples were monolithic and united in their reactions to the challenges now confronting them. Nothing could be further from the truth. Indian communities, dependent upon discussion and consensus, were riven by questions of war or negotiation, alliance or neutrality. While they disagreed among themselves on how best to conduct their relations with their European neighbours, their goal remained the same. They were not concerned with American independence or the integrity of the British empire except as those issues affected their own way of life. Parallel to the American War for Independence was the Indians' own independence struggle.[9]

The Indians divided

While both sides accused the other of inciting the Indians to war, neither initially sought active Native American involvement. In the Pittsburgh treaty of September 1775, the western tribes joined in a pledge of peace, friendship and neutrality with the American Congress.[10] The British Indian Superintendents, Sir William Johnson and John Stuart, also counselled the Indians to avoid a white man's quarrel. Stuart believed that indiscriminate Indian raids, uncoordinated with British military operations, would do little good and would drive white frontiersmen into the hands of the rebels. Although General Thomas Gage, cooped up in Boston, urged that Indians be unleashed upon the rebels, General Carleton at Quebec attempted to restrict the movement of Canadian Indians to the south.[11] During the summer of 1775, the Colonial Secretary, Lord Dartmouth urged commanders to raise armed forces from Indians and slaves, but his successor Lord George Germain was reluctant to employ Indians until the rebels did.[12] British authorities were divided between those who wanted to crush the rebellion by fire and sword and those who hoped for negotiation. British regular officers also disagreed over the military value of the Indians and how they might be best employed.

These considerations were irrelevant to the Indians themselves. White land hunger and the pressure of white settlement, exacerbated by shady dealings and the failure of the imperial governments to enforce regulations protecting the Indians, remained smouldering issues on the frontier. The Ohio Indians were particularly angered by the Treaty of Fort Stanwix between the British Indian Superintendent Sir William Johnson and the Iroquois. Asserting the Covenant Chain and the myth of their supremacy over the western Indians, the Iroquois ceded hunting grounds west of the Alleghenies to white settlement. Tensions between settlers and Indians erupted in Lord Dunmore's War of 1774, the first stage in the Indians' parallel war of independence. The Virginia Governor Lord Dunmore led a militia army against the western Indians and defeated them in the battle of Point Pleasant. Dunmore's force included a new element, riflemen under Daniel Morgan, an indication that frontier settlers had begun to adapt to the Indian way of war. The militia claimed to have taken 20 Indian scalps, hardly the sign of an overwhelming victory, and Colonel Andrew Lewis who commanded one wing of the army was killed in the fighting.[13] Lord Dunmore's War meant that the Ohio River rather than the Alleghenies was the effective boundary between the Ohio Indians and the settlers. Dunmore recognized the futility of negotiating frontiers to limit white expansion. He wrote of the settlers:

> they do not conceive that Government has any right to forbid their taking possession of a Vast tract of Country, either uninhabited, or which serves only as a Shelter to a few Scattered Tribes of Indians. Nor can they be easily brought to entertain any belief of the permanent obligation of Treaties made with those People whom they consider as but little removed from brute Creation.[14]

Ironically, the Indians are often referred to as a stateless people. Chiefs who negotiated treaties often did not speak for the entire community and their

agreements were sometimes repudiated. Nevertheless, European–Indian relations had long been governed by formal diplomatic relations and treaties.
White settlement in the west created crises in colonial societies when settlers
rejected or ignored the authority of established government, a problem that
continued after the American Revolution and the establishment of the United
States. In the settlers, the Indians now confronted a people who were, in a
sense, stateless. The frontier thus became a very unstable place and the
potential for violence almost unlimited.

Eastern land speculators also undermined the authority of the government
and drove some Indians to arms in order to protect their interests. Especially
notorious was the Sycamore Shoals land bargain of March 1775 between the
North Carolina based Transylvania Company and the Cherokees, whose
leaders ceded the area of present-day Kentucky and middle Tennessee in
return for a few wagon-loads of goods. Superintendent Stuart and Governor
Josiah Martin of North Carolina intervened in an attempt to block settlement,
but they were ignored by speculators. This transaction angered other Indians,
who believed that the Cherokees had no right to make such a cession, and this
created a crisis among the Cherokees. Older chiefs who had participated in the
bargain lost credibility and young warriors such as Dragging Canoe, who
warned that settlement would turn the land "dark and bloody", gained
prominence.[15] The collapse of imperial authority and the outbreak of the
American Revolution provoked an Indian war on the southern frontier despite
Stuart's attempts to stop it. Encouraged by a multi-tribal delegation of
northern Indians to join in pan-Indian resistance to white expansion, the
Cherokees went to war to protect their land and independence when all other
measures seem to have failed. The result was a disaster for the Cherokee
people. British authorities were unable to provide tangible assistance. The
Cherokees' hopes for support from other Indian nations were dashed particularly when the neighbouring Creeks refused to participate in the border war.
The Cherokees raided the new settlements and fought skirmishes with frontiersmen during the summer of 1776, but provoked a large retaliatory expedition by the southern states, whose militia forces ravaged Cherokee towns and
burned crops. State authorities were eager to claim the lands of the Cherokees
as a defeated people and the older chiefs were forced to trade land for peace.
But there was to be no secure peace for the Cherokees. Undefeated in battle,
Dragging Canoe and his warlike followers withdrew to Chickamauga Creek
to continue their war against the Americans. But the punitive expeditions
against the Cherokees may be considered an American strategic success. James
O'Donnell, the expert on the southern Indians, believes that the example of
the Cherokees was the most important explanation for their general reluctance
to participate in the conflict between Britain and her colonists.[16]

4. *War on the frontier during the American Revolution*

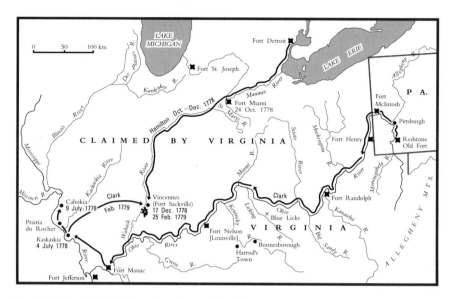

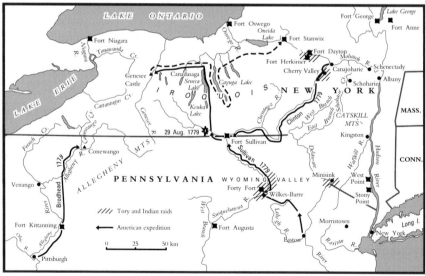

The Cherokee case typifies the crisis that the Revolution provoked in Indian communities. The civil war among white neighbours confronted Indian peoples with chaos and uncertainty. Communities were deeply and sometimes bitterly divided over how best to meet the challenges to their future. The outcome of the war was obviously of great significance to the Indians. Often they were confronted with stark choices: to fight on one side or the other, to remain neutral, or to withdraw from the area of conflict altogether. The latter course was not practicable for all Indian peoples, but the Revolution did set in motion a vast westward migration of Native Americans. Few Indian communities reached consensus. As in the case of the Cherokees, war meant generational conflict between older chiefs accustomed to peaceful accommodation with white people and fiery young spirits such as Dragging Canoe. The result could be a complete schism: the Iroquois confederacy collapsed with warriors fighting on both sides in the white civil war and others unsuccessfully seeking neutrality. The war saw communities torn asunder and remade in new forms and in new locations. While the Indian military effort may have been, as some historians believe, of marginal significance to the outcome of the Revolutionary War, the war and its outcome was hardly marginal to the Indian peoples.

In retrospect, few Indian peoples had any real choice between the apparent alternatives. The Indians of Stockbridge, Massachusetts seem to have been genuinely inspired by revolutionary ideals of liberty and fought on the American side with distinction. This community's experience in frontier warfare as part of Rogers' Rangers in the previous war provided the Americans with an important military asset. The Catawbas of the South Carolina piedmont had also furnished warriors for the Anglo-American cause during the Seven Years War and provided important service for the Americans during the Revolution. On the other hand, surrounded as they were by white communities in rebellion against the Crown, it does not seem that loyalty would have been a realistic choice. Some Indian leaders who sought neutrality or peaceful relations with the Americans would also find this an unrealistic alternative. The Delaware leader White Eyes and the Shawnee chief Cornstalk both sought good relations with the Americans. Both were murdered by American frontiersmen and the pro-British war parties among their peoples gained ascendancy. The principal threat to most Indian peoples was lawless settlers against whom American authorities could offer no protection. War also disrupted Indian trade connections with American suppliers. The American government was too poor to provide the accustomed presents necessary to cement Indian alliances and frontier settlers often barred Indian access to vital ammunition supplies.[17]

Indians determined to resist settler conquest turned to British alliances out

117

of necessity. In many ways the British empire in the west resembled the old French system. Pontiac's War had convinced commanders such as General Gage that British claims depended more upon diplomacy than force. Although the British enjoyed excellent water communications to the west, their presence was restricted primarily to garrisons at Niagara, Detroit, and Michilimackinac. They had no substantial armed force in the west that might be used against the Americans, but neither were they a threat to the Indians. For western Indians the British were the only reliable source of trade goods, arms and ammunition. Only the British government had the means to oil its diplomacy with presents. Finally, British forts offered sanctuaries to Indian families displaced by American settlers and military invasion. Many Indians made the choice of a British alliance reluctantly, but for most, there was no real alternative.

The key to understanding Indian participation in the war is the word "alliance". Indians made their decisions based upon their own self-interest and fought for objectives of their own. As in the case of the Cherokees, they began to fight before the British wanted them to, and some, undefeated in war, continued to defend themselves when Britain made peace. Neither Britain nor America was capable of arming, unifying and directing the Indian peoples to become a decisive factor in the war. The Indians, however, were a formidable presence in the war that interested them most: the war of the frontiers. By 1781, the year of the British defeat at Yorktown, it was a war that the Indians could claim to be winning.

British–Indian alliances

Indian warfare became part of British strategy to subdue America in 1777. Indian warriors accompanied General John Burgoyne's army on its ill-fated march from Canada to New York and comprised the largest part of Lt Colonel Barry St Leger's expedition to the Mohawk valley. There had been intermittent warfare between settlers and Indians on the western frontier beginning with Lord Dunmore's War in 1774. As early as 1775 Shawnees had begun to contest the new settlements in Kentucky, an area that they regarded as their own hunting preserve. Lord George Germain now became committed to raising Indian allies against the frontiers. Lieutenant Governor Henry Hamilton at Detroit was now ordered to send raiders against the frontiers of Pennsylvania and Virginia; Superintendent John Stuart received similar orders: "The Distress and Alarm so general an Attack on the frontiers of the Southern Provinces must occasion cannot fail of assisting Sir William Howe's operations to the Northward during the Summer, and of giving facility to any enterprise he may direct against the Carolinas in the winter."[18] Germain seems to have had great faith that the threat of Indian terror would bring colonists to their senses. He wrote to Burgoyne that "The dread the people of New England, etc., have of a war with the savages proves the expediency of our holding that scourge over them."[19] British policy now coincided with the views of those Indian leaders who concluded that force was the only realistic means to resist white American expansion.

Now indeed the land would become dark and bloody. Following the failures in 1777 of the expeditions of Burgoyne and St Leger, both of whom blamed their Indian partners for their defeat, 1778 saw extensive Indian attacks on frontier settlements. The new post at Boonesborough, Kentucky was besieged and Tory Rangers and Indians led by Walter Butler and the Mohawk chief Joseph Brant, carried out celebrated raids on settlements in the Wyoming and Cherry Valleys of Pennsylvania in July and November 1778. These events predictably provoked American retaliation. During the year 1779 the American frontier offensive was aimed at ravaging Indian towns and crops and destroying their bases and sanctuaries at Niagara and Detroit. Generals John Sullivan and James Clinton, and Colonel Daniel Brodhead, carried out great destruction in the Cayuga and Seneca towns of western New York, but failed to reach Niagara. Thus they exposed hostile Iroquois to poverty and hardship, increasing their dependence on the British, but did not eliminate them as a military threat. In 1778 George Rogers Clark invaded the Illinois Country in retaliation for raids on Kentucky. The Illinois tribes were not the source of those raids, but Clark hoped to eliminate the Indian threat by the capture of Detroit. Although he defeated and captured Governor Hamilton at Vincennes on 25 February 1779, he failed to take Detroit. American campaigns were thus strategic failures although Clark's invasion disrupted attempts to create a pan-Indian alliance of northerners and southerners. Indian resistance increased along with the level of indiscriminate violence on both sides. The frontier militia, often organized as mounted riflemen, demonstrated a new ability to strike into the Indian lands across the Ohio, but they were by no means masters of the field. Militia under Colonel William Crawford were routed near Sandusky in June 1781. The Indians, infuriated by a recent militia attack on defenceless Delaware Christian converts, slaughtered many militiamen and burned Crawford at the stake. On 19 August 1781, Indian raiders in Kentucky lured a pursuing force, including such experienced woodsmen as Daniel Boone, into a disastrous ambush at Blue Licks on the Licking River. The Americans were far from winning a decisive military victory in the west. Cornwallis's surrender at Yorktown imperiled Indian independence more than any American military action on the frontier.

Germain also included the southern Indians in his strategy for 1777. He was to be disappointed in his hopes, and by 1779 complained that despite the Indian Department assurances that the Indians were out on the frontiers, British officers could not contact them. Germain seems to have gone from hoping that the Indians would be a cheap way to end the war to finding them a useless expense.[20] Nevertheless, between 1779 and 1781 most Indians between the Great Lakes and the Gulf of Mexico were united in opposition to the Americans. Communication and supply difficulties plagued British efforts to co-ordinate Indian activity with their military operations in the south. John Stuart's death in 1779 created confusion over authority in the Indian Department. Orders often arrived late and when the Indians did march to join the British troops in 1779, they received reports of British defeats which sent many of them home.[21] Southern Indians joined the new Indian Superintendent and ranger commander Thomas Brown in war in the southern backcountry. Brown's biographer Edward Cashin finds him to have been an able commander who conducted Indian affairs skilfully. Nevertheless, Brown's Indian allies drove the settlers into the American fold at a time when they were becoming more skilled in frontier warfare. Consequently both Britain and the Indians would lose the war in the backcountry.[22] While Britain's southern Indian strategy failed to achieve expected results, southern Indians nevertheless provided important aid. Without Indian support, the British position in east and west Florida would have completely collapsed.

Perhaps no Indian people were more confused by the conflict between the white inhabitants of British North America than the western Abenakis, many of whom resided at the rebuilt mission town of St Francis.[23] These former French allies, the scourge of the New England frontier, had little enthusiasm for either side in the war. Strategically located between Canada and the New England–New York frontier, they were regarded with suspicion by British and Americans alike and found neutrality a difficult posture to maintain. Small parties of Abenaki warriors served on both sides and about 400 were coerced into joining Burgoyne's army in 1777. Their lack of enthusiasm explains what British authorities came to regard as their unreliability. American and British opponents of the government seized upon Burgoyne's Indian force as a propaganda issue. Burgoyne did not help matters by his rhetoric: "I have but to give stretch to the Indian Forces under my direction, and they amount to thousands to overtake the harden'd enemies of Great Britain. . . . The messengers of justice and wrath await them in the Field, and devastation, famine, and every concomitant horror".[24] This was all bluster, considering that Burgoyne commanded a few hundred reluctant allies rather than thousands of vengeful winged monkeys. Britain's old enemy La Corne St Luc, now thoroughly reconciled to the new order, was given command of the Indians. This in itself would have been enough to alarm the frontiersmen. He told New York Governor Tryon that he would unleash "les sauvages" against the rebels and terrorize the frontiers. It was necessary, he said, to brutalize "les affaires".[25] La Corne was referring to a style of war with which he was familiar from service in two previous conflicts: the Indian way of war. Like his Indian followers, he knew no other way. Burgoyne later said of his own words that he "spoke daggers, but employed none".[26] Indeed, Burgoyne was no terrorist, but the issue of terror should be placed in context. It should be remembered that Indians did not draw a fine distinction between war and murder of enemies or between combatants and non-combatants. Several settler families were surprised and slain by Indians operating with Burgoyne's army. Burgoyne was naïve if he thought that he could transform Indian allies into European soldiers by issuing a few orders. La Corne would have had few illusions in this regard. Successful command of Indians required that they be allowed to fight in their own way. Furthermore, when he advocated terror, La Corne had plenty of company. By 1778 probably a majority of the British officer corps in America believed that the rebels should be terrorized into submission and their rhetoric could be equally blood-curdling.[27]

Bernard Sheehan has observed of Burgoyne: "One would find it difficult to conceive of a character less likely to gain insight into Indian culture or less likely to succeed in changing the native way of making war".[28] Burgoyne was embarrassed by Indian attacks on frontier settlements, but had no way to restrain them for fear that they would desert. This was his explanation for failing to punish the Indians who were accused of Jane McCrea's murder. The Indians, never enthusiastic to begin with, were demoralized by the defeat of Burgoyne's German troops at Bennington and the growing hopelessness of the campaign. Burgoyne later blamed his desertion by the Indians as a cause for his defeat, but also disparaged their value as warriors and accused them of cowardice in the fighting at Saratoga. He also blamed La Corne for not transforming them into soldiers.[29] Ironically, the American General Gates would praise the heroism of the Oneida, Tuscarora, and Caughnawaga Indians who fought on the American side at Saratoga. One observer said that they "fought like Bull dogs" until Burgoyne surrendered.[30]

St Leger also blamed his check upon his Indian allies. His foray from Oswego down the Mohawk Valley was designed to pin down American forces that might have otherwise confronted Burgoyne. His force was essentially a raiding party of loyalist rangers, Senecas and Cayugas led by Sir John Johnson and John and Walter Butler. The main obstacle to this raid was Fort Stanwix which St Leger, equipped only with light field pieces, was compelled to besiege. A relief force of American militia under General Herkimer marched to its aid, predictably ran into a classic ambush, and suffered heavy casualties. In this action, known as the Battle of Oriskany, 400 Indians with about 60 loyalist rangers overcame an American force twice its size and prevented the relief of the fort. It was a hard-fought affair and the Indians, who suffered from shortages of firearms and ammunition, also experienced losses in hand-to-hand fighting. Afterwards they were accused of torturing their prisoners. When word arrived that additional reinforcements were on the way, the Indians withdrew and St Leger was forced to break off his raid. In retrospect, it is unlikely that he could have accomplished more. A student of Indian warfare, particularly of Léry's attack on Fort Bull, would certainly have expected the Indians to depart after Oriskany rather than suffer more casualties. St Leger's raiders were not properly equipped or organized to overcome Fort Stanwix or to confront the American reinforcements led by the redoubtable Benedict Arnold. St Leger's raid did not contribute to a British victory, but raids seldom do.[31]

Frontier raiders

During the following year the Indians, supported by British at Niagara, carried out a series of deadly attacks against American frontier settlements. These raids brought to prominence the Mohawk leader Joseph Brant, brother-in-law of the late Sir William Johnson. Brant was a figure at home in both European and Indian society. He had visited London where he was lionized as an Iroquois alliance chief. He now became an active figure in frontier warfare and was, of course, demonized in American accounts of the conflict. Brant and Walter Butler, son of the Indian Department official Colonel John Butler, waged relentless campaigns to drive American settlers from what they believed to be their rightful lands and to protect their people from the frontier militia. Had Britain won the war, their reputations no doubt would be different. Nevertheless, despite continual contemporary accusations that they encouraged Indian atrocities, it appears that their fury was aimed at enemy combatants. They did their best in difficult situations to protect women, children and prisoners.[32]

Two raids in 1779 dealt a hard blow to the Pennsylvania frontier. In July Butler led a loyalist-Indian force against the flourishing farms of the Wyoming Valley. The size of Butler's party is sometimes reported to have been as large as 1,100; a loyalist ranger with the party wrote that it consisted of 70 white volunteers and 300 Indians. The local American commander is said to have had 300 to 580 men with which to face the onslaught. On Butler's arrival, the inhabitants fled into Forty Fort, one of the district's fortified posts, while the raiders proceeded to devastate the neighbouring farms. Butler had no artillery or any means of assaulting the fort and it is unlikely that he could have submitted it to a long siege. However, goaded by enemy taunts and the sight of the countryside in flames, the Americans sallied forth to meet the enemy in battle. They were promptly surrounded and wiped out. Butler's men took 227 scalps and five prisoners. Forty Fort, stripped of its defenders, now surrendered on Butler's promise of good treatment. The survivors, stunned by the loss of family members and homes, were to report the outcome as a massacre, but there is no evidence that defenceless people were harmed.[33]

Brant joined Butler in a raid on Cherry Valley on 11 November. The careless American commander and his officers were caught outside the gates of the fort and many inhabitants failed to gain its protection. The raiders' leaders were unable to prevent indiscriminate attacks and women and children were seized as prisoners. On this occasion the Indians appear to have acted in retaliation for white settler attacks on Indian families during the summer. Cherry Valley was a more serious episode than that at Wyoming. It represents a rising level of unrestrained violence in retaliation for atrocities on both sides. Nevertheless, whites taken prisoner by Indians had a better chance for survival and good treatment as adoptees than Indians seized by whites. Francis Jennings has raised an interesting question about the absence of references to Indian prisoners in accounts of the frontier wars.[34]

These accounts suggest that many American militia commanders had learned very little about Indian warfare in the hundred years following King Philip's War. American soldiers were brave, but lacked caution and discipline. Indian warriors and their white allies retained tactical superiority in most encounters of the early years of the Revolution. The white response, as it had been since the Powhatan War, was to destroy the economic base of Indian warfare, burning crops and rendering the Native Americans homeless. Campaigns such as these either forced the Indians to fight on unequal terms, to make peace, or to depart for other lands. Attacks on Cherokee food supplies had been the key to American victory in the 1776 war. In 1779 the Americans turned their attention to the Iroquois and the Indians of the midwest. Campaigns conducted by Sullivan, James Clinton, and Brodhead destroyed the rich farms of western Iroquoia and reduced the native people to poverty. However, as long as Niagara provided supplies and sanctuary, the Indians fought on. General Sullivan's campaign was thus a raid on a large scale. He wrought destruction and fought an inconclusive battle. But neither he nor other American commanders imposed a military solution on the frontier in 1779. In a sense, these expeditions validated Germain's hope that Indian raids would divert American resources to the frontier. Butler, Brant, and other British commanders had thus achieved a strategic success of a sort. That British generals in the east did not exploit this opportunity was hardly their fault.

Sullivan launched his invasion on 31 July with one of the most powerful armies ever despatched to the Indian country. It was a mix of 4,000 men including Continental regulars and militia, with a battery of artillery capable of reducing any Indian fortification. The march was covered by a light brigade which consisted of Oneida scouts, six companies of rangers, and a variety of light infantry units including Daniel Morgan's rifle corps, commanded on this occasion by Major James Parr. These troops effectively protected the column from surprise attack. The army's serious weakness lay in its logistics. By 30 August the troops were placed on half rations consisting of a daily allowance of a half pound of flour and a half pound of beef per man and no spirits. There was poor grazing for the horses and insufficient clothing for the men. One officer reported that not more than one in 12 possessed a blanket. These conditions guaranteed that Niagara was beyond Sullivan's reach. Had the army not encountered abundant food supplies in the Indian towns, the expedition would have collapsed.[35]

Sullivan succeeded in ravaging the Indians' homeland, burning 40 towns, 160,000 bushels of corn and other crops. The Americans looted burial sites and waged a campaign of terror against non-combatants. On 29 August the army fought its only battle at Newtown near Chemung. The advanced guard of riflemen was fired upon by a party of Indians, who then quickly retreated. Major Parr exercised laudable caution by carefully reconnoitering the ground and sending a man up a tree to survey the surrounding area. The latter discovered what proved to be a party of about 750 Indians and loyalists commanded by Brant and Walter Butler concealed behind breastworks. For once the Americans had avoided rushing into an ambush. Sullivan attempted to pin the enemy to their breastworks with his riflemen and artillery while turning their flank with his superior numbers. But the Indian warriors, with no stomach for defending suicidal positions, quickly departed, with Butler's Rangers soon on their heels. Butler listed his loss as five dead or captured and three wounded. Sullivan's force suffered three dead and 33 wounded. The army suffered a greater loss when a scouting party was cut off and wiped out. The American soldiers were shocked to find its commander's brutally mutilated remains. What had the expedition accomplished? "The question will naturally arise," wrote the American Major Jeremiah Fogg, "What have you to show for your exploits? Where are your prisoners? To which I reply that 'The nests are destroyed, but the birds are still on the wing.'"[36]

Parallel to Sullivan's expedition, Colonel Daniel Brodhead led 600 men from Fort Pitt to the New York border. He met little opposition in a march which lasted 33 days over 400 miles. The Americans burned Seneca fields and returned with $3,000 in plunder and without the loss of a single man.[37] These expeditions reaped little martial glory for their participants. Materially they had destroyed Indian resources without curbing their ability or will to fight. Spiritually the devastation of their homelands and burial sites was a disastrous blow to the Iroquois. It represented the ruin of more than a century of war and diplomacy dedicated to the security of their homeland. The dismemberment of the Iroquois Confederacy was completed by these campaigns. Now Senecas, Onondagas, and Cayugas, dependent on British aid, made war on Oneidas who served and were dependent on the Americans.

War in the Northwest

In 1778 George Rogers Clark had invaded Illinois with the stated objective of protecting the new Kentucky settlements from the Indian attacks. This was one of the most active theatres of the frontier war, for despite whatever bargains whites had struck with the Iroquois and Cherokees, the Shawnees north of the Ohio had no intention of ceding their claims to this vast hunting ground. The Shawnees were not reluctant participants in the war; they would have fought the Kentuckians with or without British encouragement. Historians have questioned why Clark invaded Illinois when the threat to Kentucky was centred several hundred miles to the east. He had chosen a softer target than the Ohio Indians, the Illinois Indian tribes and the French inhabitants having, at best, lukewarm loyalty to the British empire. It could also be argued that Kaskaskia in Illinois offered access to rivers which might allow an army to advance on the key British base at Detroit, although events would prove that such a campaign was far beyond the capacity of any force at Clark's disposal. Finally, Clark may have been an agent of Virginia land speculation in the west or may have been in collusion with Kaskaskia merchants seeking to exploit Kentucky trade opportunities.[38] Clark easily captured Kaskaskia in July. In response, Lieutenant Governor Henry Hamilton seized the important post of Vincennes on the Wabash River, a move that blocked the river route to Detroit and reasserted British presence in the area. Clark then carried out his most celebrated exploit. In February 1779 he set forth on a march of almost 250 miles through a flooded countryside to confront Hamilton at Vincennes. There he besieged and captured the British commander, who found himself deserted by the French militia which constituted a large part of his force. Clark's behaviour at Vincennes remains a subject of controversy, particularly his treatment of Hamilton, whom he clapped in irons and shipped to Virginia as a war criminal. Clark claimed that the "Hair Buyer General" was the senior officer responsible for Indian atrocities in the Kentucky settlements, a charge supported by Virginia Governor Thomas Jefferson who invoked a version of the doctrine of superior orders against Hamilton.[39] Clark seems to have exaggerated Hamilton's guilt as a means of establishing the significance of his victory. Hamilton was following orders when he encouraged Indian war parties to strike the frontier. There is no evidence to suggest that he treated scalps any differently than any other commander, that is as evidence that the raiders had actually met the enemy. His 1778 correspondence demonstrates that he was concerned about assaults on non-combatants and urged that the warriors act with humanity. It is unlikely that he could have changed the Indian way of making war and it is clear that the latter understood that their role was to bring in scalps and prisoners.[40] Hamilton's capture did not bring an end to the attacks. Had Clark conquered the British base at Detroit, he might have materially changed the situation. Since that was beyond his means, he settled for a "show trial" of the British governor.

Clark's rough treatment of a senior British officer flouted conventions for prisoners and General Washington eventually insisted upon his release. Clark's behaviour also contributed to the image of the rebel as a savage. He and his men dressed in Indian fashion and adopted Indian styles of warfare. British officers were shocked when Clark personally tomahawked an Indian prisoner in full view of the besieged fort at Vincennes. Hamilton recalled that when he met Clark to discuss surrender terms, "He had just come from his Indian tryumph all bloody and sweating . . . and while he washed his hands and face still reeking from the human sacrifice in which he had acted as chief priest, he told me with great exultation how he had been employed."[41] Richard White observes that Clark on this occasion had appeared in the guise of an Algonquian war leader, the embodiment of violence and death. In contrast, Hamilton had appealed to the Indians as the British father, protector of harmony and peace. He had attempted to create an Indian alliance through diplomatic measures familiar to the peoples of the region. Clark relied upon terror to cow the Indians into submission. He became an example for numerous Indian-haters, for whom murder was the only Indian policy. This of course drove Indians into the British alliance just as Indian raids forced settlers to join the rebels.[42]

Clark lacked sufficient men and resources to hold the country he had seized. He was not "the conqueror of the old Northwest". That feat was achieved by American diplomats in Paris. But he was on the cutting edge of a new style of war on the frontier, one in which Americans adopted Indian ways of war. The small settlements west of the Appalachians were nurseries of these American warriors, many of whom gained experience as "long-hunters", men who spent much of their lives on extended hunts which might last for months or years at a time. These hunters could carry little food and depended upon their woodcraft and marksmanship for survival. It is not surprising that their weapon of choice was what is usually referred to as the Pennsylvania or Kentucky long rifle, a firearm equally popular with Indian hunter-warriors. Although they became inveterate enemies, the American frontiersmen and Indians came more and more to resemble one another.

When George Roush volunteered to serve as a scout at Fort Pitt in 1777, he was assigned to the company of Captain Samuel Brady, a skilled woodsman and confirmed Indian-hater. Roush was ordered to tan his thighs and legs with wild cherry and white oak bark and to dress in breechcloth, leather leggings, moccasins, and a cap made from raccoon skin and topped with hawk feathers. His face was painted red with three black stripes, an Indian sign for war. Brady's company was one of several that Colonel Brodhead despatched on raids into Indian territory, accompanied by friendly Delawares, who because of their willingness to bring in native scalps were known as "pet Indians". Roush recalled many scouting expeditions using skulking tactics reminiscent of those employed by Benjamin Church. On one occasion he crawled through the night with Brady and 15 men to attack an Indian hunting camp. They killed two men and a woman on their first fire and lured a boy within range whom they also shot. No line had been drawn between combatants and non-combatants. Despite a furious Indian pursuit, the party escaped with the loss of one dead and two wounded.[43] Such murderous small actions would become a common occurrence in the frontier war.

The most famous of the long hunter-frontier warriors was Daniel Boone, the legendary figure who helped lead the settlement of Kentucky. More at home in the forest than in established settlements, he departed on frequent long hunts, leaving his wife to attend to farm and family. It was a way of life familiar to his Indian opponents, who respected Boone for his strength, endurance, woodcraft and marksmanship. His arrival in Kentucky placed him at odds with the Shawnees and other Indian hunters determined to turn the land "dark and bloody" for the settlers. Despite his well deserved fame, Boone's success in the frontier war was mixed. He was captured twice; on one occasion he escaped and on the other was released. He carried out a famous rescue of a daughter kidnapped by an Indian party, but two of his sons were killed at his side in engagements with Indians. One of these deaths occurred at the disastrous Battle of Blue Licks in which Boone served as an officer. Boone differed from many frontiersmen in that he does not seem to have been an Indian-hater. The Shawnee war chief Blackfish adopted Boone into his family and regarded him with genuine affection, which he apparently returned. Blackfish seems to have been more saddened than angered by

127

Boone's escape and did not hold it against him. Boone and Blackfish fought to preserve their families and their rights to the land. The larger issues of the War of Independence meant little to them; indeed, Boone was suspected by some settlers of holding Tory sympathies. This is but another example that suggests that the frontier conflict was not simply a footnote to the War of Independence, but a parallel war in its own right.[44]

Although they adopted the Indian style of war, Boone and most frontiersmen held themselves distinct from Indian culture. Pursuing a life which offered escape from the bonds of European society, they retained roots within white culture. Nevertheless, they were a fiercely independent new breed removed from the traditional political, religious and moral authority of colonial establishments. While they continued to consider themselves Christians, they were heirs of the Great Awakening which had undermined formal church structures. It is difficult to recapture the moral universe of these settlers in the wilderness, for whom survival was a daily struggle. This harsh view of life necessarily shaped their view of war. This does not mean that their approach to war was any more cruel than that of seventeenth-century Puritans whose just war theories sanctioned many horrors. But it does suggest that they viewed war, as they viewed life, as a simple struggle for survival free of a moral context.

The Indian warrior inhabited a different moral world shaped by a ritualistic approach to war. Indian cultures also allowed brutal treatment of the hapless victims of war, including torture, mutilation and cannibalism. There was no fine distinction between war and murder. Nevertheless, the Indian warrior's culture provided other means by which he could reclaim his humanity. These rituals were strained by the demands of the frontier war of this period, but they were not eliminated. Thus they continued to make war with the object of taking captives who after appropriate rituals, might be adopted into their families. Indian culture continued to possess some means of limiting the horrors of war. The settlers seem to have inhabited a harder world and to have been equipped with very insecure moral anchors. The step to total war was easier for them than it was for their Indian opponents.

While frontiersmen acquired many Indian military skills, one trait above all separated them from their opponents: lack of caution. The record demonstrates that Indians were reluctant to expose themselves to needless casualties and avoided the bloody frontal assaults which were a familiar part of European warfare. Indians admired bravery, but deplored rashness. This explains why Indian warriors often withdrew when their towns were invaded by armies with superior numbers. Discretion was no disgrace. White frontiersmen, however, regarded bravery against the odds as the ultimate test of manhood. It explains many of the foolish sorties which led settlers straight into disastrous ambushes. Boone's biographer John Mack Faragher has referred to this attitude as "fool-brave"; frontiersmen feared that any expression of caution was likely to raise questions about one's manhood among one's peers. This was a flaw which the Indians exploited on more than one occasion and it was central to the Kentuckians' devastating defeat at Blue Licks on 19 August 1782. Kentucky suffered numerous Indian raids during that summer and, in August, a large Indian force accompanied by British officers and the "white Indian" Simon Girty, laid siege to the fort at Bryan's Station north of the Kentucky River; 182 militiamen from neighbouring settlements, including 45 under Boone's command, rushed to its relief. On finding that the enemy had departed, the officers debated whether to follow in hot pursuit or to await several hundred reinforcements known to be on the way. When an officer named Hugh McGary urged delay, he was silenced by scornful references to his timidity and it was resolved to begin pursuit on the following day. The Americans followed an extremely clear trail to Blue Licks, a well known salt lick on the Licking River where Boone had once been captured. Here the Americans saw a few Indians walking about casually on the hill on the opposite bank. Boone recognized the signs of an ambush, but McGary, smarting from previous insults, insisted on an immediate attack and dismissed Boone's caution with taunts of cowardice. Without waiting for orders, McGary and his detachment rushed forward to close with the enemy. Boone and the rest of the Kentuckians, including many of the most experienced frontier fighters in America, followed on their heels without any further discussion. They were cut to pieces by the Indian war party hidden in the ravines on the opposite bank.[45]

Although Indians were human and made mistakes, it seems unlikely that an Indian war party would have acted as rashly as did the Kentuckians at Blue Licks. Confident of their woodland skills and including many Indian-haters in their ranks, the Kentuckians dispensed with the service of Indian scouts. These attitudes were a recipe for disaster in forest warfare.

Blue Licks confirmed the bankruptcy of George Rogers Clark's war leadership, although he was not present. He could not capture Detroit, "conquer" the "Old Northwest", or protect Kentucky from attack. Indian forces seemed to be able to attack Kentucky virtually at will. In 1780 the British had demonstrated their ability to launch a massive raid from Detroit. Captain Henry Bird invaded Kentucky with 1,200 men and artillery which rendered settlers' forts defenceless. He quickly overcame two stations and withdrew, laden with plunder and prisoners. British officers believed that Bird would have accomplished even more had not the Indians slaughtered the cattle needed for provisions and refused to attack other posts.[46] It is likely that the Indians simply believed that they had achieved their objectives. In response Clark led almost 1,000 men against the Shawnee towns in Ohio. The Shawnees withdrew, burning their village of Chillecothe. A small party made a stand in a blockhouse in the town of Piqua, which Clark overcame by artillery fire. Indian battle casualties were light, although they included the Shawnee war chief Blackfish. However, one American reported that 73 scalps were taken and that no quarter was given. Clark's invasion was indecisive. He burned homes and crops, leaving the Shawnees impoverished but unconquered. Once the Americans burned the enemy's crops, their own logistical shortcomings forced them to withdraw.[47]

In March 1782, Indian-hating militiamen lit the fires of the last phase of the war in the midwest. They indiscriminately slaughtered peaceful Delawares at the Moravian missionary village of Gnadenhutten in Ohio, an act which roused previously friendly Delawares to seek revenge. The British commander at Detroit noted that while the Indians continued to hold prisoners taken earlier in mild captivity, they were determined to punish those they believed to be implicated in the massacre.[48] Revenge was not long in coming, when Colonel William Crawford and about 500 frontier militia marched against the Delaware town of Sandusky. In a running fight over several days, in which they were continually surrounded by Indian marksmen, some of whom were mounted, the militiamen were totally routed. Crawford and several officers were cut off from the main party and captured. Having led his men into a costly defeat, the American commander paid for the death of the Indians at Gnadenhutten by being burned at the stake.[49] By the Battle of Blue Licks the Americans were everywhere on the defensive on the western frontier.

Militarily the war in the midwest ended in a stalemate. Americans had managed to hold on to their Kentucky settlements, but had been unable to stop Indian raiders or to conquer lands north of the Ohio. The battles of 1782 had been decisively in the Indians' favor. Unfortunately for them, diplomacy was decisively against them. Their British allies had always considered them to be instruments of war of marginal value. Now the British sacrificed them by ceding virtually the entire midwest to the enemy, yielding to the Americans what had been denied them by force of arms. The Indian peoples, ravaged and impoverished by war, were deprived of the supplies and bases vital to their defence. Officers who had encouraged the Indians to fight as allies against the Americans were humiliated by this desertion. General Frederick Haldimand summed up the state of affairs exactly:

They [the Indians] must not be considered subject to Orders or easily influenced where their Interests or Resentments are concerned. Great Pains and Treasures were bestowed to bring them to act. They have suffered much in the cause of the War in their Lives and Possessions, in so much that the Mohawks who were settled in Ease and Affluence, have entirely lost their country – the rest of the Six Nations (the Oneidas excepted) have been invaded, and driven off their Settlements. They have so perpetually harassed the Enemy that they cannot look for Reconciliation upon any other terms than Abandoning the Royal Cause. They are Thunder Struck at the appearance of an accommodation so far short of their Expectation from the Language that has been held out to them, and Dread the Idea of being forsaken by us, and becoming a Sacrifice to a Vengeance which has already been raked upon them.[50]

The war and ensuing peace was a catastrophe for Native Americans. Indians were impoverished, homeless and disoriented. Their leaders, no matter what policy they had advocated, were discredited, for nothing had worked. Colin Calloway describes how Indian economies had been dislocated by the need to fight year-round, by destruction of crops and poor harvests, and by the severing of trade routes. Disease had increased among populations exposed to hunger and exposure. Indian culture had been strained by the looting of burial grounds and the disruption of ritual ceremonies. Traditional friendships and allegiances had dissolved among shifting alliances. The disruption of the Six Nations is but one poignant example. The future was clouded. Victorious Americans now claimed the lands of defeated Indians by right of conquest; a host of settlers stood ready to exploit these claims. Since the Indians had not in fact been defeated, the perils involved in American land hunger are evident. Peace between Great Britain and the United States did not mean an end to war on the frontier.[51]

The evolving nature of frontier warfare

How had frontier warfare evolved since 1675? The Indian way of war remained substantially the same. Indians continued to master European soldiers in the tactics of forest warfare. The skulking war, the commitment to marksmanship and the reluctance to risk large casualties remained hallmarks of Indian warriors. There was little in the way of technological change, but Indians equalled frontiersmen in their enthusiasm for accurate, long-range rifles. Like the frontiersmen, western Indian riflemen were often mounted and their raiding parties thus were more mobile and destructive. Eighteenth-century Indians also seem to have abandoned the wooden stockaded fortifications which had once protected their towns. Seventeenth-century experience had proven them to be death traps when surrounded by European troops equipped with artillery and determined to give no quarter. On the other hand, Indians generally lacked the ability to overcome stoutly defended forts. They seldom possessed cannon, which in any case would have burdened their raiding parties. Indian warriors might seize a fort through surprise or ruses, or attack it by tunnelling or flaming arrows and cartloads of combustibles. Their most effective technique against garrisons was to lure them into the open. In this way the Indians inflicted defeat after defeat upon their opponents.

The Indians remained vulnerable in a prolonged war. They continued to base a warrior society on a fragile economic base. Year-round war such as the War of Independence disrupted Indian hunting, which was a vital source of food and trade commodities. Indian farmlands were often contrasted favourably with those of white settlers. Sullivan's soldiers frequently commented on the prosperity of the towns that they sacked. But the Indian warriors often could not protect their farms from superior forces and had no reserves when they were lost. Sullivan and Clark could not defeat the Indians in the field, but they could impoverish them. The Indians could carry out equally destructive raids against white settlements, but despite the hardships they imposed, white society possessed reserves of capital and credit that allowed for reconstruction. Without outside support, it was difficult for Indian warriors to sustain an intensive war for more than a year. During the war the Indians were forced to turn to the British or the Americans not only for the trade goods on which they were increasingly dependent, but for weapons, ammunition, food and shelter. While Indian warriors were not mercenaries, a lengthy war inevitably compromised their independence.

Lack of unity also undermined the Indian struggle for independence. The division among the Iroquois is but the most striking example of this weakness. After the American Colonel Marinus Willet defeated a raiding party of British, loyalists and Indians at Johnstown, New York in 1781, he was joined by 60 Oneidas in his pursuit of the enemy. As the raiders crossed a river the loyalist ranger Walter Butler made a stand with the rearguard to cover the party's escape. As in the case of King Philip, this famous menace of the frontier was shot to death by an Indian.[52] Many Indian leaders recognized the evils of disunity and there is evidence of attempts to create a sense of common identity among Native Americans. During the Seven Years War Indians appear to have been increasingly unwilling to kill one another as pawns in a white man's war. The unifying spiritual messages of prophets such as Neolin were a basis for Indian unity during Pontiac's rebellion. The Cherokees opted for war in 1776 after an appeal for pan-Indian unity by northern Indians. By 1782 the native peoples of Ohio were increasingly unified in their resistance to white settlers. When Stockbridge Indians in the American service fell into the hands of the feared Abenakis, they were surprised to be kindly treated. War seems to have forged a greater sense of pan-Indian identity.[53]

Indian-style warfare had provoked emulation from whites in the seventeenth century. During the Seven Years War, regular officers had begun experiments to adapt their troops to forest war, as in the case of Gage's proposal for light infantry and the creation of the Royal Americans. The reduction of the army in 1763 meant that these innovations were short-lived. Bouquet lacked sufficient woodsmen to conduct Indian-style warfare during Pontiac's rebellion and the British army had no specially trained forest troops at the outbreak of the War for American Independence. British officers did recognize that campaigning in America presented challenges unique from those normally encountered in Europe; the army was divided between "Americans" whose previous service had inclined them to a loose order and less formal drill, and the "Germans" whose war experience had been shaped by participation in the campaigns of Prince Ferdinand of Brunswick. General Howe was chosen to command in America partly as a consequence of his familiarity with light infantry tactics in America.[54] One old frontier commander failed to achieve his former lustre. Robert Rogers received authority to reconstitute his famous Rangers, but he failed to retain Howe's confidence. Once again regular officers complained of the Rangers' lack of discipline and bad behaviour. This was a more serious charge since they were attached as light troops to the regular army rather than as Indian fighters on the frontier. In 1779 Howe disbanded them because of the scandalous conduct of their officers "in robbing and plundering many people then under the protection of His Majesty's Government". It was claimed that these officers were men of "mean extraction without any degree of education sufficient to qualify them to bear His Majesty's Commission . . . many of these Officers recommended by Lieut. Col. Rogers had been bred Mechanecks, others had kept Publick Houses, and One or Two had even kept Bawdy Houses in the City of New York".[55]

Roger's Queen's Rangers were re-established under regular officers, most notable of whom was Lieutenant Colonel J. G. Simcoe who achieved a distinguished record during the war. Simcoe, however, had no frontier experience and his Rangers continued to serve on the east coast as adjuncts to the regular army. Organized as cavalry and infantry along lines advocated by Maurice de Saxe and Turpin de Crissé, they were expert in scouting and laying ambushes for the enemy. Simcoe's Rangers thus seem to have emerged from the European light infantry manuals rather than from the frontier. Banastre Tarleton's loyalist legion was organized in a similar manner. His green-clad light infantry and cavalry routed southern militia during the British invasion of the south. Tarleton was a rash commander whose brutality contributed to the harsh nature of the southern campaigns. He was defeated by a frontier rifleman, Daniel Morgan, whose well disposed force of militia riflemen and Continental regulars smashed Tarleton's impetuous and disor-ganized charge at Cowpens on 16 January 1781. Sir Henry Clinton, a "German", blamed Tarleton's defeat on "that loose, flimsy order which had ever been too much the practice in America".[56] This does not do sufficient justice to Morgan. Cowpens was not exactly an ambush, but Morgan did lure the foolhardy Tarleton into a trap. The riflemen deployed in lines in front of the Continentals submitted Tarleton's Legion to withering volleys, but quickly gave way. Tarleton's diminished and disorganized troops were then defeated by the disciplined Continentals. Morgan's military education on the frontier was decidedly different from British officers, but it was quite effective for all that.

On 7 October 1780 the British had already suffered a serious defeat at the hands of frontiersmen seasoned in Indian warfare. Major Patrick Ferguson had led a force of about 1,100 loyalists into the backcountry of South Carolina to repress the rebellion there and to support the flank of General Cornwallis's regular army. Ferguson was an enterprising and ambitious officer. He had considerable experience in independent command, having won fame or notoriety by his bloody night-time bayonet attack on the troops of the Casimir Pulaski Legion at Little Egg Harbor, New Jersey on 15 October 1778. He was also the inventor of the breech-loading Ferguson rifle and had briefly commanded one of the first experimental rifle detachments in the British army.[57] He was, in sum, one of the rising stars of the British officer corps. Now receiving reports that large numbers of rebels were gathering to oppose him, Ferguson withdrew to a defensive position at King's Mountain in northern South Carolina. There he was surrounded by 900 mounted riflemen from the backwoods of Virginia and North Carolina and from the new settlements in Tennessee. The riflemen deployed behind trees and poured an accurate fire into the loyalists on the summit. Ferguson led three bayonet charges in an attempt to drive off the enemy, who simply fled before the assaults and returned again to continue their fire. Ferguson was killed along with 224 of his men; most of the remainder were wounded before they could surrender.[58] King's Mountain is the most clear-cut example of the application of the Indian style of war by Americans against the royal forces during the war. The mobility of the mounted riflemen had caught Ferguson completely off guard. At King's Mountain the Americans actually conformed to the myths that surround the American way of war at the time of the Revolution. They fought independently, skulking behind cover, and relied on aimed rifle fire to overcome the enemy. Like the Indians they ran before the enemy bayonets, but returned to draw the noose tighter. Patrick Ferguson, one of the most talented professional officers in the British army, had been defeated by "amateurs" trained in the Indian way of war.

British occupation of South Carolina and Georgia was resisted by guerrilla fighters, many of whom had gained experience in Indian warfare. The conflict between American and loyalist partisans was one of the most cruel episodes of the war. It was a civil war fought without regard for the rules. However, civil wars fought between peoples of a common culture are often limited by that culture's familiar restraints.[59] Why then was this conflict so savage? One expert concludes that the southern militia who fought the loyalists for the control of the countryside had performed a duel function since the beginning of the Revolution: suppression of political dissent and protection of the frontier.[60] Guerrilla leaders such as Thomas Sumter and Francis Marion came from this hard school where civil war and Indian war merged.[61] Reliance on Indian warriors by Tory leaders such as Thomas Brown also encouraged the guerrillas to retaliate against the loyalists as if they were Indians. In many cases southerners seem to have lost sight of the difference between war and murder.

What part does this play in the American military tradition? Had the Americans relied upon guerrilla tactics as the primary defence against the British army, the frontier way of war might have become that of America. The American General Charles Lee had advocated such an approach. However, George Washington, as intent on preserving the institutions of his society as he was on founding a new state, based the defence of the United States on a regular army which in many ways was a mirror image of the British regulars.[62] This was the army that won the war and became the core of the American military experience. Washington, of course, had had considerable frontier experience during the Seven Years War. Ironically, his mentor in that conflict was Major General Edward Braddock.

5. Conflict in the Old Northwest, 1783–1815

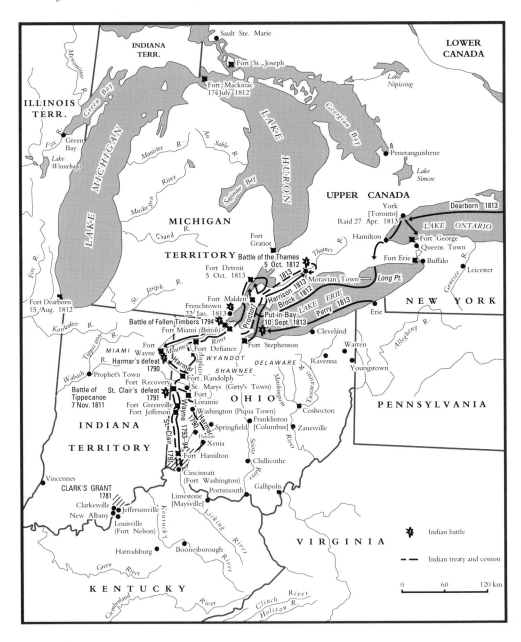

Chapter Seven

Last stands: the defeat of Indian resistance in the Old Northwest, 1783–1815

The Old Northwest

Indian military power was broken in the lands claimed by the United States east of the Mississippi by 1 January 1815. While the Treaty of Ghent, which concluded the War of 1812, restored the *status quo ante bellum* and included an article reinstating the Indians of the Old Northwest to their situation in 1811, the reality remained a decisive defeat of armed Indian resistance to American expansion. The great Shawnee warrior Tecumseh had fallen at the Battle of the Thames on 5 October 1813; with him died the dream of pan-Indian unity in opposition to the United States. Embers of that dream were extinguished on 27 March 1814 when General Andrew Jackson destroyed an army of Creek militants, the southern Indians most receptive to Tecumseh's appeal, at the Battle of Horseshoe Bend. From 1783 to 1815, Native American peoples had grappled with the problem of how to respond to the new American power. For decades their communities had been divided between those who sought peaceful accommodation and those who advocated armed defence of lands and rights. The debate was now ended, but accommodation without the alternative of force was a bankrupt policy as well. The way was now open for the removal of the Native American peoples from their homelands.[1]

Armed resistance had frustrated American ambition for three decades. Indian warfare was the first major challenge to the new republic's military institutions. In 1790–91 Indian confederate forces north of the Ohio River humiliated American armies and barred American expansion into their homelands. During the War of 1812, British military weakness, which appeared to open the way to an easy American conquest of Canada, was offset by powerful Indian allies, who inflicted stinging American reverses on the Detroit frontier. The pattern of Indian tactical superiority, evident throughout the period covered by this study, remained unbroken. It enabled Indian leaders to resist an enemy endowed with far greater numbers and material resources. Nevertheless, the Indians remained fatally dependent for their survival on European allies who could supply them with weapons, ammunition, food, and sanctuary. Thus their fate became entangled in broader diplomatic disputes between the United States and European powers which inevitably treated their interests as secondary. In 1815 Indians might ponder whether they owed their defeat more to their unreliable British ally than to their implacable American enemy.

After 1783 the Old Northwest, encompassing the modern states of Ohio, Indiana, Illinois, Michigan and Wisconsin, was of crucial concern to the new American government. American leaders believed that those lands belonged to the United States by right of conquest as acknowledged by the Treaty of Paris. Thus they represented an endowment for the almost bankrupt nation, one that might be used to settle veterans' claims and war debts. Individual states and private speculators also coveted these western riches. However, the lands remained occupied by Indian peoples, who had retained the military advantage at the end of the American War of Independence and who had gained wide experience in confederate action against a common enemy. They had been "thunderstruck" by the news of the Peace of Paris, but their British "father" continued his presence in their world. Unconvinced that the American state could long survive and hopeful of retaining a western trading empire, the British were reluctant to honour their treaty obligation to hand over the key western posts of Detroit, Michilimackinac and Niagara. As long as they retained access to these places of safety and supply, the northwestern Indians remained a formidable military force in the heart of a region critical to the future development of the United States.

The problem for the government was how to secure these valuable lands without an Indian war, which could complete the nation's financial ruin. Initially the Confederation government was able to capitalize on the prestige of its recent victory and Indian demoralization at their apparent desertion by the British. By bullying, and by exploiting divisions among individual tribes, American commissioners dictated three treaties to Indian councils during 1784–6 which ceded eastern and southern Ohio to American settlement. As usual there were questions about the legitimacy of such treaties. Individual tribal leaders who ceded their people's lands, often at a personal profit, were likely to be rejected by their followers. And all too often one tribal leadership was quick to concede rights to someone else's land, as in the case of the Iroquois who, in a last shake of the rusty Covenant Chain, yielded their shadowy claims to the west at the Treaty of Fort Stanwix. These shady dealings, coupled with a stream of settlers into Kentucky and eastern and southern Ohio, inevitably provoked renewed Indian resistance. Border war broke out again in 1786. George Rogers Clark led another, but spectacularly unsuccessful, expedition to Vincennes, and Colonel Benjamin Logan raided Shawnee towns on the Great Miami River. These raids poisoned relations already gone sour. They also demonstrated that no matter what Indian policies the national government might adopt, local authorities and settlers could provoke an Indian war. 1786 also saw the renewal of concerted action by the northwestern Indians. In November and December 1786, a general council of tribes meeting at the mouth of the Detroit River agreed that land cessions would be recognized as legitimate only if approved by the entire confederacy that was now developing. It was clear that American claims to the west would not be easily enforced.[2]

Nevertheless, expansion into the Northwest was embodied in the most significant legislative act of the Confederation Congress: the Northwest Ordinance of July 1787, which reaffirmed American ownership of the region and provided for the establishment of new states therein. Article III of the Ordinance assured the Indians that they would not be deprived of their lands without consent, nor would their rights be invaded "unless in just and lawful wars authorized by Congress". The hollowness of this piety rapidly became evident when Congress began the sale of Ohio lands still claimed by the Indian confederacy. There remained the problem of convincing the Indians to yield these lands peacefully. This was very much the concern of Secretary of War William Knox, who recognized the government's unreadiness for an Indian war. Knox believed that a new Northwest treaty was required which would secure the western lands by purchase rather than by the principle of conquest. The question remained whether Indian refusal to sell such land would be cause for a "just war".[3]

The Governor of the Northwest Territory, the veteran Revolutionary War General Arthur St Clair, was now authorized to negotiate a treaty which would secure by purchase the lands ceded in the treaties of 1784–6. St Clair's instructions were unrealistic and his conduct of negotiations inept. The Indian confederacy lacked unity and there were opportunities for a skilled diplomat to isolate the hardliners, notably the unconquered western Algonquian peoples such as the Shawnees, Miamis and Kickapoos. The confederacy also included Indians prepared for peace at any price and a moderate faction of Iroquois and Great Lakes Indians led by Joseph Brant. Brant sought to avoid war by conceding an area of eastern Ohio already penetrated by American settlement. St Clair, however, conducted the negotiations with a high hand and succeeded only in driving the leadership of the confederacy into the hands of the hardliners. Brant withdrew from the negotiations in disgust. At Fort

Harmar in January 1789, two groups of Indians signed treaties which confirmed the earlier cessions in return for a purchase price. But they did not speak for the entire confederacy and the legitimacy of the treaties was thus compromised in Indian eyes. The militants continued to regard the Ohio as the boundary between American settlement and Indian country, and they were prepared to fight to keep it so.[4]

The year 1789 marked the beginning of the new American federal government under the presidency of George Washington. It also marked a period in which "a remarkable unity of purpose bound borderland Indians from the Gulf of Mexico to the Great Lakes".[5] Indian unity was fuelled by opposition to American expansionism and nurtured by nativist spiritual leaders who provided cultural substance to pan-Indian identity. Despite the hopes of Washington and Secretary of War Knox for a "moral" and peaceful Indian policy which would allow a gradual and civilizing American expansion, events on the frontier favoured Indian militants. Indian neutralist leaders were murdered by white frontiersmen and the stream of American settlers pouring down the Ohio River made a mockery of a policy of gradualism. Indian attacks on immigrants on the river and raids on Kentucky settlements gave these events a momentum that federal policy could neither channel nor contain. St Clair observed that the United States was at peace with the Indians, but that the Indians were at war with the people of Kentucky.[6]

The small regular army, which was stationed almost entirely on the frontier, could not regulate the tide of settlement or protect the settlers from Indian attack. After the fiasco of Clark's 1786 raid on the Wabash villages, Major John Hamtramck and a small detachment of regulars were directed to occupy the old French town of Vincennes to preserve the peace between whites and Indians, and between Vincennes' French and American inhabitants. It was an humiliating experience for Hamtramck. Indians cut off his supply boats on the Wabash and threatened the garrison with starvation. White marauders flouted his authority. In August 1788, a Kentucky Indian fighter, Major Patrick Brown, appeared in the neighbourhood with 60 men, killing Indians and stealing horses. He ignored Hamtramck's order to depart and the latter, with only nine men fit for duty, was powerless to impose order. The regular army was reduced to the role of an almost passive observer of frontier developments.[7]

This presented the federal government with a major crisis, one which earlier imperial governors would have found ironically familiar. Western settlements had always strained the authority of colonial governments. Now failure to protect trans-Appalachian settlements could undermine their allegiance to the United States. They were already under the influence of powerful centrifugal forces provided by the great rivers that bore their trade west and south to New Orleans. Spain, which controlled their access to that port, and Britain, intent on preserving its own western empire, encouraged the westerners' independence. The new constitution gave the federal government the potential for a vigorous western policy, but the immediate situation was almost beyond its capacity. On 29 September 1789, Congress authorized the President to call out state militias to defend the frontiers. After conducting an unsuccessful peace mission to the militant Indians on the Wabash during the winter of 1789–90, Governor St Clair warned that a punitive expedition to the Northwest might be necessary. Secretary Knox does not seem to have grasped the implications of St Clair's warning; he ordered preparations to stamp out Indian "banditti" who he believed represented only a minority of the Indians. In doing so, he provoked a major Indian war, the first war in United States history.[8]

It was a war that the United States was woefully unprepared to fight. The regular army in 1789 consisted of only 672 men actually in service, with no more than 300 to 400 men available to General Josiah Harmar in command on the Ohio. Inadequate supplies, brutal discipline, and bad morale made it difficult to retain even that number in the ranks. When Congress voted to increase the army to 1,216 in 1790, it maintained the defence budget by cutting pay in half. By any measure the United States Army was inferior in numbers and quality to the military forces available to the Indian confederacy in the Northwest. The bulk of any military expedition launched against the Northwest Indians would have to be drawn from volunteers or militia, soldiers clearly inferior to the Indian warriors who awaited them. The ground for the American military disasters of 1790–91 was thus well prepared.[9]

In July 1790, St Clair and Harmar met to develop a plan to strike at the Shawnee and Miami villages located near the Maumee and Wabash Rivers. The offensive was to be delivered by two separate columns. The main force commanded by Harmar, consisting of 300 regulars and 1,200 Kentucky and Pennsylvania militia, would march from Fort Washington (modern Cincinnati) directly to the Miami Village (Fort Wayne, Indiana). A diversionary force under Major John Hamtramck, commander of the American garrison at Vincennes, with 100 regulars and 400 militia, would attack the Wea and Vermillion villages along the Wabash. The object was to "chastise" the Indians rather than to seize their territory. Knox rejected the idea of a fort at the Miami Village, whose garrison and communications would require more men than the American Army possessed.[10] Nevertheless, these raids were an ambitious undertaking for such a weak and inexperienced force. The Kentucky militia which reported to Harmar in September was a severe disappointment. Far from being the famed frontier fighters of legend, many were paid substitutes entirely without military experience and many were

141

without arms. The Pennsylvanians proved to be in even worse condition. Quarrels among the militia officers over precedence in command added to the confusion.[11]

Harmar began his ill-conceived expedition on 26 September 1790. Any possibility of surprising the hostile Indians was lost when St Clair, in obedience to Knox's instructions, warned the British commander at Detroit and friendly Indians of the mission's intent and destination. Although Harmar seems to have undertaken precautions for march and camp security, green and undisciplined militiamen undermined his arrangements. Wiley Sword concludes that "the character of the army's march thus seemed more to resemble a herd of elephants tramping through the underbrush than the stealthy approach of a raiding column intent upon surprising their enemy."[12]

On 29 October, Governor St Clair reported Harmar's "successful" attack upon the Indian towns on the Miami and St Joseph's Rivers. Five villages had been burned and quantities of corn and other crops had been destroyed. Unfortunately for the Americans, the old tactic of forcing the Indians to fight for their homes and food supplies had backfired. The Indians, led by the able Miami war leader Little Turtle, had twice surprised and defeated detachments of Harmar's force. St Clair's declaration of "victory" listed three officers and 150 men killed in action.[13]

Both regular and militia officers blamed the poorly disciplined militia for the debacle. Finding the first Indian towns abandoned, the militia soon turned their attention to loot. Harmar was initially buoyed by this bloodless triumph and considered expanding the scope of his raid until lurking Indians drove off a number of his packhorses and cavalry mounts. On 18 October, he despatched 300 regulars and militia on a reconnaissance, whose scouts encountered an Indian party, but the detachment returned to camp without engaging the enemy. On the following day, Colonel John Hardin of Kentucky pursued the same route with 180 men. Hardin was unpopular with his men and disregarded march security. His column extended for almost half a mile when he rode with the vanguard into a small meadow surrounded by heavy timber, the site of an ambush prepared by Little Turtle and 150 warriors. When firing erupted from the woods, the regulars stood their ground and the militia fled. The former were perfect targets for the aimed fire of the Indians, who soon attacked and overwhelmed them in hand-to-hand combat. They had saved the lives of many of the fleeing militiamen, but relations between regulars and militia did not recover from this incident. On 22 October, Harmar attempted to redeem the fortunes of his command. Learning that the Indians had reoccupied the previously deserted village of Kekionga, he arranged a complex three-pronged attack to trap and destroy the enemy. The command of this 400-man force was given to the regular officer Major John Palsgrove

Wyllys, but, with only 60 regulars available, the attack was dangerously dependent on the unreliable militia and their officers. The event would demonstrate that a co-ordinated movement of three columns, difficult enough for experienced troops, was beyond their capacity. Instead they fell victim to a sophisticated double ambush devised by Little Turtle, clearly the most gifted commander on the field. Once again the regular troops stood their ground in hand-to-hand combat and lost 83 per cent of their men. The militia, quicker to take to their heels, nevertheless suffered heavy losses and were in no mood to continue the campaign. The Americans had lost the first round of the Indian war. Major Hamtramck's expedition had fared better only in that it was able to burn a few villages without having to fight anyone.[14]

In 1790 the United States lacked the means to carry out a successful war. Harmar's defeat revealed many deficiencies. Although he was exonerated by the Court of Inquiry, there were questions about his leadership. He was unable to control militia officers, much less their men, he was too quick to divide his army in the face of an enemy about whom he knew little, and he was not present at either action. His officers stoutly rejected suggestions that he was frequently intoxicated, but he had failed to exercise effective command in critical situations. Despite the Court's judgement, Harmar had lost Washington's confidence and was replaced as commander by St Clair. He was but the first of a long line of United States officers whose military reputation would be buried in the Indian country.

Harmar's defeat demonstrated the need for disciplined full-time soldiers. The regulars had fought bravely, but they were not trained in frontier warfare tactics. Their casualty rate suggests that they remained committed to close order and the bayonet. The regular army retained a preference for muskets over rifles and Knox had urged that the latter be exchanged for the former whenever possible. American strategy was restricted by the means at hand. Knox had believed that he was faced with a few banditti whom a punitive expedition might quell. He had clung to the hope that a "sensible" majority of Indians would peacefully negotiate the surrender of their homelands. Instead, by despatching armies into the Indian country, he had committed the Indian confederacy to a general war. If the United States was to force the Indians to terms, such raids were not enough. As Major Hamtramck observed, only military occupation in the form of forts and strong garrisons could accomplish such a goal.[15] Part-time, self-willed militia could not be counted upon for such a war of conquest. Suitable for home defence, their quality quickly eroded when called upon to desert their farms for lengthy periods, thus the hiring of untrained substitutes. A larger, properly trained army was required, but did not exist in 1790.

Knox retained the hope that peace might be negotiated with moderates

among the Indians who would see the American point of view. He despatched Colonel Thomas Proctor to the Indians on the Maumee and Wabash
Rivers, but the mission was a fiasco. American diplomatic and military
missions to the Northwest were continually hampered by British control of
the Great Lakes during this period. British authorities at Niagara refused
Proctor permission to travel farther west and he had to content himself with
reaffirming friendship with the Six Nations. Harmar's defeat had empowered
confederacy militants, who did not see the American point of view at all and
were insistent on maintaining the Ohio boundary. Although the British
government feared a wider war, which would threaten their possession of the
western posts, they encouraged the idea of an Indian buffer state which would
shield their western empire. British authorities hoped for a peaceful resolution, but many Canadian fur traders such as the loyalist Simon Girty encouraged the Indians to armed resistance. The British posts might provide Indian
warriors with supplies and sanctuaries, but British support was not as firm as
that provided in the late War of Independence. While some public figures
such as Sir Henry Clinton advocated force to confine the United States east
of the Appalachians, in the end Britain would not risk war with the United
States to defend the Indian confederacy. British inconstancy would be the
Indians' greatest weakness in the war that was now underway.[16]

St Clair's defeat

Knox also prepared to renew the war. He now believed that only a fort
established in the heartland of the militant confederacy, the Miami villages on
the Maumee River, would force the recalcitrant Indians to terms. Such a
change in strategy required a far more powerful force than that which had
accompanied Harmar: an army of 3,000 men, which he believed would
outnumber the available Indian warriors by three-to-two. As a first step
towards providing such an army, the regular establishment was increased to
2,128 with the provision of a new unit: the Second United States Regiment.
Even so, the regular army would have insufficient men for the campaign ahead.
Knox intended to make up the difference by the expedient of recruiting 2,000
six-month levies. These temporary soldiers, he hoped, would be superior to
militia, for they would be subject to regular command and discipline. This was
an economical measure undertaken by an impoverished government and it
seemed to guarantee the numerical superiority that Knox deemed necessary for
success. Six-month levies, however, suggested a rapid campaign. It was unclear
how such troops would gain even the rudiments of the training and discipline

which Knox believed to be the other crucial American advantage over the Indians. Knox does not seem to have considered that sending such a force of raw and untrained men against the Indians was a death sentence. Veteran officers found that even the newly enrolled Second US Regiment included mainly urban "riffraff" unsuited for frontier war. In neither case was there time to bring the troops up to a decent standard. Regular officers scorned the professional qualifications of many of their colleagues. Adjutant Winthrop Sargent observed of Colonel Darke of the levies that "in action, he is most passionately intent upon Indian-killing himself, but inadequate to performing it by battalion, or even by platoon".[17] Furthermore, recruitment fell short of expectations and St Clair was authorized to call up the Kentucky and Pennsylvania militia to make up the difference.[18]

As this ramshackle force assembled at Fort Washington, Major Ebenezer Denny, who had served on Harmar's staff, decided to follow his chief into retirement, but his resignation from the service was rejected. Harmar was a better administrator than field commander, but he sensed a disaster in the making as he viewed the condition of the new army. Denny recalled that Harmar "conversed frequently and freely with a few of his friends on the probable result of the campaign; predicted a defeat. He suspected a disposition in me to resign; discouraged the idea. 'you must', said he, 'go on the campaign; some will escape and you may be among the number.'"[19] At some level Harmar may have relished the thought that the army would fare no better under a new leader, but his comments did little for Denny's morale. Other experienced officers may have felt similar unease at the outset of the campaign.

There was much to be discouraged about as the army began its march north from Fort Washington in mid-September. The weakness of American military institutions became more evident every day. The logistical system seemed on the verge of breakdown. Flour continually ran short and overtaxed convoys of packhorses were never able to provide more than a few days' margin at best. Food shortages provoked desertion among the militia and demands for discharge among the levies. In any event St Clair feared that all of the levies would be gone by the termination of their enlistments on 3 November. Regulars had to be assigned to prevent desertion and protect convoys from mutinous soldiers. The First US Regiment, detached on such duty, would miss the ensuing battle entirely. Bad clothing and inadequate tents led to widespread illness; construction of supply depots at Fort Hamilton on the Great Miami River and Fort Jefferson further north was hampered by shortages of axes and other essential tools. Packhorses and cavalry horses wandered off because the horsemaster had not thought to provide them with bells and hobbles.

Little had been done to prepare the soldiers for the campaign ahead. St

Clair agreed to an arrangement with Lt Colonel Oldham of the militia by which the latter were to provide all of the army's scouts "for which service they were much fitter than the troops, a great part of which had never been in the woods in their lives, and many never fired a gun, and that the militia should be excused from all fatigue duties, which they submitted to with the utmost reluctance".[20] Arthur St Clair referred to all of these deficiencies when he explained his unsuccessful campaign. Clearly he was well served neither by the men nor the material assigned to him. St Clair was a brave man and an experienced soldier whose service dated to the Seven Years War. But one wonders whether the army would have disintegrated under a more dynamic commander. Something could have been done to have brought the troops to a higher level of readiness before the march and more could have been done to inspire them on the way. But nothing was taken in hand to dispel the pessimism associated with Harmar's grim forecast.

Another glaring weakness was almost total lack of intelligence. St Clair had no knowledge of Indian strength, location, and intentions. During the summer, Kentucky militia had conducted two separate raids against Indian villages on the Wabash. The raiders burned houses, destroyed crops, and captured women and children, but encountered few warriors.[21] As St Clair's column struggled north in October, it too encountered few traces of Indians. Once again there was hope that the mission could be accomplished without resistance. But St Clair was frustrated by lack of information. Only on 29 October was he able to despatch a party of newly arrived Chickasaw Indian scouts in search of the elusive enemy. By contrast, the Indian confederate army was well informed about St Clair and they had every intention of fighting him under conditions of their own choosing.

Thus on 4 November 1791 the US Army suffered the most severe defeat at the hands of the Indians in its history. It was a defeat on a scale with that inflicted on Braddock and many of the ingredients were the same. Experienced forest warriors, under excellent tactical leadership and well equipped with rifled firearms, routed green, ill-trained, badly disciplined soldiers whose weapons proved ineffective under the conditions of frontier warfare. Both Knox and St Clair had been confident that superior numbers and discipline would prevail against the Indians. It was an over-confidence shared by American military leaders since the days of King Philip's War. The repetitive nature of American defeats at the hands of Indian warriors is perhaps the clearest argument for the value of military history in the education of military and political leaders.

On 3 November, the army pitched camp on high ground near the Wabash River. The rectangular site proved to be too small for the entire force, which now reduced to about 1,450 men and a number of women and children camp followers. As a result, the militia were sent across the river to occupy an old Indian camp ground. In addition to dividing his army, St Clair failed to order the preparation of defensive works despite reports of Indians lurking in the area. Throughout the night sentries fired at figures of Indians moving through the darkness, but officers dismissed reports of war parties as being simply horse thieves. Poorly disciplined sentries often fire at shadows and officers were likely not to have taken the firing seriously. On the morning of 4 November the army stood to arms before sunrise as usual, but, since the weather was clear and all appeared quiet, the troops were soon dismissed for breakfast and to round up scattered horses. It was then that the Indian confederate army of 1,040 Wyandots, Mingos, Shawnees, Miamis, Delawares, Ottawas, Chippewas, Potawatomis and Cherokees burst upon them. They routed the Kentuckians across the river, who fled into the main camp in disorder. Under the direction of Little Turtle, the Indians deployed in their classic half-moon to surround the camp and cut off its retreat. The experienced warriors, moving from one concealment to another, unleashed a devastating aimed fire on the hapless Americans struggling to form ranks. American musket fire was ineffective against opponents firing from cover, and the artillery, upon which the defence was centred, constantly fired its canister shot over the heads of the enemy. The gun crews of these short-range, smooth-bore cannon were perfect targets for Indian riflemen and suffered particularly high loss of life. As the Indians began to penetrate the camp, American commanders organized bayonet charges to drive them back, only to find that the enemy quickly eluded them and returned to cut them off. Soon the Indians penetrated the camp, killing the remaining gunners and many of the camp followers. After having several horses shot from under him while trying to rally the men, St Clair lost control of the situation. By mid-morning the army could no longer offer organized resistance. A body of survivors broke out to the east of the camp and fled into the woods, carrying their unfortunate general with them. The Indian army paused to take possession of the field. There they found over 600 American dead and vast quantities of military stores. The Indians had gained this astonishing victory at the cost of 21 killed and 40 wounded. It was the high point of the Indian confederacy.[22]

Denny later returned to Harmar's prediction of disaster:

He saw with what material the bulk of the army was composed; men collected from the streets and prisons of the cities, hurried out into the enemy's country, and with the officers totally unacquainted the business in which they were engaged; it was utterly impossible they could be otherwise. Besides not any one department was sufficiently prepared; both quartermaster and contractors extremely deficient. It was a matter

of astonishment to him that a commanding general who was acknowledged to be perfectly competent should think of hazarding with such
people, and under such circumstances, his reputation and life and the
lives of so many others, knowing too, as both did, the enemy with
whom he was going to contend; an enemy brought up from infancy to
war, and perhaps superior to an equal number of the best men that could
be brought against them.[23]

General John Armstrong, commenting on St Clair's defeat, believed that it
demonstrated the need for greater adaptability to the Indian way of war:

It seems probable that too much attachment to regular or military rule,
or too great a confidence in artillery (which it seems, formed a part of
the line, and had a tendency to render the troops stationary) must have
been the motives which led to the adopted order of action. I call it
adopted because the General does not speak of having intended any
other, whereby he presented a large and visible object, perhaps in too
close order too, to an enemy near enough to destroy, but from their
known modes of action comparatively invisible; whereby we may readily
infer that five hundred Indians were sufficient to do us all the injury we
have sustained, nor can I conceive them to have been many more.[24]

St Clair's defeat had wide ramifications. The policy of Indian militants now
appeared to be justified and Indians previously in the accomodationist camp
united behind the confederacy. Among the Shawnees and southern
Cherokees and Chickamaugas, native spiritualism was bolstered by the victory
over the white men. Prospects for a powerful border confederacy embracing
northern and southern Indians appeared bright. British authorities, continually
fearful of American expansion and threats to the western posts, were reminded
that the Indians were an asset that might shield their western empire. It also
seemed to offer Britain a unique opportunity to mediate between Americans
and Indians to Britain's advantage.

St Clair's defeat also demonstrated that American attempts to enforce
Confederation era Indian treaties with available forces were futile. New
diplomatic and military policies were necessary if America were to provide
security for expanding frontier settlement. Thus the federal government
initiated a new peace offensive aimed at assuring the Indians that the government recognized their rights and would not take their land by force. Such
diplomacy, if it did not convince the militants, might nevertheless divide the
confederacy. The government also began to construct an American army
which could take the land by force if it had to. American diplomacy dealt from
weakness and was unsuccessful. A series of emissaries, including the Mohawk

leader Joseph Brant and the Stockbridge Indian Captain Hendrick Aupaumut, were sent west to assure the Indians that the United States had no designs on Indian lands other than that obtained by fair treaties. These missions encountered many obstacles. Two envoys, Captain Peter Pond and William Steedman, were denied passage on Lake Erie by the British and could not even reach the Indian country. They were more fortunate than Captain Alexander Trueman and Colonel John Hardin, who were killed on separate peace missions to the Indians. Another emissary, Brigadier General Rufus Putnam, chose to treat with the Indians from the safety of the post at Vincennes. On 27 September 1792, he signed a treaty with a number of Wabash tribes which recognized: "That the lands originally belonged to the Indians; it is theirs, and theirs only. That they have a right to sell, and a right to refuse to sell. And that the United States will protect them in their said just rights." The treaty embodied professed American desires to deal fairly with the Indians and reflected the military realities. However, the treaty failed to provide for ultimate American sovereignty in the region and, given the tide of American settlement, it was unenforceable. In any event, the Senate rejected ratification in 1794. By that time, warriors of the Wabash Indians, seldom restrained by treaties negotiated by their elders, were violating the peace.

In 1793, a special commission was again despatched to treat with the Indian confederacy at its council on the Maumee. General Benjamin Lincoln, Beverly Randolph and Timothy Pickering were instructed to obtain confirmation of the cessions provided by the Fort Harmar treaty in return for additional financial compensation and a firm guarantee of all remaining Indian lands. Since the commissioners planned to travel to the Indian country via the lakes, they were dependent on the assistance of the profoundly anti-American governor of Upper Canada, J. G. Simcoe, who sought to manipulate the negotiations towards British interests and prevented them from reaching the Maumee. Thus they were compelled to treat with the Indians from a distance. But there was little ground for compromise. Militant Indians in the ascendance would recognize no other boundary than the Ohio River. The American negotiators, faced with the fact of land sales and settlement beyond that boundary, could accept nothing less than the cession of eastern and southern Ohio. Both sides recognized that an appeal to arms was now at hand.[25]

Fallen Timbers

Military defeat in the Northwest had dimmed the lustre of American arms in the aftermath of the triumph over Great Britain and dispelled the myth of a unique American way of war rooted in the experience of the frontier. Handfuls of ill-trained regulars supplemented by raw and undisciplined militia and volunteers had proven no match for the formidable confederate Indians. In this case defeat forced the government to reconsider the fundamentals of American military institutions. Fortunately for the United States, it possessed in George Washington and Henry Knox leaders of great military experience and ability. In 1792 they responded to the military crisis with one of the most creative reforms in American military history: the Legion of the United States, with an authorized strength of 5,190 rank and file under the command of one of the most distinguished soldiers of the War of Independence, Major General Anthony Wayne. The Legion, organized in four Sub-Legions, reflected the advanced military thought and experience of such influential eighteenth-century military writers as Maurice de Saxe and Turpin de Crissé. Each Sub-Legion was designed as a self-contained unit with one troop of dragoons, one company of artillery, two battalions of infantry, and one battalion of riflemen. It was an arrangement which offered an ideal combination of mobility and firepower, well suited for both offensive and defensive operations. Units of this type had been employed by both sides during the War of Independence. They had proven especially well suited to *petit guerre* and seemed to be an excellent organization for a regular army committed to an Indian war. Thus the new army was one of the first to be organized on truly revolutionary principles. The Legion organization, a victim of peace and economy in 1796, did not long survive the conclusion of the Indian war, but it anticipated the self-contained divisional units which emerged in Europe during the Napoleonic wars.[26]

In itself, the Legion organization could not guarantee success unless the men were trained for the conditions of frontier warfare. In this respect the Legion was fortunate in its commander. A comparison of Anthony Wayne's correspondence with that of his ill-fated predecessors reveals a general with energy, confidence, and "grip". In some respects Wayne was a soldier of the old school, prepared to enforce discipline with the lash and the firing squad and skeptical about the value of rifles in comparison to smooth-bore muskets, but he was an outstanding trainer of men. During the War of Independence, Washington had chosen him to command the Continental Army's light brigade. This unit had won praise even from British officers for its stunning night-time bayonet assault on 15 July 1779 upon the fortified position at Stony Point on the Hudson and for its humane treatment of the prisoners thereafter. It was one of the outstanding professional achievements in the history of the American army. Wayne had more than once demonstrated his ability to transform raw recruits into soldiers. Now he arrived in the west determined to provide his green Legionaries with the discipline and training that would allow them to survive and prevail in an Indian war. St Clair's army had begun to fall apart in the licentious surroundings of Fort Washington; Wayne, finding his men tempted by the taverns and brothels of frontier Pittsburgh, removed his camp to a remote site which he named Legionville. There he submitted the troops to a harsh and unrelenting regime. At the same time, he began realistic training for the campaign ahead. This included physical fitness, marksmanship and rapid fire. He organized sham battles with riflemen playing the part of Indians to accustom the men to the sounds and terrors of frontier combat. Thanks to this training, Wayne's army would be perhaps the best trained regular force despatched to the frontier in the period covered by this study.[27]

Wayne transferred his army to Fort Washington in the spring of 1793. However, he was frustrated in his hopes of beginning offensive operations that year. Knox insisted that diplomatic efforts be given the chance to succeed, particularly since there seemed little support within the country for an Indian war. Indeed, two distinguished frontier commanders, Daniel Morgan and Marinus Willet, had rejected offers to serve as brigadier generals in the Legion. Willet explained that he regarded such a war as unjust. The Legion also had to survive a formidable domestic threat from economy-minded Congressmen, who unsuccessfully tried to abolish it. The refusal of Willet and Morgan to serve was especially unfortunate, for that command now went to the unscrupulous James Wilkinson, a devious western adventurer, who did everything in his power to undermine Wayne's reputation.[28] But the latter was fortunate in his superiors. Both the President and the Secretary of War steadfastly protected him from the political machinations of his rivals. Despite these travails, Wayne continued preparations during 1793 to carry the war into the Indian country and had begun what would become a line of fortified posts extending as far as Fort Recovery on the site of St Clair's battlefield. The Legion itself went into winter quarters at Fort Greenville a short distance north of Fort Washington on the Ohio.

The collapse of diplomatic negotiations cleared the way for Wayne to take the offensive in 1794. While Wayne believed that hunger rendered the Indians most vulnerable to attack in the spring, difficulties with his own civilian supply contractors delayed the army's advance. There were shortages of rations and pack horses, and Wayne was driven to experiments such as using beef cattle as pack animals (a role for which they proved unsuited).[29] The logistical problems were overcome by the efforts of Quartermaster John O'Hara, who perhaps deserves credit for the success of the campaign second only to Wayne. The latter was now aware of a new menace awaiting him in the Northwest. In February 1794, Sir Guy Carleton, now Lord Dorchester, Governor of Lower Canada, while addressing a delegation of Six Nations

Indians, predicted that war between Britain and the United States was inevitable. War between France and Britain rendered the latter vulnerable in the west and more dependent on Indian military support. Dorchester and his colleague Simcoe urged the Indians to adhere closely to their British father. British Indian agents enthusiastically urged the confederate Indians to prepare to resist Wayne's advance and gave promises of tangible support. These assurances were backed by the construction of a new British post, Fort Miamis, on the Maumee River, thus extending British military occupation into an area ceded to the United States by the 1783 treaty. British authorities saw Fort Miamis as a forward redoubt for Detroit, but the confederate Indians assembled on the Maumee regarded it as a British guarantee for the defence of their homeland. Furthermore, Simcoe energetically promoted the recruitment of Indian warriors throughout the Great Lakes region to come to the aid of the confederacy. Thus Britain provided the confederacy with new strength and confidence. When Wayne marched north, he faced a concentration on the Maumee of about 1,700 warriors confident of victory.[30]

Indeed, the prospect of an advance against the Indian heartland was a daunting one. Wayne faced a wilderness campaign which required the army to haul its supplies by land over rough trails. One could protect supply depots by fortified posts, but convoys were especially vulnerable to Indian raiders. On 29 June 1794, a large convoy arrived at Fort Recovery at "the head of the line" with 360 packhorses bearing 1,200 kegs of flour to provide a forward depot for the army's advance. The escort of 50 dragoons and 90 riflemen camped outside the fort on the night of the 29th. On the following morning, as the pack horse drivers set forth to return to Fort Greenville, firing erupted on the road. When troops of the escort rushed to the aid of the drivers, they encountered an Indian army of around 1,100 men accompanied by British officers in native dress. The Americans were quickly overwhelmed and the survivors fled for the safety of the fort. Over-confidence now may have caused the Indian warriors to discard proven tactical wisdom. The Ottawas and Chippewas who composed the majority of the native army attempted to storm a well prepared fort equipped with artillery and protected by a stout stockade and blockhouses. Its energetic commander Captain Alexander Gibson had cleared the ground within 200 to 250 yards of the fort to provide a clear field for fire. It was the kind of field that experienced Indian warriors had always avoided, yet the Indians pressed their attack for almost four hours. Fort Recovery was invulnerable to small arms fire, but the Indians hoped to recover cannon which had been buried on the field after St Clair's defeat. One gun was found, but there was insufficient powder to bring it into action. On 1 July, the Indian army withdrew, having suffered 17 dead and as many wounded. American losses in the initial ambush had been heavier and fewer than 40 Indian casualties were in themselves no reason to regard Fort Recovery as a decisive defeat, but all authorities have believed it to be the turning point of the war. The incident opened deep fractures in the Indian confederacy. The Great Lakes Indians accused the Shawnees of holding back in the battle and even of firing on their rear. The Maumee Indian confederates responded with well founded charges of northern Indian recklessness and of bad behaviour in the Indian villages they were supposed to protect. The northerners now began to depart in disgust and the villagers on the Maumee saw their ranks dwindle as the American army began its advance.[31]

An important split now began to occur within the Indian leadership. The Miami war chief Little Turtle, architect of previous Indian victories, was sobered by the results of the Fort Recovery battle. Although he had limited political influence as a war leader and as a member of a small tribe, he possessed keen political insight. He did not believe that the Indian confederacy could prevail against the United States without direct British participation. When the British commander at Detroit failed to provide him with explicit assurances of British commitment, he inclined towards peace with the Americans. He was overruled in the confederacy's council, and leadership remained in the hands of the militant Blue Jacket and other Shawnees. Little Turtle bowed to majority sentiment, but his decline in influence was a blow to the confederacy. The rise to prominence of militants also seemed to coincide with a decline in prudence, which had been a hallmark of the successful skulking way of war.[32]

Prudence characterized Wayne's advance towards the Maumee, which began on 28 July. Unlike St Clair who had marched blindly, Wayne's path was well scouted by a special detachment dressed in Indian fashion led by Captain William Wells. These scouts, supplemented by a party of 100 Chickasaw and Choctaw warriors, kept the general well informed of enemy strength, location and intentions. As we have seen, few Anglo-American armies in North America had acquired such a degree of intelligence about their Indian adversaries. By reducing the danger of surprise, Wayne had nullified the Indians' principal advantage. To good intelligence were added careful march and camp security. Wayne fortified strategic points as he proceeded north to ensure protection for his supply convoys. The army ended its march early on each day to prepare an elaborate fortified camp secured by breastworks and bastions for crossfire. Each morning the army stood to arms until assured that all was secure. Indian scouts could report no opportunity for another attack on an American encampment. Wayne's uncontested advance to the junction of the Maumee and Auglaize Rivers, "the grand emporium of the hostile Indians of the West", was a triumph of military professionalism.[33]

In this respect, Wayne's defeat of the Indian confederate army was something of an anticlimax. The British and Indians assumed correctly that Wayne would advance along the Maumee River towards Fort Miamis and they planned to fight him in an area of fallen timber about five miles from the fort. This tangle of tree trunks, blown down in a wind storm, provided the Indians with a natural abatis suitable for their method of defence. Their left flank was secured by the Maumee and the right by Swan Creek. Had the entire Indian force been present on the day of Wayne's approach, the battle might have ended differently. However, the Indian army had fasted for two days in expectation of battle and many warriors had withdrawn to the rear for food on the morning of 20 August. As Wayne's militia vanguard approached the Indian position, they were enveloped in a blast of fire and put to rout. But no one in the Indian army seems to have exercised effective tactical control. The Ottawas and other Indians in the centre of the position rushed from the security of their abatis and pursued the fleeing militiamen. Other Indians, such as the Shawnees, and some 70 Detroit militia remained unengaged. This exposed the Indians in the centre to flank attack by Wayne's mounted troops and to bayonet attack by Legionaries in the centre who drove the Indians back from one position to the next. Wayne, a great believer in the bayonet, would have appreciated the recollection of an Ottawa chief: "We were driven by the sharp end of the guns of the Long Knives."[34] The Indian army was thus driven from the field and fled to the security of the British fort. But it was a false sanctuary; the British commander, who had no intention of beginning a war with the United States, barred the gates to his erstwhile allies. Colonel England, the British commander at Detroit, blamed the Indian defeat on panic "so great that the appearance of fifty Americans would have totally routed them".[35] He had nothing to say about the treacherous conduct of the Indians' British allies who had encouraged them to fight and who had deserted them in their time of need.

As far as major battles are concerned, Fallen Timbers was a brief and relatively bloodless affair. An American officer critical of Wayne observed that "this affair which does not deserve the name of a Battle began at 10 O'clk and the troops halted at 5 minutes after 11 O'clk." The Legion had suffered 133 casualties. The British agent Alexander McKee estimated that no more than 400 Indians had been engaged and that only 19 had been lost. The commander at Fort Miamis reported 40 Indian casualties and the loss of five Detroit militia. The critical loss for the Indians was in leadership, with eight principal chiefs killed in action.[36] As was so often the case, casualties did not represent the significance of this Indian–American battle. The Indian defeat lay in the collapse of their British alliance and in the dissolution of Indian unity. Many militant leaders were among the dead and the survivors were discredited. The party of accommodation was now ascendant, reinforced by the prestige of the great war leader Little Turtle who saw peace and co-operation with the Americans as the only hope for his people's future. Little Turtle thus turned from the path of war to the role of alliance chief and restorer of harmony. It was a crucial blow to the party of armed resistance. An even greater casualty was the dream of a great united Indian people who would keep the west as their own.[37]

The result of this defeat was the Treaty of Greenville of 3 August 1795. In this treaty the Indians confirmed the cessions of previous treaties and more. The United States acquired eastern and southern Ohio and a portion of southern Indiana plus 16 separate reservations beyond the line with rights of free passage. The Indians were guaranteed rights to the remaining land and security of the border, but these securities were ephemeral. Settlers flooded into the ceded lands and soon began to press against the border. For the moment the party of resistance was helpless to oppose them. Prospects of British support had evaporated with the Jay treaty of November 1794, which cleared the way for British evacuation of the northern posts. Indian resistance would revive after 1805 under the leadership of Tecumseh and his brother the Prophet Tenskatawata and would culminate during the War of 1812 in the last great Indian rising east of the Mississippi. But it was, concludes the historian Wiley Sword, "as anticlimactic as it was futile".[38]

Tecumseh and the revival of Indian resistance

Great changes would occur in the Northwest before the revival of Indian resistance. American immigration and settlement west of the Appalachians were accompanied by the retreat of European empires in the west. War with France weakened the grip of both Britain and Spain in North America. The Jay treaty was a symbol of Britain's need to reach an understanding with the United States. It was followed by agreements with Spain: by the 1796 Treaty of San Lorenzo the United States gained export rights down the Mississippi and gained recognition to its claims to the lands centred at the core of the Creek confederacy in modern Alabama. In 1798 Spain withdrew from its posts north of the 31st parallel and in the secret Treaty of San Ildefonso transferred Louisiana to France. The United States thrust forward into this apparent vacuum. Kentucky had gained statehood in 1792 and Tennessee entered the union in 1796. The new states drove a wedge between northern and southern Indians and disrupted pan-Indian communications. In 1800 the Northwest Territory was divided into the Ohio and Indiana territories, with

Ohio achieving statehood in 1803. The white population of Ohio would increase from 45,000 in 1800 to over 230,000 by 1810. In 1803 the Louisiana Purchase shifted the United States' gravitational centre yet further west.

These developments had enormous consequences for the Indian peoples east of the Mississippi. Deserted by British and Spanish patrons and defeated in war, they had to satisfy a power hungry for western expansion. In the Northwest the Treaty of Greenville which had established a "permanent" border between white settlement and the Indian country came under enormous pressure. President Thomas Jefferson was divided between a desire to deal justly with the Indians of the Northwest and his dreams of a great continental empire. As is so often the case, "realism" prevailed over moral scruple. Jefferson hoped to convince the Indians to adopt white civilization, that is, to take up white farming practices which offered the double advantage of improving their living standards while reducing the amount of land required for their support. Surplus land would then become available for sale to white settlers. Although Jefferson waxed eloquent about the advantages of such a scheme to visiting Indian spokesmen, there was a cynical element in his civilizing mission: he instructed US Indian agents to lure prominent Indian chiefs into debt in order to force them to sell land. Jefferson also authorized the Governor of the Indiana Territory, William Henry Harrison, to negotiate new treaties providing for sale of vast tracts of land beyond the Greenville line and for rights to establish roads throughout the region. Harrison was an aggressive negotiator and relentlessly pursued the purchase of Indian lands. By 1807, the Indians had ceded almost all of Ohio to the United States, along with large portions of southern Indiana, Illinois, Michigan and part of Wisconsin. This policy of expansion by purchase culminated with the Treaty of Fort Wayne of 30 September 1809, in which representatives of the Delawares, Potawatomis, Miamis and Eel River Indians ceded large areas of eastern and southern Indiana.[39]

All of this could not have been done without the co-operation of the Indians themselves. Former war leaders such as the Miami Little Turtle and the Shawnee Black Hoof believed that the collapse of British support made inevitable accommodation with the United States. They assumed the traditional role of alliance chiefs whose importance among their own people depended upon their control of the annuities provided by the government in exchange for land. Little Turtle was a skilled accommodationist who worked for the benefit of his people without personal enrichment. He was even prepared to entertain Jefferson's proposals for the development of agriculture. But the accommodationist position rested on quicksand. White agricultural practice required a transformation of gender roles few Indians could or would accept. Furthermore, white settlers did not share Jefferson's hope that white and Indian farmers might live together in neighbourly peace. American hunger for land, the primary source of wealth in an agricultural society, could not be reconciled easily with the protection of Indian rights. Nor was the Indian leadership unified. Accommodationist chiefs quarrelled among themselves over the rights to cede land and to collect annuities. While this served an American policy of divide and conquer, it also opened the way to new leaders who called for unified resistance to American expansion.[40]

This resistance revived in 1805 with the emergence of the Shawnee Prophet Tenskwatawa who regarded accommodation to white civilization as a surrender of Indian spiritual power. He attacked the authority of the Shawnee accommodationist Black Hoof and conducted witch-hunts among those who appeared to compromise Indian spiritual purity. Tenskwatawa's call for a return to native traditions and a rejection of white practices struck a resonant chord across the Northwest with the emergence of nativist prophets among the Ottawas and the Potawatomis. He revived a tradition of inter-tribal religious unity that dated at least to the Delaware Prophet Neolin in the 1760s. By 1808 Tenskwatawa assembled his followers at a settlement called Prophet's Town at Tippecanoe Creek near the Wabash River. From there he conducted a campaign against those chiefs who had ceded Indian lands in return for annuities, which he regarded as bribes, and who had agreed to the violation of Indian culture.[41]

The Prophet's role as a leader of nativist religious and political unity has sometimes been obscured or distorted by the emergence of his famous brother the great Shawnee warrior and political leader Tecumseh. Of all of the Indian resistance leaders discussed in this study, Tecumseh is the figure embraced in Anglo-American historical tradition as the "noble savage". He commanded the respect of Indians and whites alike. His opponent William Henry Harrison described him as

> one of those uncommon geniuses, which spring up occasionally to produce revolutions and overturn the established order of things. If it were not for the vicinity of the United States, he would perhaps be the founder of an Empire that would rival in glory that of Mexico or Peru.[42]

The distinguished British General Isaac Brock wrote that "a more sagacious or a more gallant Warrior does not I believe exist. He was the admiration of everyone who conversed with him."[43] Tecumseh's military skill coupled with his humanity in war, his political vision, his integrity and his devotion to his people qualifies him as one of the tragic heroes of American history. To some degree he has become an American myth, embodying the symbol of New World freedom, an Indian whom generations of Americans could understand, in contrast to his mystical brother whose conduct Harrison wrote that he could not account for on any "rational principle".[44] However, as his biographer R. David Edmunds points out, this view exaggerates Tecumseh's political authority and underestimates the role of the Prophet as the source of the resistance movement. Tecumseh's significance in the early years of the movement is unclear, but most authorities agree that after the 1809 Fort Wayne Treaty, Tecumseh became active in resisting the accommodationist chiefs on the ground that land cessions required the consent of all Indian peoples. Tecumseh would cast a wide net in seeking support, journeying south in 1811 to seek alliance with Creeks, Cherokees, Choctaws and Chickasaws. Some historians believe that Tecumseh converted a religious movement into a pragmatic programme of political resistance. But Gregory Evans Dowd argues convincingly that nativist religious and political movements were not easily separated. When he travelled south in 1811, Tecumseh followed in the footsteps of other Shawnee emissaries who for decades had carried appeals for unity to the southern Indians. In this case he enhanced his political message with prophecies of earthquakes, which bore fruit with the New Madrid tremors of November 1811 and January 1812. At the Battle of the Thames, Tecumseh discarded the dress and insignia provided by the British and fought clad in skins and feathers, symbols of spiritual purity and power.[45]

Tecumseh's southern venture was not a success. Chickasaws and Choctaws, not immediately exposed to the pressure of American settlement, were reluctant to ally with old enemies. Cherokees, caught between the white settlements in Georgia and Tennessee, had embraced accommodation as the only realistic policy of survival. While Tecumseh's call for resistance gained adherents among Creek militants, it was rejected by other members of the Creek confederacy.[46] The militants, known as the Red Sticks because of their war clubs, resisted American expansion by force of arms during the Creek War of 1813–14, but at a terrible cost in lives. At the battle of Holy Ground, 23 December 1813, 750 warriors out of a maximum warrior population of 4,000 were killed. "Already by the end of the battle, Red Stick casualties in the Creek War had mounted to a level proportionally comparable with that of any force in American history, including Confederate soldiers in the Civil War."[47]

The Red Sticks failed to receive timely British aid and fought against overwhelming odds. In addition to their numerical advantage, the Americans displayed advanced tactical skills. In November 1813 they twice lured Red Stick warriors into semicircular envelopments and inflicted heavy casualties. One historian has compared these tactics to those employed by Hannibal at Cannae, but it is unlikely that General Andrew Jackson and his subordinate General John Coffee drew their inspiration from ancient texts. These experienced frontier fighters had simply adopted the Indian way of war as their own.[48] Red Stick power was decisively broken at the battle of Horseshoe Bend on the Tallapoosa River on 27 March 1814, when Jackson assaulted 1,000 warriors on a fortified peninsula with an army of 3,000. Five hundred of Jackson's troops were Creek and Cherokee opponents of the Red Sticks. These Indians swam the river behind the Red Stick position, seized the canoes the latter had prepared for escape, and attacked the fortified camp from the rear. This led to a terrible slaughter; eight out of every ten defenders perished after Jackson's army penetrated their lines. Divisions among southern Indians rendered futile the Red Sticks' armed resistance. Such divisions also doomed Tecumseh's hopes for unity among all eastern Indians and contributed to the isolation of the militants in the Northwest.[49]

While Tecumseh pursued his southern mission, William Henry Harrison moved against the Prophet. Harrison recognized that the brothers' attacks on the annuity chiefs threatened the policy of accommodation on which peaceful American expansion depended. He accused Tenskwatawa of being a British agent stirring up trouble on the frontier, and in the autumn of 1811 advanced against Prophet's Town with about 1,000 regulars and militia. There he won a "famous victory", at least as far as presidential campaign slogans go. Harrison's army was encamped a few miles from Prophet's Town on 7 November 1811, when it was attacked in the night by a force of 600 to 700 warriors. Harrison was a prudent and experienced commander. His men were on the alert and there was no repetition of St Clair's debacle. There was heavy fighting until after daybreak when the Indians, who were short of ammunition, withdrew. Harrison had suffered 188 casualties and the Indians perhaps about the same number, although the British agent Matthew Elliot reported only 25 Indian dead. Harrison claimed a decisive victory at the Battle of Tippecanoe. Perhaps it might have been. Tenskwatawa had promised victory and had been discredited; his warriors had been at least temporarily scattered and his town burned. But, rather than being the last stand of Indian resistance in the Northwest, it was a prelude to the northwestern Indians' final defensive war, a war which merged with the War of 1812.[50]

Most wars defy the expectations of those who begin them and the War of 1812 was no exception to this rule. Americans confidently expected to conquer Canada, which was defended by only 6,000 British regulars, considered the cast-offs from an army heavily engaged in the war against Napoleon, and a militia of doubtful allegiance. Britain feared for Canada, which she could not reinforce, but expected to sweep the seas of American shipping. Instead, the war produced a series of astonishing American successes at sea and defeats on land. New England's opposition to the war and the weakness of American military institutions undermined the American offensive effort on the Canadian frontier. The bright promise of a professional and innovative military force embodied in the Legion of the United States had fallen victim in 1796 to peacetime economy and suspicions of standing armies. During 1812, the Americans suffered sharp reverses, particularly in the Northwest. Rather than an easy conquest of the province of Upper Canada, the Americans experienced humiliating defeat and the loss of the frontier posts of Detroit, Michilimackinac and Fort Dearborn on Lake Michigan, the site of modern Chicago. Reginald Horsman, a leading historian of the War of 1812, attributes British success to the steadfastness of the regulars and better-than-expected performance of the militia. Although it is apparent in his narrative of the war, he nevertheless fails to give sufficient credit to Britain's Indian allies who, under the outstanding leadership of Tecumseh, were Britain's chief military asset in the Northwest.[51]

During 1812, British warships controlled Lakes Ontario and Erie and thus dominated the most important communication and supply route to the Northwest, leaving the American posts there dangerously isolated. Michilimackinac was picked off before its garrison realized that the war had begun. They surrendered on 17 July 1812 without firing a shot to a force of 50 British regulars, 180 militia, and 300 Indians. One British observer believed that if they had not done so "not a soul of them would have been saved."[52] The surrender of this strategic post excited fears of a general Indian insurrection in the Northwest. General William Hull, the American commander in the Northwest, feared for the safety of the garrison of Fort Dearborn at Chicago, for it could no longer be supplied by water. Under orders from Hull and assured of safe conduct by neighbouring Indians, the American commander at Fort Dearborn evacuated his post. His column of 96 people, escorted by 30 friendly Miamis, was ambushed and overwhelmed by 500 Indians, mainly Potawatomis. Fifty-three Americans were killed and many were taken prisoner. British officers expressed dismay at this episode, which had occurred without their knowledge. However, this incident demonstrates once again that the Indians fought quite independently of their European allies. It was indeed an uneasy alliance, for the Indians had not forgotten previous British betrayals. Nor, despite Tecumseh's towering prestige, was the Indian confederacy under tight central leadership. Tecumseh's discipline and concern for humane conduct were manifest only when he was personally present. When he was not, Indian warriors followed their own interests and customs.[53]

The greatest American disaster of 1812 was the fall of Detroit. General Hull was demoralized by the fall of Michilimackinac and fearful of his isolation at the end of a precarious line of roads and trails running through woods and swamps and thus vulnerable to Indian attack. Although he advanced into Upper Canada to attack the British Fort Malden, Tecumseh's ambush of a supply convoy at Brownstown convinced Hull that he was safer at Detroit. There he found his communications imperilled by Indian ambushes, and surrendered Detroit without a fight to Major General Isaac Brock when the latter threatened him with an Indian massacre. The fruitful collaboration of Brock and Tecumseh had produced the British–Indian alliance's most significant victory.[54]

After their success at Chicago, the Potawatomis and other militants concentrated against Fort Wayne, the American post at the forks of the Maumee, but the Indians lacked the means to capture a fort whose garrison could not be surprised or frightened into surrender. The British despatched a column equipped with artillery to their aid, but it failed to appear before the fort was relieved by William Henry Harrison, the energetic and determined newly appointed American commander-in-chief in the Northwest. During the autumn, Harrison despatched forces to ravage the villages of friendly and unfriendly Indians alike, including those of the deceased accommodationist Little Turtle. But as long as militant Indians could count upon supplies and sanctuary at Detroit, they remained a threat to the American position in the Northwest. This was brought home in January 1813 when General James Winchester marched to the River Raisin near Detroit in hopes of encouraging French Canadian settlers in the area to rise against the British. Winchester's advance guard defeated a small British–Indian party at Frenchtown on 18 January and he arrived with his main force two days later. The initial victory may have contributed to American carelessness, for only part of their camp was fortified and the roads from Detroit were unguarded. When General Henry Procter advanced from Malden with 600 to 700 white and 800 Indian troops he caught the Americans unprepared. Winchester surrendered when the Indians and Canadian militia outflanked the unfortified part of his camp. Procter departed the field with 500 American prisoners, leaving the wounded in the hands of the Indians and a few interpreters. Procter reported that "I had much Difficulty in bringing the Indians to consent to the sparing of their lives." The Indians, who drank a cask of American whisky, killed 30 or 40 of the wounded Americans and thus another "massacre" was recorded in the annals of white–Indian warfare. The Americans justly denounced Procter for failure to protect the wounded, but it is important to recall that the "massacre" occurred against the background of indiscriminate American scorched earth tactics in the Indian villages.[55]

Frustrated in his hope of retaking Detroit during the autumn and winter of 1812, Harrison began the construction of Fort Meigs at the rapids of the Maumee. Recognizing the danger that such a post represented to Malden and Detroit, Procter moved against it with 1,000 white troops and 1,200 Indian allies. He arrived by water in April and began formal siege operations.

However, the British suffered from a shortage of big guns in the west, particularly since the Lake Erie flotilla competed for those which were available, and Procter's pieces proved too light to make an impression on the fort's earthworks. The besiegers' moment of success occurred when 1,200 Kentucky militia arrived to relieve the fort. Harrison ordered them to attack the British batteries and spike the guns before joining him, but in the ensuing action on 5 May, the British and Indians killed 150 and captured 500 Kentuckians. In spite of this success, Procter lacked the staying power to carry out a successful siege. This was the business of regulars and he had too few of them. The Indians who constituted a majority of his force had no intention of storming the defences; furthermore, their success on 5 May convinced many that they had achieved their objective and they began to depart for home. They were accompanied by many of the militia anxious to begin their spring planting and, on 9 May, Procter was forced to abandon the siege. Procter spent the summer in another vain attempt on Fort Meigs and on Fort Stephenson on the Sandusky. Again the Indians would not undertake frontal attacks, Procter's guns were too light for siege work, and at Fort Stephenson his regulars were decimated by canister from the fort's single gun and rifle fire when they attempted a frontal assault. The British offensive had thus broken its teeth on the American forts, but the British–Indian alliance in the Northwest was placed in mortal peril by the decisive American naval victory on Lake Erie on 9 September 1813.[56]

Now it was Procter's turn to find himself isolated in western Upper Canada. The Americans could move against him by means of the lake, turn his flank at will, and cut his supply lines. Observers believed that Procter was seized by panic when he ordered a hasty evacuation of the western posts. While such a retreat may have been unavoidable from a strategic point of view, Tecumseh and other Indian warriors denounced this abandonment of their homeland after their services and the British promise to help them regain their land: "We must compare our father's conduct to a fat animal, that carries its tail upon its back, but when affrighted, it drops it between its legs, and runs off."[57] Faced with the loss of British supplies and bases, many Indians departed for their homes. Tecumseh and a diminished group of warriors and their families accompanied Procter's disorganized retreat, delayed because of quarrels between the allies. Fewer than 1,000 fighting men, the majority of them Indians, remained with Procter when Harrison's pursuing force of 3,000 (including 260 Delawares, Shawnees, Wyandots and Iroquois) caught up with him on the Thames River near Moravian Town on 5 October. Procter's left flank was protected by the Thames and his right by thick woods occupied by 500 Indians under Tecumseh. But the British commander had too few troops to protect his centre and formed the 280 regulars of his first line in loose order to cover the ground between the river and the woods. Although Harrison had originally planned an infantry advance, he recognized the vulnerability of the British and ordered his Kentucky mounted riflemen to charge them. He later reported that:

> the measure was not sanctioned by anything that I had seen or heard of, but I was fully convinced that it would succeed. The American backwoodsmen ride better in the woods than any other people. A musket or a rifle is no impediment to them, being accustomed to carry them on horseback from their earliest youth. I was persuaded, too, that the enemy would be unprepared for the shock, and that they could not resist it.[58]

He was exactly right. Cavalry charges were rare in North America and the terrain was not particularly favourable on this occasion. However, the proper formation for infantry to receive a cavalry assault was a square; troops caught in loose order were at the mercy of such an onslaught. Harrison's mounted troops easily penetrated the British lines and put them to rout. They then surrounded the Indians, who put up a desperate resistance, but broke and fled when Tecumseh was killed in the struggle. Procter's regulars lost 18 killed and 25 wounded, with over 600 eventually taken prisoner as a result of the defeat. The Americans suffered 7 dead and 22 wounded. Thirty-three Indians were found slain on the field, from which the Kentuckians carried strips of skin which they claimed to have taken from Tecumseh's body.[59]

Procter was subsequently court-martialed and disgraced, but this was little compared to the loss of the Indians' great leader. Thus the Battle of the Thames was a decisive victory. While the historian Harry L. Coles has discounted the significance of American gains against the *British* in 1813, the Americans had defeated their most dangerous enemy in the Northwest.[60] Canada would not be subjected to American conquest, but by the end of 1813 the way was open for American expansion to the Mississippi. After 1815, with the exception of Florida's Seminoles who merged with the Red Stick survivors, the era of armed resistance east of the great river was at an end. The era of the removal of the Indian peoples was at hand.

Indian resistance overcome

Tecumseh had failed to achieve pan-Indian unity and even the Indians of the Northwest failed to make common cause in the manner of the early 1790s.

Nevertheless, the scope of the Indian war effort should not be underestimated. Indians made up the majority of the forces that fought on the side of the Crown in the Northwest in 1812–13 and their role was central to the surprising reversals suffered by the Americans. Indian battle tactics reflected those of earlier generations and, in woodland conditions, often remained superior to the efforts of inexperienced American regulars and militia. Famous American victories such as Fallen Timbers, Tippecanoe, and the Battle of the Thames resulted in relatively few Indian casualties. Of course, the Indian definitions of what represented "a few" might differ from those of European observers and the loss of leaders who fought in the forefront of the battle could be especially demoralizing. But, in nearly every case, the Indians were ill served by their allies. Tecumseh's confederate army achieved all that could be expected of warriors trained in the Indian way of war. But Britain, strained by challenges elsewhere, could not provide the aid required if Indian warriors were to withstand the power of the American republic. One is tempted to speculate that more regulars, more trained seamen, more heavy artillery pieces, and a British commander as able as Tecumseh might have achieved different results and that the Indian country might have remained secure for another generation.

However, such a conclusion would not do justice to the development of American skill in frontier warfare by 1815. While Harmar, St Clair and Hull floundered, Wayne, Harrison and Jackson succeeded. The latter displayed a grasp of the Indian way of war and developed tactics to counter it. They combined the ability to discipline disorderly frontiersmen with a realistic training for forest warfare. In addition, they achieved a successful mix of arms and a flexible approach to their use. Their forces included US regulars, militia, volunteers (most notably the mounted riflemen) and Indian warriors and scouts. Jackson's envelopment tactics in the Creek War might have been designed by Little Turtle or Tecumseh. But Jackson surpassed both of these skilled commanders in his instinct for the total destruction of the enemy. William Tecumseh Sherman was not the first destroyer to cut a swath through the south. Wayne and Harrison demonstrated that true professionals could succeed in frontier warfare. Harrison wrote admiringly of Wayne that:

> If General Wayne had marched his army in close columns instead of those long flexible files which enabled him to penetrate the woods with facility and to present a very long extended front to the enemy on every point of attack, if he had neglected to reconnoiter the country in every direction as he advanced to prevent an attack from the enemy before he completed his disposition to receive them, or if, instead of putting them up with the bayonet and keeping up the charge until they were entirely

broken and dispersed, he had permitted them to exercise their skill in distant shooting from behind trees, – the 20th of August, 1794, would now have produced as melancholy recollections as the 4th of November, 1791.[61]

Harrison shared Wayne's energy and resolution. Both demonstrated *coup d'oeil*, the ability to grasp immediately the tactical situation and to know what to do. Harrison valued the rifle more highly than did Wayne and seems to have had a better appreciation of the strengths of Kentucky frontier fighters. He regarded the Kentucky mounted riflemen as an indispensable part of his northwestern army and recruited Kentucky Governor Isaac Shelby, a veteran of King's Mountain, to accompany them. Like Jackson, he was able to temper their reckless courage with discipline. Thus by 1815, the United States had begun to match its population and material resources with the tactical skill required to prevail on the frontier. Against such a combination, the Indian confederacy, even with British assistance, could not have long prevailed.

Chapter Eight

Conclusion

The continuities in European–Indian warfare in the period 1675–1815 are readily apparent. There was little change in weapons, technology, or tactics. A soldier or warrior of King Philip's War would not have been out of place in the conditions of the War of 1812. Indian skulking tactics – concealment and surprise, moving fire, envelopment and, when the enemy's ranks were broken, hand-to-hand combat – remained the cardinal features of Native American warfare. The superb training and formidable physical endurance of Indian warriors continued to provide them with advantages that often offset inferiority in numbers. In their wars against the United States, they produced military leaders such as Little Turtle and Tecumseh who demonstrated extraordinary tactical skill and, in the latter's case at least, strategic vision. We know much less about the Indian military leaders of King Philip's War, but the continuities evident in the Indian way of war imply that they possessed similar skills.

Native Americans failed to overcome inherent weaknesses which crippled their societies' ability to resist the European "invasion". These were partly economic and technical weaknesses. During King Philip's War, Indians were able to maintain and repair firearms, but they could not manufacture them, nor could they produce gunpowder. This remained true until 1815, leaving them dependent on European suppliers. By 1675, Indians had begun to adapt their fortifications to European models, but they could not withstand onslaughts by European troops equipped with cannon. Instead, they tended to abandon their towns and food supplies rather than to fight for them. On the other hand, the lack of artillery rendered any well designed and garrisoned fort invulnerable to Indian attack if its defenders were not surprised or frightened into submission. The Indians were well informed about European forts and on occasion employed fire arrows, carts of combustibles, and mining in attempts to overcome them. But their respect for the strength of such places is evident

167

in their common refusal to storm well defended positions. Indian tactical superiority in the woods was offset by the European advantage in fortification and artillery.

European soldiers frequently encountered flourishing Native American agriculture when they raided towns in the Indian country. Many Indian communities were as prosperous as any found on the white frontier. But this was a fragile prosperity, easily disrupted by raiding forces who destroyed crops and food reserves. Indian peoples lacked independent means to recover from such catastrophes. King Philip's War demonstrated that they could not sustain a major war in their own country for more than a year. War quickly exposed them to the related evils of famine and disease, and sapped their ability to resist, if not their will. As we have seen, a prolonged war required a European ally who could provide economic and technical assistance, and sanctuary for families driven from their homes. This was often a fatal dependency, for it rendered the Indians pawns in larger imperial struggles in which their interests were secondary.

Perhaps a more serious disadvantage was political. Despite the efforts of leaders from Philip to Tecumseh, Native Americans were never able to present a united front to European enemies. Old rivalries among Indians often counted for as much as hostility to whites. War often divided Indian societies between older peace chiefs and younger war leaders, thereby diminishing the collective response to military threats. During 1790–94, many Indians of the Northwest joined a confederacy to resist American expansion and they were joined by many southerners. But such confederacies were unstable. Many Indians sought accommodation rather than war; others disagreed over strategy and tactics. Under these conditions, war leaders were ephemeral and warriors joined and departed as they saw fit. A confederacy could quickly collapse when discredited by military defeat or could fall prey to divisive diplomacy. In addition to weakening Indian military resistance, such disunity added to the forces of the enemy. From King Philip's War to the battles of the Thames and Horseshoe Bend, most successful European commanders on the frontier included substantial numbers of Indian warriors in their forces. These Indian allies sometimes allowed European commanders to neutralize Native American tactical advantages.

Nevertheless, from the outbreak of King Philip's War, it took the European powers 140 years to complete the military conquest of the Indian peoples east of the Mississippi. One may partly explain this fact by the very size of the territory the Europeans had to digest. As we have seen, they consumed it in incremental bites. Southern New England was reduced by 1676, but northern New England was conquered only in the Seven Years War. Divisions among the Europeans slowed their advance. Although they played a weaker hand, Indian diplomats could be quite astute in playing one imperial power off against the other. The War of 1812 which opened the west to a unified American empire was thus the decisive event in this struggle.

European military institutions did not adapt well to frontier warfare conditions. Militias generally failed to provide the training required to meet the Indians on equal terms; militiamen tried to avoid long service and even the Kentucky militia hired poorly trained substitutes to serve in campaigns far from home. Americans remained committed to militia institutions, which conformed to social rather than military needs. The exception to this rule was the French Canadian militia, the product of a different social and economic system, which adopted the Indian way of war as its own. From the time of King Philip's War to the War of 1812, volunteers were raised to make up the deficiencies in the militia. From the American War of Independence, Tennessee and Kentucky volunteers, usually mounted riflemen, won fame in frontier warfare. Of all American troops, these came closest to adopting the Indian style of warfare. However, they were often plagued by bad discipline and rashness, which culminated in disastrous defeats as well as victories. The battles of King's Mountain and the Thames showed these volunteers at their best. In the latter case, Harrison, a professional officer, employed them with skill. On the other hand, the Blue Licks disaster revealed the inherent weakness of such troops, who lacked Indian military discipline and caution. One advantage of volunteers was that Indians often served in that capacity, thus increasing the odds for the Europeans.

European professionals adapted to North American conditions slowly. Experiments with light troops, which began during the War of the Austrian Succession, did not necessarily prepare European troops for frontier combat. At best, a European commander such as Henry Bouquet could protect his men against ambush while marching in the forest, but he found that his regulars were helpless in the forest without experienced woodsmen or Indian allies. While European military revolutions provided states with the means to project power into the interior of North America, they did not provide troops with the appropriate training and tactics to succeed on the frontier. Regulars had a place in this form of war, but as we have seen, commanders such as Church, Léry, Wayne, Jackson, and Harrison succeeded with a mix of regular, irregular and Indian troops. The continuity between war as practised by Church and by Harrison is clear, the exception being the introduction first of European and then United States regulars. During the 140-year period beginning in 1675, the features of frontier warfare remained stable, with only a slow evolution in weapons and tactics. If there was a military revolution in North America, it thus occurred before 1675 with the introduction of firearms and the transformation of the Indian style of war.

Notes

Chapter One

1. This account of Léry's expedition is based on: "Capture of Fort Bull by M. Léry, 27 March, 1756", in *Documents relative to the colonial history of the State of New-York procured in Holland, England and France, by John R. Brodhead*, E. B. O'Callaghan (ed.), X (Albany, 1858), pp. 403–5; "Journal de la campagne de M. de Léry . . .", in Francois Gaston duc de Lévis, *Collections des manuscrits du Maréchal de Lévis* [12 vols] (Montreal, 1889–95), X: *Relations et journaux des differentes expeditions faites durant les annees 1755–56–57–58–59–60* (1895), pp. 53–64; and "Journal . . . de l'expedition de M. de Léry . . .", *Ibid.*, VII: *Journal du Marquis du Montcalm* (1895), pp. 114–18. For Léry, who was promoted to captain and awarded the Cross of Saint Louis for this exploit, see F. J. Thorpe, "Gasparde-Joseph Chaussegros de Léry", *Dictionary of Canadian biography*, III, Frances G. Halpenny (ed.) (Toronto: University of Toronto Press, 1979), pp. 145–7.

2. For Rogers' account see his *Journals of Major Robert Rogers* (Readex Microprint, 1966), p. 147. For his appreciation of the Indian way of life see his *A concise narrative of North America . . .* (London, 1763), especially pp. 151–237. J. R. Cuneo, *Robert Rogers of the Rangers* (New York: Oxford University Press, 1959) is a positive biography which may be contrasted with the comments of Francis Jennings who in *Empire of fortune: crowns, colonies and tribes in the Seven Years War in America* (New York: W. W. Norton, 1988) dismisses Rogers as a "depraved" boaster. Rogers had the advantage of publishing his account of the raid, but the St Francis Indians preserved their own oral record of the raid. See G. M. Day, "Rogers' raid in Indian tradition", *Historical New Hampshire* **XVII** (June 1962), pp. 3–17. Also see C. G. Calloway, *The western Abenakis of Vermont, 1600–1800* (Norman: University of Oklahoma Press, 1990), pp. 174–80. For Armstrong's raid see W. A. Hunter, "Victory at Kittanning", *Pennsylvania History* **XXIII** (1956), pp. 367–407.

3. The term "invasion" seems to have originated with F. Jennings with his *The invasion of America: Indians, colonialism, and the cant of conquest* (Chapel Hill: University of North Carolina Press, 1975). See also I. K. Steele, *Warpaths: invasions of North America* (New York: Oxford University Press, 1994).

4. See F. Parkman, *France and England in North America*, 2 vols (New York, 1983). In the twentieth century, the view of a benign and progressive Anglo-American empire was

171

advanced by L. H. Gipson, *The British empire before the American Revolution* [15 vols] (Caldwell, Id.: Caxton Printers, 1936–70). This may be contrasted with G. Fregault, *Canada: the war of the conquest*, trans. M. M. Cameron (Toronto: Oxford University Press, 1969). For an assessment of Gipson's history, see J. Shy, "The Empire remembered: Lawrence Gipson, historian", *A people numerous and armed* (New York: Oxford University Press, 1976), pp. 109–31.

5. See W. J. Eccles, "The history of New France according to Francis Parkman", *William and Mary Quarterly*, Third Series, **XVIII**(2), April 1961, pp. 163–75. For a discussion of Canadian historiography on the subject of Indian peoples see D. B. Smith, *Le sauvage / The native people in Quebec historical writing on the heroic period (1534–1663) of New France* (Ottawa: National Museum of Canada, 1974).

6. For a discussion of the historiographical issues in Native American history, see R. D. Edmunds, "Native Americans, new voices: American Indian history", *American Historical Review* **C** (3), 1995, pp. 717–40. Francis Parkman's most severe critic is Francis Jennings. In addition to *The invasion of America* and *Empire of fortune* already cited, see his "Francis Parkman: a Brahmin among Untouchables", *William and Mary Quarterly*, Third Series, **XLII,** July 1985, pp. 305–28. He is a revisionist scholar who writes with the passion of an advocate. For an exploration of the Indian as the dark "other" in the American imagination see R. Slotkin, *Regeneration through violence: mythology of the American frontier, 1600–1860* (Middlettown, Conn.: Wesleyan University Press, 1973) and B. W. Sheehan, "Images: the Indian in the Revolution", *The American Indian experience, a profile: 1524 to the present*, P. Weeks (ed.) (Arlington, Ill., 1988), pp. 66–80.

7. For population estimates see J. D. Daniels, "The Indian population of North America in 1492", *William and Mary Quarterly* **XLIX**, 1992, pp. 298–320. For critical consideration of the disease theory of conquest see G. Raudzens, "Why did Amerindian defences fail? Parallels in the European invasions of Hispaniola, Virginia and beyond", *War in History*, **III**(2), 1996, pp. 331–52.

8. Francis Jennings cites the estimate of Daniel Gookin of 72,000 before 1616 and estimates the 1670 population at 52,000 Europeans and 8,600 Indians. See *The invasion of America*, p. 31. Neil Salisbury cites the higher pre-colonial figure in *Manitou and Providence: Indians, Europeans and the making of New England, 1500–1643* (New York: Oxford University Press, 1982), pp. 24–30.

9. B. G. Trigger, *The children of Aataentsic: a history of the Huron people to 1660* (Montreal: McGill–Queen's University Press, 1976), 2 vols, II, p. 602; D. K. Richter, *The ordeal of the longhouse: peoples of the Iroquois League in the era of European colonization* (Chapel Hill: University of North Carolina Press, 1992), p. 59; R. White, *The middle ground: Indians, empires, and republics in the Great Lakes region, 1650–1815* (Cambridge: Cambridge University Press, 1991), p. 41; J. H. Merrell, *The Indians' new world: Catawbas and their neighbors from European contact through the era of removal* (Chapel Hill: University of North Carolina Press, 1989), pp. 19–27.

10. Trigger, *The children of Aataentsic*, II, pp. 499–602; J. Axtell, *The invasion within: the contest of cultures in colonial North America* (New York: Oxford University Press, 1985), p. 273.

11. Richter, *The ordeal of the longhouse*, p. 109.

12. Trigger, *The children of Aataentsic*, II, pp. 721–836; D. Delage, *Bitter feast: Amerindians and Europeans in northeastern North America, 1600–1664*, trans. J. Brierly (Vancouver: UBC Press, 1993), pp. 163–224.

13. Richter, *The ordeal of the longhouse*, pp. 105–32.

14. Delage, *Bitter harvest*, pp. 78–102.

15. J. Axtell, *Beyond 1492: encounters in colonial North America* (New York: Oxford University Press, 1992), p. 131; White, *The middle ground*, pp. 127–32.

16. Trigger, *The children of Aataentsic*, II, p. 622.

17. *The America of 1750, Peter Kalm's travels in North America. The English version of 1750*, A. B. Benson (ed.) [2 vols] (New York: Wilson-Erickson, 1937), I, pp. 258–9. See also P. C. Mancall, *Deadly medicine: Indians and alcohol in early America* (Ithaca: Cornell University Press, 1995).

18. Trigger, *The children of Aataentsic*, I, p. 3.

19. General John Armstrong to President Washington, 23 December 1791, in *The St. Clair papers*, W. H. Smith (ed.) [2 vols] (Cincinnati: Robert Clarke, 1882), II, p. 277.

20. Henry Bouquet to General Jeffrey Amherst, 26 July 1763, in *The papers of Henry Bouquet*, Series 21634, Northwestern Pennsylvania Series, Prepared by Frontier Forts and Trails Survey, S. K. Stevens & D. H. Kent (eds), I (Harrisburg, 1940), p. 288.

21. This is the conclusion of I. Steele, *Guerrillas and grenadiers, the struggle for Canada, 1689–1760* (Toronto: Ryerson Press, 1969), pp. 131–3. See also his *Warpaths*, pp. 221–2.

22. This subject is best considered in W. Sword, *President Washington's Indian war: the struggle for the Old Northwest, 1790–1795* (Norman: University of Oklahoma Press, 1985).

23. This was Parkman's theme and was essentially embraced by the prominent twentieth-century scholar, Howard Peckham. See the latter's *The colonial wars 1689–1762* (Chicago: University of Chicago Press, 1964).

24. The traditional view of Clark is provided by J. Bakeless, *Background to glory: the life of George Rogers Clark* (Lincoln: University of Nebraska Press, 1957, 1992). J. P. Ronda's introduction to the 1992 edition places Clark within the context of recent scholarship. See also the essays of G. C. Chalou, G. M. Waller & D. L. Smith in *The French, the Indians and George Rogers Clark in the Illinois country*, Proceedings of an Indiana American Revolution Bicentennial Symposium (Indianapolis: Indiana Historical Society, 1977). They portray Clark's victories in the Northwest as ephemeral.

25. J. Axtell, *The European and the Indian: essays in the ethnohistory of colonial America* (New York: Oxford University Press, 1981), p. 240.

26. Francis Jennings is an example of a revisionist historian who is especially censorious of the behaviour of European colonists and governments. His work is well researched, but he seems to look for the worst in European behavior and is seldom disappointed. He disagrees with the more cautious approach of B. W. Sheehan in "The problem of moral judgements in history", *South Atlantic Quarterly* **84**, 1985, pp. 37–50. The general question of moral responsibility in war is most ably dealt with by M. Walzer, *Just and unjust wars: a moral argument with historical illustrations*, 2nd ed. (Basic Books, 1992). Also see H. E. Selesky, "Colonial America", in *The laws of war: constraints on warfare in the Western world*, M. Howard, G. J. Andreopoulos & M. R. Shulman (eds) (New Haven: Yale University Press, 1994), pp. 59–85.

Chapter Two

1. J. Smith, *Scoouwa: James Smith's Indian captivity narrative* (Columbus, Ohio: Ohio Historical Society, 1978), p. 161.

2. *Ibid.*, p. 65.

3. *Ibid.*, pp. 85, 108–13.

4. For a full discussion of this concept see B. W. Sheehan, "Images: the Indian in the Revolution", *The American Indian experience, a profile: 1524 to the present*, P. Weeks (ed.) (Arlington, Ill., 1988), pp. 66–80.
5. For example, S. P. Adye, *A treatise in courts martial and military discipline . . .*, 3rd edn (London, 1786), especially pp. 283–4; B. Cuthbertson, *A system for the complete interior management and oeconomy of a battalion of infantry* (1776), p. 121; C. Dalrymple, *A military essay . . .* (London, 1761), pp. 48–9; R. Stevenson, *Military instructions for officers . . . for carrying on the petite guerre* (Philadelphia, 1775), pp. 33–53. See also the writers discussed by D. Gates, *The British light infantry arm c. 1790–1815: its creation, training, and operational role* (London: B. T. Batsford, 1987).
6. J. Smith, *Scoouwa*, p. 167.
7. Smith's account of the Indian way of war is supported by many informed observers including Robert Rogers. See his *A concise narrative of North America* (London, 1763), pp. 229–35. See also the comment of the experienced frontier diplomat Conrad Weiser in P. A. W. Wallace, *Conrad Weiser 1696–1760, friend of colonist and Mohawk* (Philadelphia: University of Pennsylvania Press, 1945), p. 201.
8. C. H. Lincoln, *Narratives of the Indian wars 1675–1695* (ed.), (New York: Scribner's, 1913), p. 167.
9. Rogers, *A concise narrative*, p. 229.
10. Forbes to Henry Bouquet, 27 June 1758, *The writings of General John Forbes pertaining to his service in North America*, A. P. James (ed.) (Menosha, Wis.: Collegiate Press, 1938), p. 125.
11. D. Gookin, "Historical collections of the Indians in New England", *Massachusetts Historical Society Collections*, 1st Series, **I**, 1792, p. 153.
12. My discussion of Indian technology is based primarily upon P. Malone, *The skulking way of war: technology and tactics among the New England Indians* (Lanham, Md.: Madison Books, 1991).
13. D. K. Richter, *The ordeal of the longhouse: the peoples of the Iroquois League in the era of European colonization* (Chapel Hill: University of North Carolina Press, 1992), p. 55; B. G. Trigger, *The children of Aataentsic: a history of the Huron people to 1660* (Montreal: McGill–Queen's University Press, 1976) [2 vols], I, p. 417; R. White, *The middle ground: Indians, empires and republics in the Great Lakes Region, 1650–1815* (Cambridge: Cambridge University Press, 1991), pp. 2–3.
14. For Champlain's account of his encounter, see *Voyages of Samuel de Champlain*, trans. C. Pomeroy (New York: Burt Franklin, 1880), XI, pp. 91–6. In addition to Malone, see T. B. Abler, "European technology and the art of war in Iroquoia", *Cultures in conflict: current archeological perspectives*, D. C. Tkaczuk and B. C. Vivian (eds), Proceedings of the Twentieth Annual Conference of the Archaeological Association of the University of Calgary (1989), pp. 273–82; and B. J. Given, "The Iroquois and native firearms", in *Native peoples, native lands: Canadian Indians, Inuit and Metis*, Carleton Library Series No. 142, B. A. Cox (ed.) (Ottawa: Carleton University Press, 1987), pp. 3–13. The standard work on firearms for the period covered by this study is M. L. Brown, *Firearms in colonial America: the impact on history and technology 1492–1792* (Washington: Smithsonian Institution Press, 1980).
15. Trigger, *The children of Aataentsic*, II, p. 629.
16. Abler, "European technology", p. 10.
17. J. A. H. de Guibert, *A general essay on tactics*, trans. by an Officer (London, 1781), p. 157.
18. Malone, *The skulking way of war*, p. 31. Like Given, Malone tested the musket against the bow, but drew different conclusions.

19. There are numerous references to this preference in *The writings of General John Forbes pertaining to his service in North America.*

20. "Colonel Bradstreet's thoughts on Indian affairs", *Documents relative to the colonial history of New York*, E. B. O'Callaghan (ed.), VII (1856), p. 692. See also the reference to rifles in the *Massachusetts Gazette and Boston News-Letter*, No. 3111, 12 August 1763.

21. *Boston Weekly Newsletter*, No. 2874, 4 August 1757.

22. Malone, *The skulking way of war*, p. 60.

23. M. de Saxe, *Reveries on the art of war*, trans. T. R. Phillips (Harrisburg, 1944), p. 32; Frederick the Great, *Instructions for his generals*, trans. T. R. Phillips (Harrisburg, 1960), p. 92; Sieur de Folard, *Nouvelles decuvertes sur la guerre* (Paris, 1762), pp. 83, 253–74. The best modern discussion of eighteenth-century military thought is by A. Gat, *The origins of military thought from the Enlightenment to Clausewitz* (Oxford, 1989).

24. L. V. Eid, "'A kind of running fight': Indian battlefield tactics in the late eighteenth century", *Western Pennsylvania Historical Magazine* **LXXI**, 1988, pp. 147–71.

25. Malone, *The skulking way of war*, pp. 42–51; J. H. Merrell, *The Indians' new world: Catawbas and their neighbors from European contact through the era of removal* (Chapel Hill: University of North Carolina Press, 1989), p. 59. That the Great Lakes Indians were well equipped with firearms will be demonstrated in Chapter Five.

26. Malone, *The skulking way of war*, pp. 71–2; M. N. McConnell, *A country between; the Upper Ohio Valley and its peoples, 1724–1774* (Lincoln: University of Nebraska Press, 1992), p. 218.

27. The Bouquet Papers, British Library Add. Mss. 21, 6,500, pp. 126, 140–42. For a discussion of gunpowder manufacture see J. West, *Gunpowder, government and war in the mid-eighteenth century* (Royal Historical Society: Boydell Press, 1991).

28. I. K. Steele, *Warpaths: Invasions of North America* (New York: Oxford University Press, 1994), p. 53.

29. For discussion of some native fortifications and their modification, see Trigger, *The children of Aataentsic*, I, p. 43 and II, p. 772; Merrell, *The Indians' new world*, p. 125.

30. For the traditional warfare practice of the Hurons and the Iroquois see Richter, *The ordeal of the longhouse*, p. 35, and Trigger, *The children of Aataentsic*, I, p. 70.

31. J. Axtell, *Beyond 1492: encounters in colonial North America* (New York: Oxford University Press, 1992), pp. 141–2.

32. For example see Richter, *The ordeal of the longhouse*, pp. 62, 98.

33. For example see J. E. Ferling, *A wilderness of miseries: war and warriors in early America*, Contributions in Military History, No. 22 (Westport, Conn.: Greenwood Press, 1980), p. 21.

34. Steele, *Warpaths*, pp. 92–3; A. J. Hirsch, "The collision of military cultures in seventeenth-century New England", *Journal of American History*, **74**, 1997–8, pp. 1187–1212; N. Salisbury, *Manitou and Providence: Indians, Europeans, and the making of New England, 1500–1643* (New York: Oxford University Press, 1982), pp. 221–5.

35. D. Richter, "War and culture: the Iroquois experience", *William and Mary Quarterly*, Third Series, **40**, 1983, pp. 528–59 and *The ordeal of the longhouse*, pp. 32–3, 148; Trigger, *The children of Aataentsic*, I, p. 103; Merrell, *The Indians' new world*, p. 121.

36. T. Taylor, *The anatomy of the Nuremberg trials: a personal memoir* (New York: A. Knopf, 1992), p. 253.

37. R. Rogers, *Journals of Major Robert Rogers* (Readex Microprint, 1966), pp. 128, 145; R. Rogers, "Journal of a scout", 25 January 1757, Huntington Library, San Marino, Cal.,

Loudon Papers, LO 2704 A&B; William Eyre to Major General Abercromby, 28 January 1757, Loudon Papers, LO 2718.

38. I have based this paragraph on V. D. Hanson, *The Western way of war: infantry battle in classical Greece* (New York, 1989) and M. van Creveld, *Technology and war from 2000 B.C. to the present* (New York, 1989), pp. 18–20. I have elaborated on this point in my article "Paoli to Stony Point: military ethics and weaponry during the American Revolution", *Journal of Military History* **58**(1), January 1994, pp. 7–27. Braddock's defeat will be discussed in a later chapter. For Fontenoy see F. H. Skrine, *Fontenoy and Great Britain's share in the War of the Austrian Succession 1741–1748* (Edinburgh, 1906).

39. W. Smith, *An historical account of the expedition against the Ohio Indians in the year MDCCLXIV under the command of Henry Bouquet* . . . (Philadelphia, 1766), p. 38. Smith based this account on information provided by Bouquet.

40. For the Indian "rites of war" see G. E. Dowd, *A spirited resistance: the North American struggle for Indian unity 1745–1815* (Baltimore: Johns Hopkins University Press, 1992), pp. 9–22.

41. R. White, *The middle ground: Indians, empires, and republics in the Great Lakes Region, 1650–1815* (Cambridge: Cambridge University Press, 1991), p. 80.

42. Trigger, *The children of Aataentsic*, II, p. 660; Dowd, *A spirited resistance*. James Axtell believes that Indian men may have simply found European women unattractive; see *The European and the Indian: essays in the ethnohistory of colonial America* (New York: Oxford University Press, 1981), p. 152.

43. Great Britain, Historical Manuscripts Commission, *Report on the manuscripts of the late Reginald Rawdon Hastings*, 4 vols (London, 1934), III, p. 179.

44. "Melanges et documents: La Campagne de 1761 en Westphale d'apres les lettres du Maréchal de Crissé au Prince de Saxe", *Revue Historique*, May–August 1910, p. 323.

45. F. Jennings, *The invasion of America: Indians, colonialism, and the cant of conquest* (Chapel Hill: University of North Carolina Press, 1975), p. 169.

46. I have developed this point in my article "War and culture, a case study: the Enlightenment and the conduct of the British army in America, 1755–1781", *War and Society* **8**(1), May 1990, pp. 1–28.

47. *Campagnes de Mercoyral de Beaulieu, 1743–1763*, Societe de l'histoire de France, Vol. 370, p. 323.

48. H. Peckham, "Thomas Gist's Indian captivity 1756–1759", *The Pennsylvania Magazine of History and Biography* **80**(3) (July 1956), p. 299.

49. This was the explanation of British observers. See *The George Rogers Clark papers 1781–1784. Collections of the Illinois State Historical Library*, XIX, *Virginia Series*, IV, J. A. James (ed.) (Springfield, Ill., 1924), pp. 78–80.

50. Trigger, *The children of Aataentsic*, I, p. 162; Jennings, *The invasion of America*, pp. 160–63.

51. White, *The middle ground*, p. 325. Also see C. Calloway, *The western Abenakis of Vermont, 1600–1800* (Norman: University of Oklahoma Press, 1990), 27; Richter, *The ordeal of the longhouse*, pp. 65–6.

52. White, *The middle ground*, pp. 299–300; "Journal of a detachment of the 42nd Regiment going from Fort Pitt down the Ohio to the country of the 'Illinoise' . . .", Scottish Reconds Office, Hunter, Harvey, Webster and Will Collection, G. D. 296\196, pp. 144–5.

53. R. D. Edmunds, *Tecumseh and the quest for Indian leadership* (Boston: Little Brown and Co., 1984), p. 73.

54. J. Axtell & W. C. Sturtevant, "The unkindest cut, or who invented scalping?", *William and Mary Quarterly*, Third Series, **37**(3), July 1980, pp. 451–72.

55. P. A. W. Wallace, *Conrad Weiser, 1696–1760, friend of colonist and Mohawk* (Philadelphia: University of Pennsylvania Press, 1945), p. 434.

56. For this correspondence see *Frontier advance on the Upper Ohio, 1778–1779*, L. P. Kellogg (ed.), *Publications of the State Historical Society of Wisconsin* (Madison, 1916) **XXIII**, p. 385; and *Frontier retreat on the Upper Ohio, 1779–1781*, L. P. Kellogg (ed.), *Publications of the State Historical Society of Wisconsin Collections* (Madison, 1917) **XXIV**, Draper Series, V, pp. 183–4.

57. R. C. Johnson, "The search for a usable Indian: an aspect of the defense of colonial New England", *Journal of American History* **64**, 1977, pp. 623–51.

58. "Journal of an expedition against the rebels on the frontiers of East Florida . . . by David Holmes, Esq. Captain and Acting Commissary . . .", Public Record Office CO/5/80, p. 42.

59. "Journal of a detachment of the 42nd Regiment", p. 21 and also pp. 29 and 45.

60. *Adventure in the wilderness: the American journals of Louis Antoine de Bougainville, 1756–1760*, E. F. Hamilton (trans. and ed.) (Norman: University of Oklaloma Press, 1964).

61. I. Steele, *Betrayals: Fort William Henry and the "Massacre"* (New York, 1993), pp. 184–5.

62. Merrell, *The Indians' new world*, p. 78.

63. See Richter, *The ordeal of the longhouse*, especially Chapters 2 and 3.

64. In addition to Richter, I have based my generalizations about Indian government on Trigger, *The children of Aataentsic*, I, pp. 54–62; McConnell, *A country between*, pp. 27–31; and White, *The middle ground*, p. 188.

65. See L. V. Eid, "National war among Indians of northeastern North America", *Canadian Review of American Studies* **16**(2), Summer 1985, pp. 125–54.

66. Steele, *Warpaths*, pp. 216–17.

67. Dowd, *A spirited resistance*, p. 36.

Chapter Three

1. M. Roberts, *The military revolution 1560–1660. An inaugural lecture delivered before the Queen's University of Belfast* (Belfast, 1956), p. 32. See also G. Parker, *The military revolution: military innovation and the rise of the West* (Cambridge: Cambridge University Press, 1988). As his title suggests, Parker develops the global implications of the "military revolution". The principal critic of the Roberts–Parker thesis is Jeremy Black. See his *A military revolution? Military change and European society 1550–1800* (Atlantic Highlands, NJ: Humanities Press International, 1991).

2. For the concept of the "fiscal-military state", see J. Brewer, *The sinews of power: war, money, and the English state, 1688–1783* (New York: Knopf, 1988).

3. For an example of the "nationalist" point of view, see H. Peckham, *The colonial wars 1689–1762* (Chicago: University of Chicago Press, 1964). On the subject of the relationship between European military thought and frontier warfare, see P. Paret, "Colonial experience and European military reform at the end of the eighteenth century", *Bulletin of the Institute of Historical Research* **37**, 1964, pp. 47–9, and the same author's "The relationship between the Revolutionary War and European military thought and practice in the second half of the eighteenth century", in *Reconsiderations on the Revolutionary War: selected essays*, D. Higginbotham (ed.), Contributions on Military History, No. 14. (Westport, Conn.: Greenwood Press, 1978), pp. 144–57. Also see P. Russell, "Redcoats in the wilderness:

British officers and irregular warfare in Europe, 1740 to 1760", *William and Mary Quarterly*, Third Series, **XXXV**(4), October 1978, pp. 629–52.

4. For Elizabethan military institutions and practices see C. G. Cruikshank, *Elizabeth's army*, 2nd edn (Oxford: Oxford University Press, 1966); L. Boynton, *The Elizabethan militia* (London, 1967); and J. S. Nolan, "The militarization of the Elizabethan state", *Journal of Military History* **58**(3), July 1994, pp. 391–420. Nolan provides the most positive view of Elizabethan military developments.

5. Whatever view one takes of the military revolution debate, most agree that sixteenth-century England did not experience one. See B. M. Downing, *The military revolution and political change: origins of democracy and autocracy in early modern Europe* (Princeton: Princeton University Press, 1992), p. 163 and Nolan, "The militarization of the Elizabethan state", pp. 419–20. The latter perceives Tudor developments as an elaboration of traditional practice, but laying the groundwork for the struggles of the seventeenth century.

6. For a reprint of the laws drawn up between 1609 and 1612, see "For the colony in Virginea Britannia lawes divine, morall and martiall, etc." (A Jamestown Document), compiled by W. Strachey, D. H. Flaherty (ed.) (Charlottesville: The University of Virginia Press, n.d.). It may be compared to "Leicester's disciplinary code" in Cruikshank, *Elizabeth's army*, Appendix 12, pp. 296–303. For the development of the Virginia militia, see W. L. Shea, *The Virginia militia in the seventeenth century* (Baton Rouge: Louisiana State University Press, 1983). Shea provides a good discussion of the war with the Powhatan Indians, as does I. K. Steele, *Warpaths: invasions of North America* (New York: Oxford University Press, 1994), Chapter 3, and J. L. Wright, Jr, *The only land they knew: the tragic story of the American Indians in the old south* (New York: The Free Press, 1981), pp. 60–86.

7. Shea, *The Virginia militia*, p. 140.

8. C. Falls, *Elizabeth's Irish wars* (New York: Barnes and Noble, 1970). See also N. P. Canny, *The Elizabethan conquest of Ireland: a pattern established 1565–1576* (New York: Harper and Row, 1976). Canny finds "the colonists in Virginia using the same pretexts for the extermination of the Amerindians as their counterparts had used in the 1560's and 1570's for the slaughter of segments of the native Irish population", p. 160.

9. J. Shy, "A new look at the colonial militia", in *A people numerous and armed, reflections on the military struggle for American independence* (New York: Oxford University Press, 1976), Chapter 2.

10. I. Steele, *Guerrillas and grenadiers, the struggle for Canada, 1689–1760* (Toronto: Ryesson Press, 1969), pp. 16–17; W. J. Eccles, "The French forces in North America during the Seven Years War", *Dictionary of Canadian biography*, III, *1741 to 1770*, F. G. Halpenny (ed.) (Toronto: University of Toronto Press, 1974), p. xvii.

11. For the life of La Corne Saint-Luc, see the article by P. Tousignant and M. Dionne-Tousignant in *Dictionary of Canadian biography*, IV, *1771 to 1800* (Toronto: University of Toronto Press, 1979), pp. 425–428. La Corne's experience may be contrasted with that of Massachusetts provincial troops as described by F. Anderson, *A people's army: Massachusetts soldiers and society in the Seven Years War* (Chapel Hill: University of North Carolina Press, 1982).

12. Steele, *Guerrillas and grenadiers*, p. 26.

13. H. Bland, *A treatise of military discipline: in which is laid down and explained the duty of the officer and soldier, through the several branches of the service*, 9th edn (London, 1762).

14. R. C. Alberts, *The most extraordinary adventures of Major Robert Stobo* (Boston: Houghton Mifflin, 1965); W. E. Wright, *Colonel Ephraim Williams, a documentary life* (Pittsfield, Mass.: Berkshire County Historical Society, 1970).

15. Bland, *A treatise*, pp. 283–4.

16. S. Pargellis, "Braddock's defeat", *American Historical Review* **XLI**(2), January 1936, pp. 253–69.

17. Lancelot, Comte Turpin de Crissé, *Essai sur l'art de la guerre* [2 vols] (Paris, 1754); Capitaine [Hector] de Grandmaison, *La petite guerre* (Paris, 1756); Mr de Jeney, *Le Partisan ou l'art de faire la petite guerre* (1759). According to Peter Paret, the earliest of these treatises on irregular war appeared in 1752; he has identified 50 such works published in the period 1752–1800. See his "Colonial experience and European military reform", p. 57.

18. See in particular P. Russell, "Redcoats in the wilderness: British officers and irregular warfare in Europe, 1740 to 1760", *William and Mary Quarterly*, Third Series, **XXXV**(4), October 1978, pp. 629–52.

19. M. Van Creveld, *Supplying war: logistics from Wallenstein to Patton* (Cambridge: Cambridge University Press, 1977), pp. 36–7. For the most complete discussion of European warfare in the period, see J. Black, *European warfare 1660–1815* (London: UCL Press, 1994).

20. *Frederick the Great on the art of war*, J. Luvaas (ed. and trans.) (New York: The Free Press, 1966), p. 128.

21. R. Parker & Comte de Merode-Westerloo, *The Marlborough wars*, D. Chandler (ed.) (Hamden, Conn.: Archon Books, 1968), p. 160.

22. A.-R. Mopinot de la Chapotte, *Sous Louis Le Bien Amé, correspondance amoureuse et militaire d'un officier pendant La Guerre De Sept-Ans (1757–1765)*, J. Lemoine (ed.) (Paris: Calmann-Levy, 1905), pp. 370–1.

23. For Corsica, see T. E. Hall, *France and the eighteenth century Corsican question* (New York: New York University Press, 1971). There is a large literature on the Jacobite risings in Scotland, particularly the '45. The best recent discussion is that of J. Black, *Culloden and the '45* (New York: St Martin's Press, 1990). For Jacobite military tactics, see J. M. Hill, *Celtic warfare 1595–1763* (Edinburgh: John Donald, 1986).

24. *Writings of General John Forbes pertaining to his service in North America*, A. P. James (ed.) (Menosha, Wis: Collegiate Press, 1938), pp. 117, 191, 198.

25. Henry Bouquet to General Amherst, 26 July 1763, and to Lieut. Colonel Robertson on the same date, in "Before and after the Battle of Edge Hill [Bushy Run]", D. Brymner, *Report on the Canadian Archives* (1889), Note D (Ottawa, 1890), pp. 61–2.

26. *Governor's messages and letters: messages and letters of William Henry Harrison*, L. Esarey (ed.) [2 vols] (Indianapolis: Indiana Historical Commission, 1922), I, p. 409.

27. Trenck's life was written by a kinsman who tried to be sympathetic, but portrayed him as a rash and violent man. See "History of Francis Baron Trenck, a partisan colonel, and Commander in Chief of the Pandours in the service of Her Majesty the Empress-Queen, written by Frederick Baron Trenck as a necessary supplement to his own history", in *The life of Frederick Baron von der Trenck* (Boston, 1828). Ironically, in his last illness, Trenck sought to be canonized: "He had lived a tyrant and enemy of men, and died a sanctified imposter", p. 94. Some observers drew a distinction between the lawless Trenck and the somewhat more respectable Mentzel although the results were usually the same. See C. Duffy, *The army of Maria Theresa: the armed forces of Imperial Austria, 1740–1780* (New York: Hippocrene Books, 1977), pp. 67–8.

28. "Letters of Lieut. Col. Charles Russell", in Historical Manuscripts Commission, *Report on the manuscripts of Mrs. Frankland Russell-Astley* (London, 1900), p. 282. See also *"To Mr. Davenport" being letters of Major Richard Davenport (1719–1760) to his brother during service in the 4th Troop of Horse Guards and 10th Dragoons, 1742–1760*, C. W. Frearson (ed.), Society

for Army Historical Research, Special Publication No. 9 (London and Aldershot, 1968), pp. 39–40.

29. C. von Clausewitz, *On war*, M. Howard & P. Paret (eds and trans.) (Princeton: Princeton University Press, 1976), p. 632.

30. See J. Ewald, *Diary of the American War: a Hessian journal*, J. P. Tustin (trans.) (New Haven, 1979), and J. G. Simcoe, *Simcoe's military journal, a history of the operations of the Queen's Rangers commanded by Lieut. Col. J. G. Simcoe, during the War of the American Revolution* (New York, 1884; repr. New York, 1968).

31. For this development, see D. Gates, *The British Light Infantry Arm* (London: B. T. Batsford, 1987).

32. I differ on this point with the conclusions of Peter Russell, "Redcoats in the wilderness".

33. *Campagnes de Mercoyrol de Beaulieu, 1743–1763*, Societe de l'histoire de France, Vol. 370, p. 8.

34. See R. Rogers, "Methods used in disciplining the Rangers . . . with their manner and practices in scouting and fighting in the woods", 25 October 1757, Loudon Papers, LO 4701, and "Instructions for new rangers", 1757, in Rogers, *Journals*, pp. 56–70.

35. J. R. Cuneo, *Robert Rogers of the Rangers* (New York: Oxford University Press, 1959), p. 59.

36. *Ibid.*, pp. 59–60.

37. J. E. O. Screen, "The 'Royal Military Academy' of Lewis Lochée," *Journal of the Society for Army Historical Research*, **80** (283), 1992, p. 155. Lochée's plan of study is described in L. Lochée, *An essay on military education* (London, 1776).

38. Sir Thomas Spencer Wilson Bart to Lord Fitzmaurice, 18 May 1761, University of Michigan, William L. Clements Library, Shelburne Papers, Vol. 37, p. 47.

39. See A. Corvisier, *Armies and societies in Europe 1494–1789*, A. T. Siddall (trans.) (Bloomington: Indiana University Press, 1979). Also see his monumental study of the French army, *L'Armee Française de la fin du XVIIe siécle au ministere de Choiseul: Le Soldat* [2 vols] (Paris, 1964). An interesting comparison of seventeenth- and eighteenth-century French officer ethics is provided by J. Chaginot, "The ethics and practice of war amongst French officers during the seventeenth century", *War and Society* **10**(1), May 1992, pp. 19–36. For the outlook of French officers in America during the War of American Independence, see G. Bodiner, *Les Officiers de L'Armée Royale combattants de la guerre d'Independence des Etats-Unis de Yorktown a l'an II*, Service Historique De L'Armée De Terre (Chateau de Vincennes, 1983). I am grateful to Professor Chaginot for this reference and for guidance on French officer memoirs. For the development of professionalism in the British army, see J. A. Houlding, *Fit for service: the training of the British army, 1715–1795* (Oxford: The Clarendon Press, 1981) and A. J. Guy, *Oeconomy and discipline: officership and administration in the British army 1714–1763* (Manchester: Manchester University Press, 1985).

40. Jennings, *Empire of fortune*, p. 209. The British army has no more severe critic: "The British military system and its commanders were simply rotten", p. 211.

41. G. A. Steppler, "British military law, discipline and the conduct of courts martial in the later eighteenth century", *English Historical Review* **CII**(405), October 1987, pp. 854–86; S. Frey, *The British soldier in America: a social history of military life in the revolutionary period* (Austin, 1981), pp. 85–7. See also S. P. Adye, *A treatise in courts martial and military discipline . . .* , 3rd edn (London, 1786), pp. 241–2 and 269–71; B. Cuthbertson, *A system for the complete interior management and oeconomy of a battalion of infantry* (1776), pp. 120–22; C. Dalrymple, *A military essay . . .* (London, 1761), pp. 14–17, 48–9, 113; and R. Donkin, *Military collections and remarks* (New York, 1777), pp. 9–10.

42. Houlding, *Fit for service*, p. 167; D. Chandler, *The art of warfare in the age of Marlborough* (London, 1976).
43. This point is especially well developed by A. Gat, *The origins of military thought from the Enlightenment to Clausewitz* (Oxford, 1989).
44. For examples of the constraints imposed by professionalism, see J. Snyder, *The ideology of the offensive: military decision making and the disaster of 1914* (Ithaca: Cornell University Press, 1984), and A. J. Bacevich, "The use of force in our time", *Wilson Quarterly*, Winter 1995, pp. 50–63.
45. Montcalm to Lévis, 17 August 1756, in F. Gaston, duc de Lévis, *Journal des campagnes du Chevalier de Lévis en Canada de 1756 a 1769* (Montreal: C. O. Beauchemin et Fils, 1889), in *Collections des manuscrits du Maréchal de Lévis* [12 vols] (Montreal, 1889–95), I, p. 35.
46. Montcalm to M. de Bourlamaque, 13 June 1757, in *Lettres de M. de Bourlamaque au Chevalier de Lévis, Lévis Collections*, V (Quebec, 1891), p. 168.
47. *Adventure in the wilderness: the American journals of Louis Antoine de Bougainville, 1756–1760*, E. P. Hamilton (trans. and ed.) (Norman: University of Oklahoma Press, 1964), p. 251.
48. *Ibid.*, pp. 252–3.

Chapter Four

1. B. Church, *Diary of King Philip's War 1675–1676*, A. M. Simpson (eds) (Chester, Conn.: The Pequot Press, 1975), pp. 151–6.
2. See D. Leach, *Flintlock and tomahawk: New England in King Philip's War* (New York: Macmillan, 1958), pp. 228–9. This remains the standard account of the war. See also the introduction provided by Alan and Mary Simpson to their introduction to Church's *Diary of King Philip's War*, pp. 1–63. P. Malone, *The skulking way of war: technology and tactics among the New England Indians* (Lanham, Maryland: Madison Books, 1991) is an indispensable guide to the conduct of the war. The leading revisionist account is that of F. Jennings, *The invasion of America, Indians, colonialism and the cant of conquest* (Chapel Hill: University of North Carolina Press, 1975). One should also consider R. Bourne, *The red king's rebellion: racial politics in New England 1675–1678* (New York: Atheneum, 1990). In addition to Church's diary, contemporary accounts of the war were provided by W. Hubbard, *A narrative of the troubles with the Indians in New England . . .* (London, 1677); I. Mather, *A brief history of the warr with the Indians of New England . . .* (Boston, 1676); and D. Gookin, *An historical account of the doings and sufferings of the Christian Indians in New England in the years 1675, 1676, 1677*, in *Archaelogica Americana, Transactions and Collections of the American Antiquarian Society*, II (Cambridge, 1836). Important narratives and documents are to be found in S. G. Drake, *The old Indian chronicle* (Boston, 1836, 1867) and C. H. Lincoln, *Narratives of the Indian wars, 1675–1699* (New York: Scribner's, 1913)
3. Hubbard, *A narrative of the troubles*, p. 104.
4. Bourne, *The red king's rebellion*, emphasizes peaceful white–Indian relations in the period prior to 1660. Jennings, *The invasion of America*, however, provides a picture of almost unrelieved Puritan aggression against the Indians in which the Pequot war was no exception.
5. Bourne, *The red king's rebellion*, pp. 26–8. See also N. Salisbury, "Indians and colonists in southern New England after the Pequot War. An uneasy balance", in *The Pequots in*

Southern New England: the rise and fall of an American Indian nation, L. M. Hauptman & J. D. (eds) Wherry (Norman: University of Oklahoma Press, 1990), pp. 81–95.

6. Jennings, *The invasion of America*, pp. 254–81.

7. See R. Slotkin, *Regeneration through violence: mythology of the American frontier, 1600–1860* (Middleton, Conn.: Wesleyan University Press, 1973), Chapter 2.

8. A. T. Vaughn, *The New England frontier: Puritans and Indians, 1620–1675* (Boston: Little, Brown, 1965), p. 303. Vaughn insists that the Puritans' religion ensured that they were fair and just in their dealings with the Indians.

9. Jennings, *The invasion of America*, p. 298. Just as his *Empire of fortune* is a vigorous assault on history according to Francis Parkman, Jennings characterizes this book as a "detailed refutation" of the account of the contemporary Puritan writer William Hubbard (p. 185). See Hubbard's *A narrative of the troubles*.

10. Jennings, *The invasion of America*, pp. 212–13.

11. See J. Axtell, *The invasion within: the contest of cultures in colonial North America* (New York and Oxford: Oxford University Press, 1985), p. 273; and N. Salisbury, "Red Puritans: the praying Indians of Massachusetts Bay and John Eliot", *William and Mary Quarterly*, Third Series, **31**, 1974, pp. 27–54.

12. See D. Gookin's sympathetic portrayal of the "praying Indians", in *An historical account of the doings and sufferings*, pp. 450 and following.

13. Mather, *A brief history of the warr* p. 1.

14. Hubbard, *A narrative of the troubles*, p. 12.

15. See Chapter One, note 7.

16. Axtell, *The invasion within*, p. 273.

17. P. Ranlet, "Another look at the causes of King Philip's War", *New England Quarterly* **LXI**(1), March 1988, pp. 79–100. Ranlet differs from the revisionist analysis of the causes of the war and offers a detailed account of the events leading to hostilities.

18. *Ibid.* Also see Leach, *Flintlock and tomahawk*, Chapter 2. While this remains the standard account of the war, Leach's discussion of Philip's thinking during this period seems highly speculative.

19. Salisbury, "Red Puritans", p. 38.

20. "A relacion of the Indyan warre by Mr. Easton of Roade Isld., 1675", in Lincoln, *Narratives of the Indian wars*, pp. 7–17. The Plymouth authorities provided their own version of the causes of the war in "Narrative showing the manor of the begining of the present warr with the Indians at Mount Hope and Pocassett . . . 1675", in *Records of the Colony of New Plymouth* [12 vols in 13], X: "Acts of the Commissioners of New England", II, 1653–1679, D. Pulsifer (ed.) (Boston, 1859), pp. 362–4.

21. William Leete to John Winthrop, Jr, 23 September 1675, "The Winthrop papers", *Collections of the Massachusetts Historical Society* (Boston, 1865), 4th Series, **VII**, p. 579.

22. I have based this section on the work of Douglas Leach. See *Flintlock and tomahawk*, particularly Chapter 6, and "The military system of Plymouth Colony", *New England Quarterly* **XXIV**, 1951, pp. 342–64. For the Massachusetts militia, see G. M. Bodge, *Soldiers in King Philip's War* (Boston, 1891), particularly pp. 15–16.

23. "The present state of New-england with respect to the Indian War . . . from the 20th of June till the 10th of November 1675", in Drake, *The old Indian chronicle*, p. 10.

24. Bodge, *Soldiers in King Philip's War*, p. 27. For Moseley's harsh treatment of Christian Indians, see Gookin, *An historical account*, pp. 496–7.

25. Gookin, *An historical account*, p. 436.

26. "Petition of the Rev. John Eliot, August, 1675", *Records of the Colony of New Plymouth*, X, p. 451.
27. "The present state of New-england", in Drake, *The old Indian chronicle*, p. 37.
28. See "Indian affairs 1603–1705", Massachusetts Archives, Boston, Mass., Vol. 30, pp. 185b, 190, 194, 194a.
29. Gookin, *An historical account*, p. 444.
30. See the order of 31 August 1675 in "Journal of the Council of War from 1675 to 1678", *The Public Records of Connecticut from 1665 to 1678*, J. H. Trumbull (ed.) (Hartford, 1852), II, p. 359.
31. "Council of War, Oct. 6, 1675", *The Public Records of Connecticut*, 373–4; "Council of Hartford, Oct. 12, 1675", Massachusetts Archives, Vol. 67, p. 298; Leete to Winthrop, 23 September 1675, "Winthrop papers", pp. 579–80; "A continuation of the state of New-England . . . from the 10th of November, 1675 to the 8th of February, 1676" in Drake, *The old Indian chronicle*, p. 59.
32. *Ibid.*, p. 525.
33. Lieutenant Walter Tyler of Windsor, Conn., 21 October 1675, Massachusetts Archives, Vol. 68, pp. 24–6.
34. See *The Public Records of Connecticut*, pp. 361, 375, 417.
35. "The present state of New-england", in Drake, *The old Indian chronicle*, p. 14.
36. Samuel Gorton to Winthrop, 11 September 1675, "Winthrop papers", p. 630.
37. Gookin, *An historical account*, p. 441.
38. Hubbard, *A narrative of the troubles*, p. 79.
39. Gookin, *An historical account*, pp. 441–2.
40. Hubbard, *A narrative of the troubles*, pp. 38–9; Mather, *A brief history*, p. 12.
41. "A further brief and true narrative of the late wars risen in New England . . ." (Boston, 28 December 1675), in Drake, *The old Indian chronicle*, p. 318.
42. Leete to Winthrop, 23 September 1675, "Winthrop papers", p. 579.
43. See the "Commissioners of the United Colonies to William Coddington, Governor of Rhode Island Colony, Nov. 12, 1675", in *Further letters on King Philip's War . . .* (Society of Colonial Wars in the State of Rhode Island and Providence Plantations, 1923), pp. 18–19. Those who do not accept this letter at face value include: Bourne, *The red king's rebellion*, p. 152; Jennings, *The invasion of America*, pp. 304–12; Leach, *Flintlock and tomahawk*, p. 119; and I. Steele, *Warpaths* (New York: Oxford University Press, 1994), p. 102.
44. *Further letters*, p. 12.
45. "Captain Henchman, Sept. 25, 1675", Massachusetts Archives, Vol. 67, p. 269.
46. Leach, *Flintlock and tomahawk*, p. 120. I have based my discussion of this campaign on Chapter 5 of this work.
47. *Ibid.*, p. 110.
48. See the correspondence in the *Conn. Records*, pp. 394–5, which protests that the colony had suffered disproportionate losses in the Narragansett campaign and no longer had the men or food to support a new offensive.
49. Gookin, *An historical account*, pp. 488–91.
50. "New and further narrative of the state of New-England being a continued account of the bloody Indian war from March till August 1676" in Drake, *The old Indian chronicle*, p. 83. See Leach, *Flintlock and tomahawk*, Chapter 9 for an account of the Indian offensive.
51. The proposal for the stockade and the response of the towns are in the Massachusetts Archives, Vol. 68, pp. 174, 175b, 176a, 180.

52. "Petition of April, 1676 by Lieut. Samuel Niles, his sergeant, corporal and 40 men", Massauchusetts Archives, Vol. 68, p. 203.

53. "Narrative of the captivity of Mrs. Mary Rowlandson, 1682", in Lincoln, *Narratives of the Indian wars*, p. 153.

54. Gookin, *An historical account*, p. 513.

55. Jennings, *The invasion of America*, p. 316. See also C. Calloway, *The western Abenaki of Vermont, 1600–1800* (Norman: University of Oklahoma Press, 1990), p. 78.

56. "Letter from Samuel Hunting, August 10, 1676", Massachusetts Archives, Vol. 69.

57. Church, *Diary*, pp. 125–7.

58. J. Axtell, *Beyond 1492: encounters in colonial North America* (New York Oxford: Oxford University Press, 1992), p. 239.

59. "New and further narrative", in Drake, *The old Indian chronicle*, p. 101. New York secretary Edward Randolph reported that 600 men and 12 captains had been killed in action. See "Extracts form Edward Randolph's report to the Council of Trade: Seaventh Enquiry", in *Documents relative to the colonial history of the State of New York*, III (Albany, 1853), pp. 242–4. Russell Bourne has concluded that nearly 9,000 people died in the war, one-third of them English; *The red king's rebellion*, p. 36.

60. Bourne, *The red king's rebellion*, p. 36.

61. Jennings, *The invasion of America*, p. 325.

62. For the charge of rape, see "New and further narrative", in Drake, *The old Indian chronicle*, p. 102.

63. Roger Williams to Governor John Winthrop, Jr, 18 December 1675, in *The correspondence of Roger Williams*, 2 vols, G. W. LaFantasie (ed.) (Hanover and London: University Press of New England, 1988), II, p. 708.

64. "Easton's relacion", in Lincoln, *Narratives of the Indian wars*, p. 17.

65. On the question of the laws of war and their application by English settlers, see H. E. Selesky, "Colonial America", in *The laws of war: constraints on warfare in the Western world*, M. Howard, G. Andreopoulos & M. R. Shulman (eds) (New Haven: Yale University Press, 1994), p. 66.

66. For example, see C. Mather, "Decennium luctuosum", in Lincoln, *Narratives of the Indian wars*, pp. 171–300, which covers the Indian wars from 1688 to 1698.

67. For Church's account of these campaigns, see B. Church, *The history of the eastern expeditions of 1689, 1690, 1692, 1696, and 1704 against the Indians and French*, H. M. Dexter (ed.) (Boston, 1867).

68. Church, *The history of the eastern expeditions*, pp. 74–5.

69. *Ibid.*, p. 117.

Chapter Five

1. C. G. Calloway, *The western Abenakis of Vermont, 1600–1800* (Norman and London: University of Oklahoma Press, 1990), p. 113.

2. For French–Indian relations see the work of W. J. Eccles, in particular, *The Canadian frontier 1534–1760* (New York: Holt, Rinehart and Winston, 1969). The most important recent work concerning Indians of the midwest and their relations with the European empires is that of R. White, *The middle ground: Indians, empires, and republics in the Great*

Lakes region, 1650–1815 (Cambridge: Cambridge University Press, 1991) and M. N. McConnell, *A country between: the Upper Ohio Valley and its peoples, 1724–1774* (Lincoln and London: University of Nebraska Press, 1992). For the Iroquois see F. Jennings, *The ambiguous Iroquois empire* (New York and London: W. W. Norton, 1984) and his *Empire of fortune: crowns, colonies, and tribes in the Seven Years War* (New York: W. W. Norton, 1988); D. Richter, *The ordeal of the longhouse: the peoples of the Iroquois League in the era of European colonization* (Chapel Hill: University of North Carolina Press, 1992); and D. R. Snow, *The Iroquois* (Cambridge, Mass.: Blackwell, 1994). For the Hurons see B. G. Trigger, *The children of Aataentsic: a history of the Huron people to 1660* (Montreal: McGill–Queen's University Press, 1976). For the frontier between Canada and New England, see Calloway, *The western Abenakis of Vermont*.

3. Richter, *The ordeal of the longhouse*, pp. 60–1; Trigger, *The children of Aataentsic*, I, pp. 658–788; D. Delage, *Bitter feast: Amerindians and Europeans in northeastern North America, 1600–64*, J. Brierley (trans.) (Vancouver: UBC Press, 1993), pp. 142–224.

4. In addition to Jennings, *The ambigious Iroquois empire*, see Richter, *The ordeal of the longhouse*; Trigger, *The children of Aataentsic*, especially Vol. 2; Delage, *Bitter feast*.

5. "Papers relating to De Courcelle's and De Tracy's expeditions against the Mohawk Indians, Anno 1665–6", in *The documentary history of the State of New York*, E. B. O'Callaghan (ed.), 4 vols. (Albany, 1850), I, pp. 46–9; I. Steele, *Warpaths: invasions of North America* (Oxford, 1994), pp. 73–5.

6. "Papers relating to . . . expeditions against the Mohawk Indians", p. 49.

7. "Papers relating to M. de la Barre's expedition to Hungry Bay (1684)", *The documentary history of New York*, p. 84.

8. Richter, *The ordeal of the longhouse*, pp. 133–89.

9. Eccles, *The Canadian frontier 1534–1760*, p. 154.

10. *Ibid.*, pp. 122–4. Frontenac who led the French war effort against the Iroquois until his death in 1698 is also the subject of a critical biography by Eccles: *Frontenac the courtier Governor* (Toronto: McClelland and Stewart, 1959). Eccles corrects Francis Parkman's admiring portrait of Frontenac, but concludes that his claim to greatness rests on three things: "under his leadership the English assault on Canada was repulsed, the Iroquois were finally humbled, and the French extended their power into the heart of the continent", p. 337.

11. Calloway, *The western Abenakis of Vermont*, p. 103; J. Williams, *The redeemed captive returning to Zion* (Northampton, 1853); C. A. Baker, *True stories of New England captives carried to Canada during the old French and Indian wars* (Cambridge, 1897; New York: Garland Press, 1976), pp. 128–54; E. Haefeli & K. Sweeney, "Revisiting *The redeemed captive*: new perspectives on the 1704 attack on Deerfield", *William and Mary Quarterly*, Fifth Series, **52**(1), 1995, pp. 3–46.

12. Calloway, *The western Abenakis of Vermont*, pp. 143–59.

13. White, *The middle ground*, p. 188; see also McConnell, *A country between*, p. 23.

14. McConnell, *A country between*, pp. 119–20.

15. F. T. Nichols, "The organization of Braddock's army", *William and Mary Quarterly*, Third Series, **IV**(2), p. 131.

16. L. H. Gipson, *The British empire before the American Revolution*, VI (New York, 1946), pp. 64–5, 77–8. Virginia Governor Robert Dinwiddie's complaints on this matter are in *The official records of Robert Dinwiddie, Collections of the Virginia Historical Society*, III (1883), pp. 364, 378.

17. Gipson, *The British empire*, VI, pp. 91–2.

18. "Anonymous letter on Braddock's campaign", 25 July 1755, in S. Pargellis, *Military affairs in North America, 1748–1765* (1936, reprinted by Archon Books, 1969), pp. 115, 117. See pp. 129–32 for the Contrecoeur's report of the battle. Pages 53–127 include many important documents on the campaign. For other documents, see *Braddock's defeat*, C. Hamilton (ed.) (Norman: University of Oklahoma Press, 1959).

19. Sir John St Clair to Robert Napier, 22 July 1755 and "Anonymous letter", Pargellis, *Military affairs*, pp. 103, 118.

20. In this case P. Kopperman, *Braddock at the Monongahela* (Pittsburgh: University of Pittsburgh Press, 1977), p. 121. Braddock's sympathetic biographer Lee McCardell also blames the troops. See *Ill-starred General: Braddock of the Coldstream Guards* (Pittsburgh: University of Pittsburgh Press, 1958), p. 259. McCardell is not convincing in his defence of Braddock: "Had Braddock been surprised? Had he done his duty? For a hundred miles he had marched by old Humphrey's [Bland] book." One needed more than Bland to succeed.

21. Gipson, *The British empire*, VI, p. 94; D. S. Freeman, *George Washington* (New York, Scribner's, 1948), II, p. 96. Failure to appreciate the Indian way of war is the crucial flaw in the article by R. L. Yaple, "Braddock's defeat: the theories and a reconsideration", *Journal of the Society for Army Historical Research* **46**, 1968, pp. 194–201. Yaple dismisses the value of "the unspeakably unreliable Indian allies" with the comment "They were not Sepoys, after all", p. 197. That is precisely the point: the Indians were not mercenaries, but allies who fought for reasons of their own. Successful frontier commanders understood this.

22. "Extract of a private letter from Boston, in New England, dated August 18", *The Public Advertiser*, 3 October 1755, in N. D. Davis, "British newspaper accounts of Braddock's defeat", *Pennsylvania Magazine of History and Biography* **23**, 1899, p. 319. For similar sentiments see the *Boston Weekly Newsletter*, 14 August 1755, no. 2771, and the *New York Mercury*, 11 August 1755.

23. See George Washington to Governor Dinwiddie, 18 July 1755, *Pennsylvania Magazine of History and Biography* **IX**, 1885, p. 238; "An unpublished autograph narrative by Washington", *Scribner's Magazine* **XIII**(5), May 1893, pp. 550–37.

24. "Journal of a British officer", in *Braddock's defeat*, p. 50.

25. For reports of the Battle of Lake George see *Documents relating to the colonial history of New York*, VI, pp. 1003–13, and X, pp. 316–99, 422–3.

26. Eccles, *The Canadian frontier*, pp. 175–6; G. Fregault, *Canada: the war of the conquest*, M. M. Cameron (trans.) (Toronto: Oxford University Press, 1969), p. 243.

27. In particular, see Jennings, *Empire of fortune*, pp. 296, 423.

28. Calloway, *The western Abenakis of Vermont*, p. 172.

29. Steele, *Warpaths*, pp. 216–17.

30. Fregault, *Canada*, pp. 120, 135; Montcalm's satisfaction with the raids is expressed in a letter to M. de Bourlamaque, 13 June 1757, in *Lettres de M. de Bourlamaque au Chevalier de Levis, collections des manuscrits du Marechal de Levis* [12 vols] (Montreal, 1889–95), V, p. 162.

31. *Writings of General John Forbes pertaining to his service in North America*, A. P. James (ed.) (Menosha, Wis.: Collegiate Press, 1938), pp. 112–234.

32. James Abercromby to Lord Loudon, 29 November 1757, Huntington Library, San Marino, Calif., Loudon Papers, LO 4915; William Haviland to Major General Abercrombie, December 1757, LO 6859.

33. *The journal of Jeffrey Amherst, recording the military career of General Amherst in America from 1758 to 1763*, J. C. Webster (ed.) (Toronto and Chicago: Riverson and University of Chicago Presses, 1931), p. 133.

34. T. Gage, "Proposal to His Excellency the Earl of Loudon for raising a regt. of light armed foot", 22 December 1757, Loudon Papers, LO 5066; see also 5038, 5074, 5072.
35. Jennings, *Empire of fortune*, pp. 207–8.
36. Calloway, *The western Abenakis of Vermont*, pp. 177–9.
37. *Adventure in the wilderness: the American journals of Louis Antoine de Bougainville, 1756–1760*, E. P. Hamilton (trans. and ed.) (Norman: University of Oklahoma Press, 1964), p. 172.
38. Lord Loudon to the Earl of Holdernesse, 16–17 August p. 1757, Huntington Library, Loudon Papers, LO 4239 A&B.
39. Loudon to the Marquis de Vaudreuil, 8 November 1757, Loudon Papers, LO 4788. This was, of course, wartime rhetoric. A British professional officer who wrote a history of the war exonerated Montcalm. See T. Mante, *The history of the late war in North America and the Islands of the West Indies* (London, 1772; repr. New York 1970), p. 91.
40. See *An historical journal of the campaigns in North America for the years 1757, 1758, 1759 and 1760 by Captain John Knox*, A. G. Doughty (ed.) [3 vols] (Freeport, New York: Books for Library Press, 1970, first published 1914–16), I, pp. 389, 438. British troops killed and scalped Canadian partisans: II, p. 45.
41. Jennings, *Empire of fortune*, p. 318.
42. I. Steele, *Betrayals: Fort William Henry and the "Massacre"* (New York and Oxford: Oxford University Press, 1990), pp. 184–5.
43. F. Parkman, *Montcalm and Wolfe in North America*, 2 vols (New York, 1983), II, p. 1492.
44. P. Pouchot, *Memoir upon the late war in North America between the French and English, 1755–1760*, F. B. Hough (trans. and ed.) [2 vols] (Roxbury, Mass., 1866), I, pp. 91, 204.
45. J. Bradstreet, *An impartial account of Lieut. Col. Bradstreet's expedition to Fort Frontenac* (Toronto: Toronto and Mann Ltd., 1940), pp. 21–2; Bougainville, *Adventure in the wilderness*, p. 276; Pouchot, *Memoir*, I, p. 264.
46. Amherst, *Journal*, pp. 239, 243. See also "George Croghan's Journal, 1759–1763", *Pennsylvania Magazine of History and Biography* **LXXXI**(1) January 1947, pp. 409–10. The Senacas told Croghan that Amherst had not allowed them "to prosecute the Warr agreeable to their own Custom and semm'd not to want their services."
47. For example, H. C. B. Rogers, *The British army of the eighteenth century* (New York: Hippocrene Books, 1977), p. 152.
48. Calloway, *The western Abenakis of Vermont*, pp. 180–85.
49. White, *The middle ground*, p. 340.
50. "The Gladwin manuscripts together with an historical sketch of the conspiracy of Pontiac", *Michigan historical commission: Michigan pioneer and historical collections* (Lansing, 1897), XXVII, p. 642.
51. See *The papers of Sir William Johnson*, IV (Albany, 1925), pp. 170, 274–7.
52. McConnell, *A country between*, p. 182. I rely upon McConnell and White, *The middle ground* for this section. H. Peckham, *Pontiac and the Indian uprising* (Princeton: Princeton University Press, 1947) provides a well researched narrative of the military events, but is dated in portraying the conflict as one of "civilization vs. savagery". A good appreciation is provided by Steele, *Warpaths*, Chapter 12.
53. Documents providing testimony concerning the seizure of the British posts are in "The Gladwin manuscripts", pp. 631–9.
54. For example, see the Indian message to Captain Ecuyer, commanding at Fort Pitt and his reply, 24 June 1763, British Library, Bouquet Papers, Add. Mss. 21655, pp. 216–17.

55. "Gladwin manuscripts", p. 653. For a discussion of the rumour that the French would return to the region, see G. E. Dowd, "The French King wakes up in Detroit: 'Pontiac's War in rumor and history'", *Ethnohistory* **XXXVII**(3), 1990, pp. 254–75.

56. *The papers of Henry Bouquet*, Series 21634, Northwestern Pennsylvania Series, Prepared by Frontier Forts and Trails Survey, S. K. Stevens & D. H. Kent (eds) (Harrisburg, 1940), p. 161. See also B. Knollenberg, "General Amherst and germ warfare", *Mississipi Valley Historical Review* **XLI**, 1954–5, pp. 489–94.

57. Bouquet Papers, p. 215

58. See E. de Vattel, *The laws of nations: or the principles of the law of nature, applied to the conduct and affairs of sovereigns*, III, *Of war*, J. Chitty (ed.) (first published in 1758: Philadelphia, 1861), p. 361; D. Hume, "Of the laws of nations", *Hume's moral and political philosophy*, H. D. Aitken (ed.) (New York, 1966), p. 125. Vattel did not believe that the laws of war should apply to fighting "savage" peoples.

59. William Grant to Bouquet, 11 April 1764, Bouquet Papers, Add. Mss. 21,650, pp. 140–42.

60. Details are provided by Peckham, *Pontiac*, pp. 204–8, 224–5, 241.

61. Bouquet's description of the battle is provided in "Before and after the Battle of Edge Hill [Bushy Run]", D. Brymner, *Report on the Canadian Archives*, 1889, Note D (Ottawa, 1890), pp. 62–5.

62. McConnell, *A country between*, p. 194.

63. Bouquet to the Governor and Commissioners of Pennsylvania, 4 June 1764, Bouquet Papers, Add. Mss. 21,653, p. 243.

64. "Disposition for march and to receive attack", 15 September 1764, Bouquet Papers, Add. Mss. 21,653, pp. 316–20.

65. Bouquet Papers, Add. Mss. 21,650, p. 350.

Chapter Six

1. *The Annual Register . . . for the Year 1777* (London, 1778), p. 157.

2. B. Burns, "Massacre or muster? Burgoyne's Indians and the militia at Bennington", *Vermont History* **45**(3), Summer 1977, pp. 133–44. See also J. Namias, *White captives: gender and ethnicity on the American frontier* (Chapel Hill: University of North Carolina Press, 1993), pp. 117–44; F. J. Hudleston, *Gentleman Johnny Burgoyne* (New York, 1927), pp. 163–6; C. Calloway, *The American Revolution in Indian country: crisis and diversity in Native American communities* (Cambridge: Cambridge University Press), pp. 295–7.

3. The *London Evening Post*, 28–30 January 1779.

4. For the most famous criticisms of the government's Indian alliance, see the "Debate on Burke's motion relative to the military employment of Indians in the Civil War in America", in W. Cobbett, *The Parliamentary history of England*, XIX, pp. 694–707. Lord Chatham's speech opposing the use of Indians is included in *The George Rogers Clark papers, collections of the Illinois State Historical Library*, VIII, *Virginia Series*, III, J. A. James (ed.) (Springfield, Ill., 1912), p. xxxix. For Germain see G. S. Brown, *The American Secretary: the colonial policy of Lord George Germain*, (Ann Arbor: University of Michigan Press, 1963), p. 62; Germain to William Knox, 1 January 1781, in "Correspondence of William Knox, chiefly in relation to American affairs, 1757–1808", *The Manuscripts of H. V. Knox*, Great

Britain, Historical Manuscripts Collection, *Report on manuscripts in various collections* (Dublin, 1909), VI, p. 175. For ministry loyalists' discomfort see *A series of letters of [James Harris] the First Earl of Malmesbury . . . from 1745 to 1820* (London, 1870), I, p. 397.

5. *Letters of Hugh Earl Percy from Boston and New York, 1774–1776*, C. K. Bolton (ed.) (Boston, 1902), pp. 37, 44, 51; "Observations by Benjamin Thompson (afterwards Count Rumford)", 4 November 1775, HMC, *Stopford Sackville manuscripts*, II, p. 18; D. Higginbotham, *The War of Independence: military attitudes, policies, and practices, 1763–1789* (New York: Macmillan, 1971), p. 63.

6. B. W. Sheehan, "Images: the Indian in the Revolution", in *The American Indian experience, a profile: 1524 to the present*, P. Weeks (ed.) (Arlington, Ill., 1988), pp. 66–70.

7. *The spirit of 'seventy-six: the story of the American Revolution as told by participants*, H. S. Commager & R. B. Morris (eds) [2 vols] (Indianoplis, 1958), II, p. 999.

8. J. M. Soison, *The Revolutionary frontier 1763–1783* (New York: Holt, Rinehart and Winston, 1967), p. 105.

9. The best single work on the impact of the American Revolution on the Indian peoples is Calloway, *The American Revolution in Indian country*. Also see the same author's "We have always been the frontier: the American Revolution in the Shawnee country", *American Indian Quarterly* **XVI**(1), 1992, pp. 39–52. For Indians of the midwest R. White, *The middle ground: Indians, empires, and republics in the Great Lakes region, 1650–1815* (Cambridge: Cambridge University Press, 1991), pp. 367–418, is indispensable. Also see Barbara Graymont, "The Six Nations Indians in the Revolutionary War", *The Iroquois in the American Revolution* (Rochester, New York: Research Division, Rochester Museum and Science Center, 1981), Research Records No. 14, pp. 25–36; J. H. O'Donnell, *Southern Indians in the American Revolution* (Knoxville: University of Tennessee Press, 1973); and J. H. Merrell, *The Indians' new world: Catawbas and their neighbors from European contact through the era of removal* (Chapel Hill: University of North Carolina Press, 1989), pp. 215–25.

10. *Documents relative to the colonial history of New York* (1887), VIII, pp. 605–31; *Revolution on the Upper Ohio, 1775–1777*, Compiled from the Draper Manuscripts in the Library of the Wisconsin Historical Society, R. G. Thwaites & L. P. Kellogg (eds) (1908, repr. Kennikat Press, 1970), pp. 25–127.

11. Gage to Lord Barrington, 12 June 1775, in *Sources of American Independence, selected manuscripts from the collections of the William L. Clements Library*, H. H. Peckham (ed.), 2 vols (Chicago: University of Chicago Press, 1978), I, pp. 133–4.

12. Lord Dartmouth to Gage, 2 August 1775 and to Lord Dunmore, 6 August 1775, *American archives consisting of a collection of authentic records, state papers, debates and letters . . .* , P. Force (ed.), 4th Series, III (Washington, 1840), p. 6; Lord George Germain to Governor Tonyn, 23 December 1775, University of Michigan, William L. Clements Library, Sackville Germain Papers, IV.

13. For accounts of the battle see *Documentary history of Lord Dunmore's War 1774*, R. G. Thwaites and L. P. Kellogg (eds) (Madison: Wisconsin State Historical Society, 1905), pp. 253–312. See also G. E. Dowd, *A spirited resistance: the North American Indian struggle for unity, 1745–1815* (Baltimore: The Johns Hopkins University Press, 1992), pp. 45–6.

14. *Ibid.*, p. 371.

15. O'Donnell, *Southern Indians*, p. 13; Calloway, *The American Revolution*, pp. 189–90.

16. Calloway, *The American Revolution*, pp. 182–212; O'Donnell *Southern Indians*, pp. 34–53, 142; Dowd, *A spirited resistance*, pp. 47–56.

17. *Frontier advance on the Upper Ohio, 1778–1779*, L. P. Kellogg (ed.) (Madison, 1916), p. 385. Dowd, *A spirited resistance*, pp. 75–8.

18. Extract of a letter from Germain to Stuart, 2 April 1777, Sackville Germain Papers, VI. See also Germain to General Frederick Haldimand, 26 March 1777 (copy forwarded to Hamilton on 21 May 1777), in "The Haldimand papers–copies of papers on file in the Dominion Archives at Ottawa, Canada", Michigan Historical Commission, *Michigan historical collections [Michigan pioneer collections]* (Lansing, 1886), IX, pp. 346–7.

19. Germain to Burgoyne, 23 August 1776, Sackville Germain Papers, V.

20. Germain to Stuart, 2 June 1779, Public Record Office, CO/5/80, pp. 88–90.

21. Charles Shaw to Germain, 7 August 1779, Public Record Office, CO/5/80, pp. 260–63. Dowd, *A spirited resistance*, pp. 54–60.

22. E. J. Cashin, *The King's Ranger: Thomas Brown and the American Revolution on the southern frontier* (Athens and London: University of Georgia Press, 1989), especially p. 124.

23. For the Abenaki response to the war see Calloway, *The American Revolution*, pp. 65–84.

24. J. Hadden, *A journal kept in Canada upon Burgoyne's campaign in 1776 and 1777 . . .* (Albany, 1884; repr. Freeport, NY, 1970), pp. 59–62.

25. Tryon to Secretary William Knox, 21 April 1777, *Documents relative to the colonial history of New York*, VIII, p. 707.

26. E. B. de Fonblanque, *Political and military episodes . . . from the life and correspondence of the Right Hon John Burgoyne . . .* (London, 1876), pp. 244–5.

27. S. Conway, "To subdue America: British army officers and the conduct of the Revolutionary War", *William and Mary Quarterly*, Third Series, **XLIII**(3), July 1986, pp. 405–6.

28. Sheehan, "Images", p. 70.

29. *A state of the expedition from Canada as laid before the House of Commons by Lieutenant General Burgoyne. . . . The second edition* (London, 1780; repr. Arno Press, 1969), pp. 130–32, 163.

30. Graymont, "Six Nations", p. 126.

31. Details of St Leger's expedition are in H. Swiggett, *War out of Niagara: Walter Butler and the Tory Rangers* (New York: Columbia University Press, 1933; repr. Port Washington, NY: Ira J. Friedman), pp. 82–92. Swiggett's work is flawed by his failure to appreciate the qualities of Indian warriors. See also Graymont, "Six Nations", p. 28. St Leger's account is in *A state of the expedition*, pp. lxxviii, lxxx–lxxxi. For other contemporary accounts see *Documents relative to the colonial history of New York*, VIII, pp. 718–23, 740–41.

32. For Brant see I. T. Kelsay, *Joseph Brant, 1743–1807: man of two worlds* (Syracuse, NY: Syracuse University Press, 1984); for Butler, see Swiggett, *War out of Niagara*.

33. John Butler's report to Lt Col Bolton, 8 July 1778, Public Record Office, CO/5/96, p. 107. Secondary accounts include Swiggett, *War out of Niagara*, pp. 124–30; Soisin, *The Revolutionary frontier*, p. 115; Kelsay, *Joseph Brant*, pp. 220–21.

34. Sir Henry Clinton to Germain, 11 January 1779, Sackville Germain Papers, IX; Swiggett, *War out of Niagara*, pp. 136–65; Graymont, "Six Nations", p. 34; Kelsay, *Joseph Brant*, p. 232; F. Jennings, *Empire of fortune: crowns, colonies, and tribes in the Seven Years War in America* (New York: W. W. Norton, 1988), p. 198.

35. *Journals of the military expedition of Major General John Sullivan against the Six Nations of Indians in 1779*, F. Cook (ed.) (Auburn, NY: Knapp, Peck, and Thomson, 1887), pp. 43, 60.

36. *Ibid.*, pp. 101, 7–8, 26–7, 40, 44, 75, 155–6. Also in *The spirit of 'seventy-six*, p. 1019. See Calloway, *The American Revolution*, pp. 51–2; Swiggett, *War out of Niagara*, 194–9.

37. *Frontier retreat on the Upper Ohio, 1779–1781*, L. P. Kellogg (ed.), *Publications of the State Historical Society of Wisconsin Collection*, XXIV, *Draper Series*, V (Madison, 1917), p. 57; *The spirit of 'seventy-six*, pp. 1021–4; Dowd, *A spirited resistance*, pp. 81–2.

38. See the essays by G. C. Chalou and G. M. Waller in *The French, the Indians, and George Rogers Clark in the Illinois country*, Proceedings of an Indiana American Revolution

Bicentennial Symposium (Indianapolis: Indiana Historical Society, 1977); Soisin, *The Revolutionary frontier*, pp. 140–41; J. Bakeless, *Background to glory: the life of George Rogers Clark* (Lincoln and London: University of Nebraska Press, 1957, repr. 1992) provides a useful narrative, but one should read J. P. Ronda's introduction to the 1992 edition. Documents for this campaign are published in the *George Rogers Clark papers 1771–1781, collections of the Illinois State Historical Society*, VIII, *Virginia Series*, III, J. A. James (ed.) (Springfield, 1912); *Michigan historical collections*, IX; *Frontier advance on the Upper Ohio, 1778–1779*. A useful selection is *The spirit of 'seventy-six*, pp. 1035–51.

39. *George Rogers Clark papers*, III, pp. 114–54; 347–52; *The papers of Thomas Jefferson*, J. Boyd (ed.) [24 vols] (Princeton University Press, 1951), pp. 26–97.

40. *Michigan historical collections*, IX, pp. 431–50; See also J. D. Barnhart, *Henry Hamilton and George Rogers Clark in the American Revolution with the unpublished journal of Lieut. Gov. Henry Hamilton* (Crawfordsville, Ind.: R. E. Banta, 1951), pp. 35–6, 94–5.

41. *The spirit of 'seventy-six*, p. 1050.

42. White, *The middle ground*, pp. 368, 384–6.

43. *The Revolution remembered: eyewitness accounts of the War for Independence*, J. C. Dann (ed.) (Chicago and London: University of Chicago Press, 1980), pp. 258–61; *Frontier advance on the Upper Ohio*, pp. 35–6.

44. I have relied upon the excellent biography by J. M. Faragher, *Daniel Boone: the life and legend of an American pioneer* (New York: Henry Holt: 1992), particularly pp. 68–235.

45. Faragher, *Daniel Boone*, pp. 214–24; *The spirit of 'seventy-six*, pp. 1060–61; *George Rogers Clark papers*, IV, pp. 89–110.

46. White, *The middle ground*, p. 407; *Michigan historical collections*, X, p. 416.

47. Calloway, *the American Revolution*, pp. 53–4; *The spirit of 'seventy six*, pp. 1054–6; *George Rogers Clark papers*, III, pp. 476–84.

48. A. S. De Peyster, *Miscellanies by an officer*, J. W. De Peyster (ed.), (New York, 1888), p. xxxv; Dowd, *A spirited resistance*, pp. 83–9.

49. White, *The middle ground*, pp. 389–91, 394–5; *George Rogers Clark papers*, IV, pp. 78–9; *The spirit of 'seventy six*, pp. 1058–60; *The Revolution remembered*, pp. 309–14.

50. *Michigan historical collections*, X, p. 663; De Peyster, *Miscellanies*, p. xi; White, *The middle ground*, pp. 407–18.

51. Calloway, *The American Revolution*, pp. 56–64.

52. Graymont, "Six Nations", p. 26.

53. Steele, *Warpaths*, pp. 216–17; Calloway, *The American Revolution*, p. 96; Dowd, *A spirited resistance*, pp. 36, 46–64, 75.

54. Germain to Lord Suffolk, 16 or 17 June 1775, *Stopford Sackville MSS.*, II, p. 2.

55. Papers regarding the dissolution of Robert Rogers' Queen's Rangers, 7–11 November 1779, Clements Library, Clinton Papers, 75, pp. 3–7.

56. Sir Henry Clinton, *The American Rebellion: Sir Henry Clinton's narrative of his campaigns, 1775–1782*, W. B. Willcox (ed.) (New Haven: Yale University Press, 1954), p. 247. Also see F. and M. Wickwire, *Cornwallis: the American adventure*, (Boston: Houghton Mifflin, 1970), pp. 177, 330–31, and D. Higginbotham, *Daniel Morgan: Revolutionary rifleman* (Chapel Hill: University of North Carolina Press, 1961), pp. 135–42.

57. See "An officer out of his time: correspondence of Major Patrick Ferguson, 1779–1780", H. Rankin (ed.), *Sources of American Independence: selected manuscripts from the collections of the William L. Clements Library*, H. Peckham (ed.) [2 vols] (Chicago, 1978), II.

58. J. Alden, *The American Revolution, 1775–1783* (New York: Harper and Row, 1965), p. 235.

59. See for example B. Donagan, "Codes and conduct in the English Civil War", *Past and Present*, No. 118, February 1988, pp. 65–95.

60. C. R. Ferguson, "Carolina and Georgia patriot and loyalist militia in action, 1778–1783", in *The southern experience in the American Revolution*, J. J. Crow & L. E. Tise (eds), (Chapel Hill: University of North Carolina Press, 1978), p. 184.

61. H. F. Rankin, *Francis Marion: the swamp fox* (New York: Thomas Y. Crowell, 1973); R. D. Bass, *Gamecock: the life and campaigns of General Thomas Sumter* (New York : Holt, Rinehart and Winston, 1961).

62. J. Shy, "Charles Lee: the soldier as radical", in *George Washington's generals*, G. Bilias (ed.) New York: William Morrow, 1964), p. 48.

Chapter Seven

1. For 1812–15, I have relied on R. Horsman, *The War of 1812* (New York: Knopf, 1969); H. L. Coles, *The War of 1812* (Chicago: University of Chicago Press, 1965); and D. R. Hickey, *The War of 1812: a forgotten conflict* (Urbana and Chicago: University of Illinois Press, 1989).

2. W. Sword, *President Washington's Indian war: the struggle for the old northwest, 1790–1795* (Norman: University of Oklahoma Press, 1985), pp. 1–44; R. Horsman, *Expansion and American Indian policy, 1783–1812* (East Lansing: Michigan State University Press, 1967), pp. 1–31; R. White, *The middle ground: Indians, empires and republics in the Great Lakes region, 1650–1815* (Cambridge: Cambridge University Press, 1991), pp. 426–7. Also see J. L. Wright, Jr, *Britain and the American frontier, 1783–1815* (Athens: University of Georgia Press, 1975), pp. 1–50.

3. Horsman, *Expansion*, pp. 37–44.

4. Horsman, *Expansion*, pp. 46–9; Sword, *Indian war*, pp. 54–68; for the Fort Harmar treaty see *The American state papers: Indian affairs*, 2 vols (Washington, 1832–4), I, pp. 5–7.

5. G. E. Dowd, *A spirited resistance: the North American struggle for Indian unity 1745–1815* (Baltimore: Johns Hopkins University Press, 1992), p. 99.

6. St Clair to President Washington, 14 September 1789, *American state papers: Indian affairs*, I, p. 58; see pp. 84, 86–92 for reports of Indian attacks upon Kentucky.

7. *Outpost on the Wabash, 1787–1791: letters of Brigadier General Joseph Harmar and Major John Francis Hamtramck and other letters and documents from the Harmar papers in the William L. Clements Library*, G. Thornbrough (ed.), *Indiana Historical Society publications*, IXX (Indianapolis, 1957), pp. 105, 114–17.

8. Horsman, *Expansion*, pp. 84–5; *The St. Clair Papers*, W. H. Smith (ed.) [2 vols] (Cincinnati: Robert Clarke, 1882), II, pp. 123–4, 147, 162.

9. Sword, *Indian war*, pp. 81–2; R. H. Kohn, *Eagle and sword: the Federalists and the creation of the military establishment in America, 1783–1802* (New York and London: The Free Press, 1975), pp. 60–70. *American state papers: Indian Affairs*, I, pp. 92–105.

10. *St. Clair Papers*, II, pp. 181–2.

11. Sword, *Indian war*, pp. 93–4; Kohn, *Eagle and sword*, pp. 95–106; F. P. Prucha, *The sword of the Republic: the United States army on the frontier, 1783–1846* (Toronto: Collier-Macmillan, 1969), p. 20. Regular officers and even militia officers placed much of the blame for their defeat on the poor condition and conduct of the men. They were a

convenient scapegoat, but they had not been properly trained or equipped. See "Court of Inquiry on General Harmar", *The new American state papers: military affairs*, B. F. Cooling (ed.) (Wilmington, Del.: Scholarly Resources, 1979), VIII, pp. 77–93. For other documents, see B. Meek, "General Harmar's expedition", *Ohio Archaelogical and Historical Publications* **XX**, 1911, pp. 74–108.

12. Sword, *Indian war*, p. 96. Diagrams of Harmar's dispositions are in "Court of Inquiry on General Harmar", pp. 88–90, and in Meek, "General Harmar's Expedition", pp. 80 and 83.

13. *St. Clair papers*, II, p. 188.

14. Sword, *Indian war*, pp. 101–16.

15. *St. Clair papers*, II, p. 197.

16. Horsman, *Expansion*, pp. 90–91; Wright, *Britain and the American frontier*, pp. 67–85.

17. "Winthrop Sargent's diary while with General Arthur St. Clair's expedition against the Indians", *Ohio Archaelogical and Historical Society Publications* **XXXIII**, 1924, p. 266.

18. Sword, *Indian war*, pp. 145–7; for St Clair's campaign see Chapters 16 and 17; Kohn, *Eagle and sword*, pp. 109–16; Prucha, *The sword of the Republic*, pp. 22–7. For the condition of St Clair's men, also see the reports to Congress on St Clair's defeat in *The new American state papers: military affairs*, VIII, pp. 93–9. "Winthrop Sargent's diary", pp. 237–73, is an important contemporary narrative of the campaign.

19. "The campaign in the Indian country [From the diary of Major Ebenezer Denny, Aid-de-Camp to Major General St. Clair]", *St. Clair papers*, II, p. 252.

20. *A narrative of the . . . campaign against the Indians . . . , under the command of Major General St. Clair . . .*, in *The first American frontier*, D. Van Every (ed.) (New York: Arno Press, 1971), pp. 26–7.

21. For reports of these raids, see *American state papers: Indian affairs*, I, pp. 132–5.

22. For contemporary accounts, see the *St. Clair papers*, II, pp. 258–62; *American state papers: Indian affairs*, I, pp. 136–8; "Winthrop Sargent's diary", pp. 256–73.

23. Denny diary, *St. Clair papers*, II, p. 262.

24. General John Armstrong to the President, 23 December 1791, *St. Clair papers*, II, pp. 276–7.

25. Horsman, *Expansion*, pp. 84–98; Sword, *Indian war*, pp. 223–31; Wright, *Britain and the American frontier*, pp. 86–91; Dowd, *A spirited resistance*, pp. 106–9; *American state papers: Indian affairs*, I, pp. 351–60.

26. "Organization of the army in 1792", in *The new American state papers: military affairs*, II, pp. 2–3; Kohn, *Eagle and sword*, p. 124.

27. Sword, *Indian war*, pp. 234–5; Kohn, *Eagle and sword*, pp. 125–6; for Wayne's correspondence, see *Anthony Wayne: a name in arms*, R. C. Knopf (ed.) (Pittsburgh: University of Pittsburgh Press, 1960); pp. 13–235 cover the training of the Legion and preparations for a campaign. For Wayne's life, see P. D. Nelson, *Anthony Wayne: soldier of the early Republic* (Bloomington: Indiana University Press, 1985); see pp. 222–83 for his command in the west.

28. For an example of the critical sniping that Wayne had to endure from the Wilkinson partisans among his officers, see the anonymous "From Greene Ville to Fallen Timbers: a journal of the Wayne campaign, July 28–September 14, 1794", D. L. Smith (ed.), *Indiana Historical Society Publications* **XVI**(3) (Indianapolis, 1952), pp. 239–333.

29. Sword, *Indian war*, pp. 236–7; *Anthony Wayne: a name in arms*, pp. 136, 186.

30. For British policy, see Wright, *Britain and the American frontier*, pp. 86–102. Also see Sword, *Indian war*, pp. 29–37; Kohn, *Eagle and sword*, pp. 141–74.

31. Sword, *Indian war*, pp. 272–8; *Anthony Wayne: a name in arms*, pp. 345–9.

32. Sword, *Indian war*, p. 258; D. W. H. Howard, "The Battle of Fallen Timbers as told by Chief Kin-Jo-I-No", *Northwest Ohio Quarterly* **XX**(1), January 1948, pp. 37–49.

33. Sword, *Indian war*, pp. 268–80; *Anthony Wayne: a name in arms*, pp. 280–1, 347. *American state papers: Indian affairs*, I, p. 490.

34. Howard, "The Battle of Fallen Timbers", p. 49.

35. *The correspondence of Lieut. Governor John Graves Simcoe*, E. A. Cruikshank (ed.) [5 vols] (Toronto: Ontario Historical Society, 1923–31), III, p. 21.

36. *Ibid.*, pp. 8, 118.

37. For the Battle of Fallen Timbers and its aftermath see Sword, *Indian war*, pp. 299–317; *Anthony Wayne: a name in arms*, pp. 351–7; "From Greenville to Fallen Timbers", p. 295.

38. Sword, *Indian war*, p. 336. For the Treaty of Greenville, see Horsman, *Expansion*, pp. 99–103; *American state papers: Indian affairs*, I, pp. 562–83.

39. Horsman, *Expansion*, pp. 105–66; for the 1809 Fort Wayne treaty see *Governors messages and letters: messages and letters of William Henry Harrison* [2 vols] (Indianapolis: Indiana Historical Commission, 1922) (hereafter cited as *Harrison letters*), I, pp. 359–78.

40. Dowd, *A spirited resistance*, pp. 131–6.

41. Dowd, *A spirited resistance*, pp. 136–9. There are numerous expressions of concern about the Prophet's intentions in the *Harrison letters*, I, pp. 239–417. For his life, see R. D. Edmunds, *The Shawnee Prophet* (Lincoln: University of Nebraska Press, 1983).

42. *Harrison letters*, I, p. 549.

43. *Ibid.*, II, p. 102.

44. *Ibid.*, I, p. 605.

45. Dowd, *A spirited resistance*, pp. 116–47; R. D. Edmunds, *Tecumseh and the quest for Indian leadership* (Boston: Little, Brown and Co., 1984), pp. 81–122, 223–4; Horsman, *Expansion*, pp. 105–66; L. S. Dean, "Tecumseh's prophecy: the great New Madrid Earthquakes of 1811–1812 and 1841 in Alabama", *Alabama Review* **XLVII**(3), 1994, pp. 163–71.

46. Dowd, *A spirited resistance*, pp. 170–3; R. Hassig, "Internal conflict in the Creek War of 1813–1814", *Ethnohistory* **XXI**(3), 1974, pp. 251–73.

47. Dowd, *A spirited resistance*, p. 187.

48. Coles, *The War of 1812*, p. 197. For Jackson's accounts, see *The correspondence of Andrew Jackson*, J. S. Bassett (ed.) [7 vols] (New York: Kraus Reprint, 1969), I, pp. 341, 366–7.

49. Coles, *The War of 1812*, p. 187; *The correspondence of Andrew Jackson*, I, pp. 489–92; J. Brannan, *Official letters of the military and naval officers of the United States during the war with Great Britain in the years 1812, 13, 14, 15* (Washington, 1823), pp. 319–20.

50. Edmunds, *Tecumseh*, p. 160; Wright, *Britain and the American frontier*, p. 153; Horsman, *Expansion*, pp. 168–9. Documents relative to the Tippecanoe campaign are in the *Harrison letters*, I, pp. 608–725, and II, pp. 1–27. Harrison's account of the battle is in I, pp. 614–15. The account of the British agent Matthew Elliot is in I, pp. 616–18.

51. Horsman, *The War of 1812*, p. 51; for American weaknesses, see pp. 29–32; and Coles, *The War of 1812*, pp. 69–70.

52. For the capture of Michilimackinac, see Horsman, *The War of 1812*, pp. 36–37. Documents relative to this episode are in *Select British documents of the Canadian War of 1812*, W. Wood (ed.) [3 vols] (Toronto: The Champlain Society, 1920–1928), I, pp. 432–55.

53. Horsman, *The War of 1812*, p. 41; R. D. Edmunds, *The Potawatomis: keepers of the fire* (Norman: University of Oklahoma Press, 1978), pp. 181–8; *Harrison letters*, II, p. 85; *Select British documents*, I, p. 520.

54. Coles, *The War of 1812*, pp. 45–57; Horsman, *The War of 1812*, pp. 35–41; Hickey, *The War of 1812*, pp. 80–84; *Select British documents*, I, pp. 461–79.
55. Horsman, *The War of 1812*, pp. 81–5; Coles, *The War of 1812*, pp. 113–17; Edmunds, *The Potawatomis*, pp. 189–95; *Select British documents*, II, pp. 5–8; *Harrison letters*, II, pp. 314–41; Brannan, *Official letters*, pp. 130–32.
56. Horsman, *The War of 1812*, pp. 100–6; Coles, *The War of 1812*, pp. 118–21; *Harrison letters*, II, pp. 417–47, 474–500; *Select British documents*, II, pp. 31–7, 40–46; Brannan, *Official letters*, pp. 149–59, 184–6.
57. Brannan, *Official letters*, p. 241.
58. Brannan, *Official letters*, p. 236; *Harrison letters*, II, p. 562.
59. Dowd, *A spirited resistance*, pp. 184–5; Horsman, *The War of 1812*, pp. 107–15; Coles, *The War of 1812*, pp. 129–35; *Harrison letters*, II, pp. 557–68; *Select British documents*, II, pp. 319–41. For an effort to rehabilitate Procter's reputation, see J. Sugden, *Tecumseh's last stand* (Norman: University of Oklahoma Press: 1989).
60. Coles, *The War of 1812*, p. 111.
61. Harrison to Gen. Charles Scott, 17 April 1810, *Harrison letters*, I, p. 414. This long letter concerning militia organization provides important insight to Harrison's intellectual approach to military affairs.

Select Bibliography

R. Allen, *His Majesty's Indian allies: British Indian policy in the defence of Canada, 1774–1815* (Toronto: Dundurn, 1992).

J. Axtell, *Beyond 1492: encounters in colonial North America* (New York: Oxford University Press, 1992).

J. Axtell, *European and Indian: essays in the ethnohistory of colonial America* (New York: Oxford University Press, 1981).

J. Axtell, *The invasion within: the contest of cultures in colonial North America* (New York: Oxford University Press, 1985).

R. Bourne, *The red king's rebellion: racial politics in New England, 1675–1678* (New York: Atheneum, 1990).

C. Calloway, *The American Revolution in the Indian country: crisis and diversity in Native American communities* (Cambridge: Cambridge University Press, 1995).

C. Calloway, *The western Abenakis of Vermont, 1600–1800* (Norman: University of Oklahoma Press, 1990).

B. Church, *Diary of King Philip's War, 1675–1676*, A. & M. Simpson (eds) (Chester, Conn.: The Pequot Press, 1975).

H. L. Coles, *The War of 1812* (Chicago: University of Chicago Press, 1965).

D. Delage, *Bitter feast: Amerindians and Europeans in northeastern North America, 1660–1664*, J. Brierly (trans.) (Vancouver: UBC Press, 1993).

G. Dowd, *A spirited resistance: The North American struggle for Indian unity, 1745–1815* (Baltimore: Johns Hopkins University Press, 1992).

W. J. Eccles, *The Canadian frontier, 1534–1760* (New York: Holt, Rinehart and Winston, 1969).

W. J. Eccles, *Frontenac: The courtier Governor* (Toronto: McClelland and Stewart, 1959).

R. D. Edmunds, *The Potawatomis: keepers of the fire* (Norman: University of Oklahoma Press, 1978).

R. D. Edmunds, *The Shawnee Prophet* (Norman: University of Oklahoma Press, 1983).

R. D. Edmunds, *Tecumseh and the quest for Indian leadership* (Boston: Little, Brown, 1984).

L. V. Eid, "A kind of running fight: Indian battlefield tactics in the late eighteenth century", *Western Pennsylvania Historical Magazine* **LXXI**, 1988, pp. 147–71.

J. M. Faragher, *Daniel Boone: the life and legend of an American pioneer* (New York: Henry Holt, 1992).

197

J. Ferling, *A wilderness of miseries: war and warriors in early America* (Westport, Conn.: Greenwood Press, 1980).

G. Fregault, *Canada: the war of the conquest*, M. M. Cameron (trans.) (Toronto: Oxford University Press, 1969).

L. H. Gipson, *The British empire before the American Revolution*, 15 vols (Caldwell, Id.: Caxton Printers, 1936–70).

B. Graymont, "The Six Nations Indians in the Revolutionary War", in *The Iroquois in the American Revolution* (Rochester: Rochester Museum and Science Center, 1981).

R. Horsman, *Expansion and American Indian policy, 1783–1812* (East Lansing: Michigan State University Press, 1967).

R. Horsman, *The War of 1812* (New York: Knopf, 1969).

R. D. Hurt, *The Ohio frontier: crucible of the old northwest, 1720–1830* (Bloomington: Indiana University Press, 1996).

F. Jennings, *The ambigious Iroquois empire* (New York: Norton, 1984).

F. Jennings, *Empire of fortune: crowns, colonies, and tribes in the Seven Years War* (New York: Norton, 1988).

F. Jennings, *The invasion of America: Indians, colonialism, and the cant of conquest* (Chapel Hill: University of North Carolina Press, 1975).

I. Kelsay, *Joseph Brant, 1743–1807: man of two worlds* (Syracuse: Syracuse University Press, 1984).

R. Kohn, *Eagle and sword: the Federalists and the creation of the military establishment in America, 1783–1802* (New York: The Free Press, 1975).

P. Kopperman, *Braddock at the Monongahela* (Pittsburgh: University of Pittsburgh Press, 1977).

D. Leach, *Flintlock and tomahawk: New England in King Philip's War* (New York: Macmillan, 1958).

P. Malone, *The skulking way of war: technology and tactics among the New England Indians* (Lanham, Md.: Madison Books, 1991).

M. McConnell, *A country between: the Upper Ohio Valley and its peoples, 1724–1774* (Lincoln: University of Nebraska Press, 1992).

J. Merrell, *The Indians' new world: Catawbas and their neighbors from European contact through the era of removal* (Chapel Hill: University of North Carolina Press, 1989).

P. Nelson, *Anthony Wayne: soldier of the early Republic* (Bloomington: Indiana University Press, 1985).

J. O'Donnell, *Southern Indians in the American Revolution* (Knoxville: University of Tennessee Press, 1973).

S. Pargellis, *Military affairs in North America, 1748–1765* (1936, repr. Archon Books, 1969).

F. Parkman, *France and England in North America*, 2 vols (New York, 1983).

H. Peckham, *The colonial wars 1689–1762* (Chicago: University of Chicago Press, 1964).

H. Peckham, *Pontiac and the Indian uprising* (Princeton: Princeton University Press, 1947).

F. Prucha, *The sword of the Republic: the United States army on the frontier, 1783–1846* (Toronto: Collier-Macmillan, 1969).

D. Richter, *The ordeal of the longhouse: peoples of the Iroquois League in the era of European colonization* (Chapel Hill: University of North Carolina Press, 1992).

N. Salisbury, *Manitou and Providence: Indians, Europeans and the making of New England, 1500–1643* (New York: Oxford University Press, 1982).

W. Shea, *The Virginia militia in the seventeenth century* (Baton Rouge: Louisiana State University Press, 1983).

J. Shy, *A people numerous and armed; reflections on the military struggle for American independence* (New York: Oxford University Press, 1976).

R. Slotkin, *Regeneration through violence: mythology of the American frontier, 1600–1860* (Middletown, Conn.: Wesleyan University Press, 1973).

J. Soison, *The Revolutionary frontier, 1763–1783* (New York: Holt, Rinehart and Winston, 1967).

I. Steele, *Betrayals: Fort William Henry and the "Massacre"* (New York: Oxford University Press, 1990).

I. Steele, *Guerrillas and grenadiers, the struggle for Canada, 1689–1760* (Toronto: Ryerson Press, 1969).

I. Steele, *Warpaths: invasions of North America* (New York: Oxford University Press, 1994).

H. Swiggert, *War out of Niagara: Walter Butler and the Tory Rangers* (New York: Columbia University Press, 1933).

W. Sword, *President Washington's Indian war: the struggle for the old northwest, 1790–1795* (Norman: University of Oklahoma Press, 1985).

B. Trigger, *The children of Aataentsic: a history of the Huron people to 1660*, 2 vols (Montreal: McGill–Queen's University Press, 1976).

A. Vaughn, *The New England frontier: Puritans and Indians, 1620–1675* (Boston: Little, Brown, 1965).

R. White, *The middle ground. Indians, empires, and republics in the Great Lakes region, 1650–1815* (Cambridge: Cambridge University Press, 1991).

J. L. Wright, Jr, *Britain and the American frontier, 1783–1815* (Athens: University of Georgia Press, 1975).

J. L. Wright, *The only land they knew: the tragic story of the American Indians in the old south* (New York: The Free Press, 1981).

Index

Note: "n." after a page reference indicates the number of a note on that page.